C.H.

BATTLES OF THE FALKLANDS WAR

BATTLES OF THE FALKLANDS WAR

GORDON SMITH

LONDON

IAN ALLAN LTD

First published 1989

ISBN 0 7110 1792 1

Published by Ian Allan Ltd, Shepperton, Surrey; and
printed by Ian Allan Printing Ltd at their works at
Coombelands in Runnymede, England

Contents

SAN CARLOS LANDINGS AND CONSOLIDATION

THE APPROACH TO AND BATTLE FOR STANLEY

VICTORY

Abbreviations

Abbreviations

[a]	Argentine (Argentine aircraft lost)
AA	Anti-aircraft
AAC	Army Air Corps
AAM	Air-to-air missile
AB	Able Seaman
ACM	Air Chief Marshall
ADC	Aide-de-Camp
Adm	Admiral
AFC	Air Force Cross
AM	Air Marshall
ammo	ammunition
ARA	*Armada Republica Argentina* (Argentine Navy)
Arty Bty	Artillery Battery
Asst	Assistant
ASW	Anti-submarine warfare
[b]	British (British aircraft lost)
BAS	British Antarctic Survey
Bde	Brigade
Bdr	Bombardier
BEM	British Empire Medal
Brig	Brigadier
Brig-Gen	Brigadier-General
Btn	Battalion
Bty, bty	Battery, battery
c	circa
CAB	*Battalion de Aviacion de Combate* (Combat Aviation Battalion of Argentine Army)
CANA	*Comando Aviacion Naval Argentina* (Argentine Naval Aviation Command)
CAP	Combat air patrol
Capt	Captain
Casevac	Casualty evacuation
CB	Companion of the Bath
CBAS	Commando Brigade Air Squadron
CBE	Commander of Order of British Empire
CBU	Cluster bomb unit
Cdo	Commando
Cdo Bde	Commando Brigade (British 3)
Cdo Regt	Commando Regiment
CGM	Conspicious Gallantry Medal
Ch	Chartered
Cdr	Commander
Cdre	Commodore
CSgt	Colour Sergeant
CO	Commanding Officer
Col	Colonel
Coy, coy	Company, company
Cpl	Corporal
CPO	Chief Petty Officer
CV	Aircraft carrier
CVBG	Carrier Battle Group
DCM	Distinguished Conduct Medal
DD	Destroyer
DFC	Distinguished Flying Cross
DFM	Distinguished Flying Medal
DSC	Distinguished Service Cross
DSM	Distinguished Service Medal
DSO	Companion of Distinguished Service Order
ECM	Electronic counter-measures
EEC	European Economic Community
EOD	Explosive Ordnance Disposal
Eng Offr	Engineering Officer
Esc	*Escuadrilla* (CANA squadron)
F	Fighter
FAA	Fleet Air Arm (Royal Navy)
FAA	*Fuerza Aerea Argentina* (Argentine Air Force)
Flt	Flight
Flt Lt	Flight Lieutenant
Flt Sgt	Flight Sergeant
FOB	Forward operating base
FOO	Forward Observation Officer
FR	Frigate
FSB	Forward support base
GBE	Knight Grand Cross of British Empire
Gdsmn	Guardsman
Gen	General
GM	George Medal
Gp Capt	Group Captain
GPMG	General purpose machine gun (7.62mm)
grt	Gross registered tonnage
H	Helipad
HAS	Anti-submarine helicopters (primarily)
HC	Assault helicopters (primarily)
HMS	Her Majesty's Ship
HQ	Headquarters
HU	Assault/utility helicopters (primarily)
I/C	In Command
2i/c	Second in Command
Ind Cdo Sqn	Independent Commando Squadron
Inf Bde	Infantry Brigade (British 5th)
Inf Regt	Infantry Regiment
IPV	Ice patrol vessel (HMS *Endurance*)

KBE	Knight Commander of Order of British Empire	Paras	Paratroopers
KCB	Knight Commander of Order of the Bath	PNA	*Prefectura Naval Argentina* (Argentine Coastguard)
LAW	Light anti-armour weapon (66mm)	PNG	Passive Night Goggles
		PO	Petty Officer
L/Cpl	Lance Corporal	Post	Posthumous
LCU	Landing craft, utility	POW	Prisoner-of-war
LCVP	Landing craft, vehicle and personnel	Pte	Private
		QGM	Queen's Gallantry Medal
Ldg	Leading	RA	Royal Artillery
LS	Leading Seaman	RAF	Royal Air Force
L/Sgt	Lance Sergeant	RAOC	Royal Army Ordnance Corps
LSL	Landing ship, logistic	RAPC	Royal Army Pay Corps
LST	Landing ship, tank	RAS	Replenishment-at-sea
Lt	Lieutenant	RCB	Red Cross Box (to north of Falklands)
Lt-Cdr	Lieutenant Commander	RCT	Royal Corps of Transport
Lt-Col	Lieutenant Colonel	RE	Royal Engineers
Lt-Gen	Lieutenant-General	Rear-Adm	Rear-Admiral
LVTP	Landing vehicle, tracked, personnel	Recce	Reconnaissance
		Regt, regt	Regiment, regiment
Maj	Major	REME	Royal Electrical and Mechanical Engineers
Maj-Gen	Major-General		
M & AW Cadre	Mountain and Arctic Warfare Cadre (Royal Marines)	Req	Requisitioned
		RFA	Royal Fleet Auxiliary
MAW	Medium anti-armour weapon (84mm Carl Gustav)	RM	Royal Marine(s)
		RMAS	Royal Maritime Auxiliary Service
MBE	Member of British Empire Order	RMP	Royal Military Police
MC	Military Cross	RN	Royal Navy
MCMS	Mine Countermeasures Squadron	RO-RO	Roll-on, roll-off
		SAM	Surface-to-air missile
MEA (M)	Marine Engineering Artificer (Mechanical)	SAR	Search and rescue
		SAS	Special Air Service
MEM (M)	Marine Engineering Mechanic (Mechanical)	SBS	Special Boat Squadron
		SC(Satcom)	Satellite communication
MEZ	Maritime exclusion zone (excludes Argentine naval vessels from zone 200 nautical miles in radius from Falkland Islands as from 12 April 1982)	Sgt	Sergeant
		SN(Satnav)	Satellite navigation
		Sqn, sqn	Squadron, squadron
		Sqn Ldr	Squadron Leader
		SS	Submarine — conventionally-powered
MID	Mention in Despatches	SSgt	Staff Sergeant
MM	Military Medal	SSM	Surface-to-surface missile
MN	Merchant Navy	SSN	Submarine — nuclear-powered
Mne	Marine		
MR	Maritime reconnaissance	STUFT	Ships taken up from trade
MVO	Member of Royal Victorian Order	STWS	Ships torpedo weapon system
NAS	Naval Air Squadron	Sub-Lt	Sub-Lieutenant
NATO	North Atlantic Treaty Organisation	Tac HQ	Tactical Headquarters
		TB	Torpedo Bomber
NCO	Non-commissioned officer	TEZ	Total exclusion zone (excludes all Argentine vessels and aircraft from zone 200 nautical miles in radius from the Falkland Islands as from 30 April 1982; and outside 12 nautical mile zone from Argentine coast from 7 May)
NGFO	Naval Gunfire Forward Observer		
NP	Naval Party		
OAS	Organisation of American States		
OBE	Officer of Order of British Empire		
Offr	Officer		
Para	Parachute Battalion	TF	Task Force

TG	Task Group	
TRALA	Tug, Repair and Logistic Area	
	(to east of the Falklands)	
UK	United Kingdom	
UN	United Nations	
US	United States (of America)	
UXB	Unexploded bomb	
vertrep	Vertical replenishment (by	
	helicopter)	
VC	Victoria Cross	
Vice-Adm	Vice-Admiral	
Wg Cdr	Wing Commander	
WO1/2	Warrant Officer Class 1, 2	

Distances, times and the maps

All distances are quoted in statute miles, unless stated otherwise. All times are local.

The British forces operated on Greenwich Mean Time or 'Zulu' time, 3-4hr ahead of the Falklands and Argentina. Few books are consistent or clear on the subject, and there will no doubt be discrepancies in this one. However, the aim has been to use a local time for the Falklands equal to 'Zulu' minus 3hr.

Groups of ships and their tracks, especially on the 'Task Force Movements' maps are approximate only. The aim is to give the reader an idea of which ships operated together in the same area or role for the period in question, and the direction they were moving in.

Wherever possible, gallantry awards (in brackets) are listed on the most relevant map, or in the text, although some recipients will be found twice.

Introduction

The definitive battlefield atlas of the Falklands War will have to wait some years or even decades for the release of full British information and the publication and analysis of much more from Argentina. In the meantime, this one pulls together much of the data published in the UK, not so much in greater detail, but as an accurate-as-possible, step-by-step picture of how the war progressed from incident to Argentine invasion and on to British response and victory.

Like many human events, the Falklands War can best be treated like a jigsaw puzzle, but one neither so big that most of the ships, land forces and aircraft squadrons taking part, gallantry awards earned, cannot be included, nor so specialised that it cannot be treated as a total war of the conventional variety. In telling the story in the battlefield atlas form, the build-up is slow as the British Task Force progresses south, but as the great logistics success the South Atlantic campaign was, it perhaps deserves to be told in this way. And like any jigsaw, a lot of pieces have to be sorted, so that first the border can be established and then a small group collected together here, and another there, until a fuller picture emerges. The appendices are included for the sake of completeness, and thought was given to an additional one listing the British war dead by date and action. However many families and servicemen will not want to see their men and comrades listed yet again. So even though the dead and the wounded are a major part of the price paid for the liberation of the Falklands, it was decided to omit this information. However, it should be remembered that what to many readers may be a fascinating military and logistics story, is, to more than 250 families in Britain (and over 1,000 in Argentina) still a cause for mourning.

Acknowledgements

An early decision was taken to rely as far as possible on existing publications and those used are listed in the Bibliography; but for some, a special word of appreciation is due. For the most comprehensive accounts of the war, *The Battle for the Falklands* by Max Hastings and Simon Jenkins and the later *Task Force* by Martin Middlebrook can not be bettered. *No Picnic* by Brigadier Julian Thompson covers the land campaign at all levels in depth and feeling. *The Forces Postal History of the Falklands Islands and the Task Force* by John Davies is a real mine of information, and the more recently published *The Royal Navy and the Falklands War* by David Brown was most timely and helpful. But the all-round accolade for basic information on the air and to a slightly lesser extent, the sea and some land actions, and for its scholarship and helpfulness must go to *Falklands: The Air War* by members of the British Aviation Research Group. These include Rodney Burden, Michael Draper, Douglas Rough, Colin Smith and David Wilton. To them I am particularly grateful.

Some of the publications used as well as other sources of information were supplied by a number of people, whom I would like to thank, including Bill Burkett; Mr A. L. Carter, BP Shipping Ltd; Bosun R. Cartwright of the Royal Fleet Auxiliary Service; Captain S. J. Crowsley, Gurkha Rifles; Colonel W. T. Dennison, Royal Engineers; Mardie Esterkin, P & O Group; Philip Forbes, Major J. I. Grant, Scots Guards; Brigadier R. J. Lewendon Royal Artillery; John Miller, Captain A. G. Newing Royal Marines and Chris Newman.

For the photographs, Mr F. R. Andrews, Royal Fleet Auxiliary Service; Lieutenant-Commander C. W. Beattie RN, RNAS Yeovilton; Matthew Little, Royal Marines Museum; Major G. Norton, Airborne Forces Museum; Alison Pickard, United Towing Ltd; Brigadier J. F. Rickett, Welsh Guards; Commander T. J. K. Sloane RN, MOD (Navy); Group Captain G. Thorburn RAF, MOD (RAF) and Major D. R. d'A Willis, 7th Duke of Edinburgh's Own Gurkha Rifles.

Most importantly, my sincere thanks go to Nicholas Smith, Michael Smith, Alex and Jane Welby and David and Betty Chapman. Without their support at crucial stages, the book would not have been completed.

Gordon Smith
Penarth 1988

INVASION AND TASK FORCE DEPARTURE

MAP 1

The Falkland Islands and Argentina

Falkland Islands

Some 8,000 miles (7,000 nautical miles) from Britain, nearly two-thirds the size of Wales and often compared with the western isles of Scotland, the Falklands are the only major island group in the South Atlantic and lie 300 miles to the east of the Strait of Magellan. The main islands of West and East Falkland and more than 100 smaller ones total over 4,700 sq miles in area. They are chiefly moorland, treeless and the highest point is Mount Usborne on East Falkland. The climate is cool, damp and often windy with mean monthly temperatures varying between 49°F in January (summer) and 36°F in July (winter). The air temperature rarely exceeds 70°F or falls below 12°F.

The total population at the 1980 census numbered 1,813 with just over 1,000 living in Stanley on the east coast of East Falkland, the capital and only town in the colony. The remainder live outside in the 'camp' where there are no roads, although some of the settlements have an airstrip. Most of the people are of British extraction and mainly engaged in farming the 600,000 sheep which occupy much of the land. In 1980, exports to Britain of wool and hides totalled £2.8 million and imports including food, manufactured goods, timber and machinery, were valued at £2 million. The Governor (later Sir) Rex Hunt is President of the mainly nominated and advisory Executive Council and also of the partly elected Legislative Council which includes six people's representatives. The Government balanced public revenue and expenditure at around £2.4 million in 1981-82, and also administers two dependencies:

South Georgia

Lying 900 miles east-southeast of the Falklands, the 100-mile-long island of South Georgia is completely mountainous, covered with glaciers and is likened to a partly submerged stretch of the Swiss Alps. With an area of 1,450 sq miles, conditions are near Antarctic, and by now its only regular population are the 20 or so staff of the British Antarctic Survey based at King Edward Point near the old whaling station of Grytviken.

South Sandwich Islands

Some 350 miles further on is the start of this 150-mile-long island chain which continues down to Southern Thule. Normally uninhabited and actively volcanic, the islands are totally Antarctic in climate.

Argentina

This huge country occupies most of the southern part of South America, and stretches a total of 2,300 miles from Bolivia in the north to near Cape Horn far away to the south. Just smaller than India and the eighth largest country in the world, Argentina covers a total area of 1,080,000 sq miles. To the west, bordering the length of Chile, are the Andes Mountains and to the east of them, down to the Atlantic, are the great plains and pampas. The climate ranges from sub-tropical to cold temperate.

Out of a 1980 population of 27,900,000, nearly 10 million people live in and around the seaport capital of Buenos Aires on the River Plate estuary. The great majority of the people

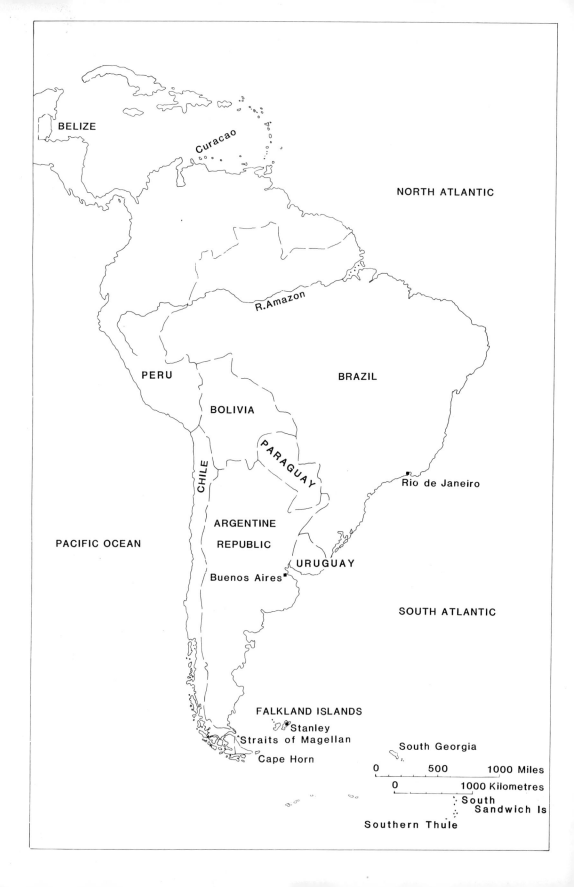

BELIZE

Curacao

NORTH ATLANTIC

R.Amazon

PERU

BRAZIL

BOLIVIA

PARAGUAY

CHILE

Rio de Janeiro

ARGENTINE

REPUBLIC

PACIFIC OCEAN

URUGUAY

Buenos Aires

SOUTH ATLANTIC

FALKLAND ISLANDS

Stanley

Straits of Magellan

South Georgia

Cape Horn

0   500   1000 Miles

0   1000 Kilometres

South
Sandwich Is

Southern Thule

are of European origin, mainly from Spain and Italy, and the native Indian population is small. Their language is Spanish, the main religion Roman Catholic and much of the country's culture is 'European Mediterranean' in character. Agriculture and livestock have long been an important part of the country's economy, and the meat-packing and food processing industries reflect this. Apart from oil and mineral production, there has been a considerable growth in recent years in the textile, plastics, machine tool, car and steel product industries. Exports to Britain in 1980 were worth £144 million, and imports £173 million. Communications by rail, road and airline, and through the medium of television and radio are well developed. Education is compulsory between the ages of six and 13, with facilities for secondary education up to the age of 17 plus available in most of the big cities and towns. Literature flourishes, and around 450 newspapers are published throughout the country.

The Spanish first went ashore in what was to become Argentina in 1515. Following three centuries of colonisation, a six-year struggle led by Gen José de San Martin brought independence in 1816. Then a long period of dictatorship by Juan de Rosas was ended in 1852, Buenos Aires became the seat of federal government, and the country developed rapidly. The military took over in 1930. Juan Peron was elected President in 1945 with the strong support of his wife Evita who died in 1952 and he was ousted three years later. Political and economic instability over the next 18 years led to Peron being recalled from exile and becoming President again in 1973, but he died within a year. Further difficulties brought about a bloodless military coup in 1976 along with repressive and often brutal government by a junta made up of the commanders of the armed forces. Lt-Gen Videla served as the first President until 1981, but after a few months, his successor Viola was moved out and replaced in December by Army Gen Leopoldo Galtieri, with the support of the other members — Air Force Brig-Gen Basilio Lami Dozo and Adm Jorge Anaya.

As the 150th anniversary of British control over the Falklands nears, the junta gives priority to the recovery of the *Islas Malvinas*, if necessary by force. Argentina will thus resolve what to them is a major and long-standing territorial dispute, but to Britain a distant and almost forgotten remnant of empire.

MAP 2

The Falklands in Dispute

Claims for the first sightings of these uninhabited islands include those by the Italian Amerigo Vespucci in 1502 and the expedition of Portuguese-born Ferdinand Magellan in 1520. Thereafter three firsts are generally accepted — Capt John Davis makes the first British sighting in 1592, Dutchman Sebald de Weert first accurately plots the westerly Jason Islands in 1600, and the first British landing is made in 1690 on the north coast by Capt John Strong who names Falkland Sound after Lord Falkland of the Admiralty.

The Treaty of Utrecht of 1713 confirms Spain's continued control of her traditional territories in the Americas, including the offshore islands, but by now the French, many from St Malo, are visiting the islands from which they receive the name *Les Iles Malouines*, subsequently the Spanish *Islas Malvinas*. In the 1740s, Adm Lord Anson, back from his voyage around the world, recommends them as a naval base because of their strategic position near Cape Horn.

The first settlement is established in 1764 at Port Louis in Berkeley Sound by the French under Antoine de Bougainville, who claims the colony in the name of the King of France, a step which brings strong protests from allied Spain. Next year British Capt John Byron arrives to survey the north coast, goes ashore on Saunders Island off West Falkland and in turn claims the islands for Britain, naming Port Egmont before sailing away. Capt John McBride follows him there in 1766 to set up a permanent colony, and that same year tries to eject the French from Port Louis, but unknown to both of them, de Bougainville has already sold out to Spain.

He formally hands over the French colony in 1767 and Port Louis is renamed Puerto Soledad. A Spanish governor is appointed under the Captain-General of mainland Buenos

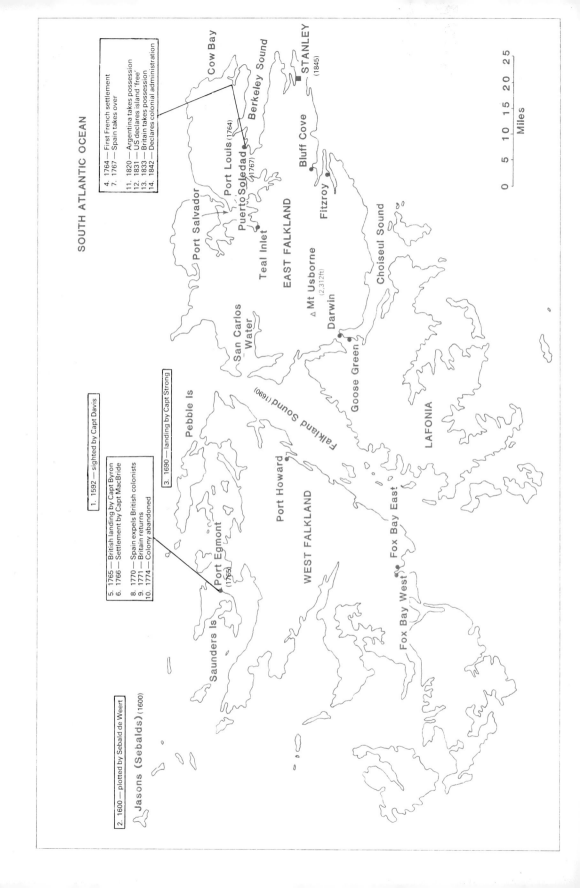

SOUTH ATLANTIC OCEAN

1. 1592 — sighted by Capt Davis

2. 1600 — plotted by Sebald de Weert

Jasons (Sebalds) (1600)

3. 1690 — landing by Capt Strong

4. 1764 — First French settlement
7. 1767 — Spain takes over

11. 1820 — Argentina takes possession
12. 1831 — US declares island 'free'
13. 1833 — Britain takes possession
14. 1842 — Declares colonial administration

5. 1765 — British landing by Capt Byron
6. 1766 — Settlement by Capt MacBride

8. 1770 — Spain expels British colonists
9. 1771 — Britain returns
10. 1774 — Colony abandoned

Cow Bay

Berkeley Sound

STANLEY (1845)

Port Louis (1764)

Puerto Soledad (1767)

Port Salvador

Bluff Cove

Teal Inlet

Fitzroy

EAST FALKLAND

△ Mt Usborne (2,312ft)

Darwin

San Carlos Water

Choiseul Sound

Goose Green

Pebble Is

Falkland Sound (1690)

LAFONIA

Port Howard

WEST FALKLAND

Fox Bay East

Saunders Is

Port Egmont (1765)

Fox Bay West

Miles

0 5 10 15 20 25

Aires, but both the British on West Falkland and Spanish on East Falkland carry on until 1769 when each tries to get the other to leave. Next year, on orders from Buenos Aires, five Spanish ships with 1,400 troops arrive and the small marine garrison at Port Egmont is forced to leave in a move which nearly leads to war between the two countries. In 1771, after intensive negotiations Spain agrees to Britain returning to Port Egmont, but reserves the right to sovereignty. She also claims Britain has secretly agreed to pull out and indeed the settlement is abandoned three years later in 1774. Until the early 19th century, the Falklands remain the Spanish colony of *Islas Malvinas*.

Following independence from Spain in 1816, the future state of Argentina lays claim to the previous colonial territories and in 1820 sends a frigate to take possession of the Falklands. In 1826, Louis Vernet of French origin establishes himself and a number of colonists at Puerto Soledad to develop fishing, farming and trade and, as Governor from 1828, attempts to control the widespread sealing. Waking up to developments, Britain's Consul General in Buenos Aires protests in 1829 against the appointment of a governor and reasserts claims to sovereignty.

In 1831, after arresting American sealers accused of poaching, Vernet sails in one of them for Buenos Aires where the captain is to stand trial. In reprisal, the US warship *Lexington* arrives off Puerto Soledad, destroys the fortifications, arrests some of the people and declares the islands free of government before sailing away. Argentina and the United States argue furiously over each other's high-handed behaviour and the following year a new governor is appointed but then murdered by rebellious colonists. As Argentine forces attempt to restore order, Royal Navy warships *Clio* and *Tyne*, under the command of Capt Onslow, arrive in early 1833, force them to leave and claim the Falklands for Britain. Argentina protests strongly, but the British Government maintains that all rights to sovereignty were retained during the negotiations with Spain in 1770.

Britain later starts to settle the islands and formally declares a colonial administration in 1842, although Argentina continues to press her claim and, from the 1960s onwards, with increasing vigour. By this time, Britain's right to ownership rests mainly on her peaceful and continuous possession over a long period of time. When serious negotiations begin, they become dominated by the islanders' desire to remain British.

After a period of Argentine lobbying, the United Nations passes Resolution 2065 in 1965 specifying the Falklands/*Malvinas* as a colonial problem and calling on Britain and Argentina to find a peaceful solution. Talks continue on and off for the next 17 years under both British Labour and Conservative Governments. Britain initially appears flexible over the question of sovereignty and by 1971 the Argentines are agreeing to concentrate on economic development and support. But thereafter, the position of both sides hardens. The Argentines will accept nothing less than full sovereignty and in late 1980 the islanders reject the one remaining solution of lease-back for a fixed period. Argentina sets up a scientific base on Southern Thule in the South Sandwich Islands in 1976 and stays put, and in 1982 her forces find themselves about to land on South Georgia and to invade and hold the Falkland Islands themselves.

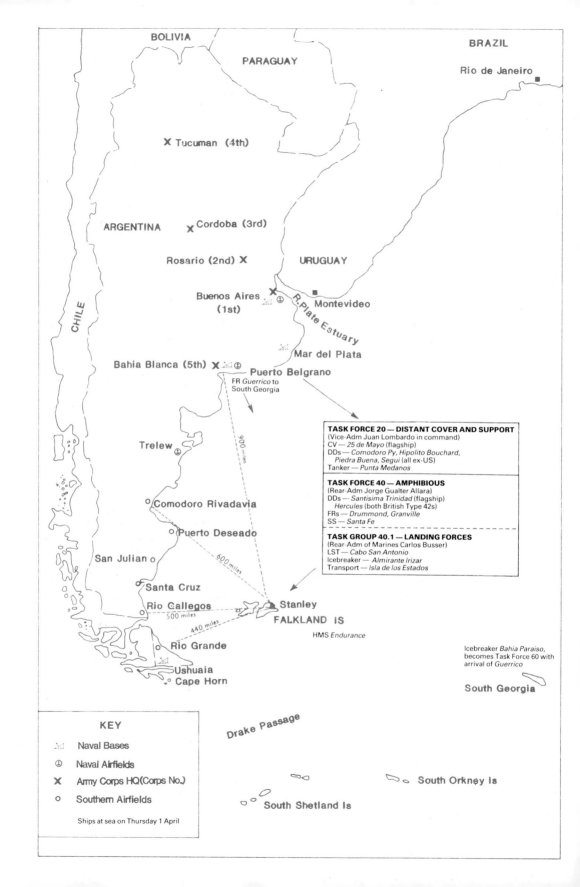

BOLIVIA

PARAGUAY

BRAZIL

Rio de Janeiro

X Tucuman (4th)

ARGENTINA   **X** Cordoba (3rd)

Rosario (2nd) **X**   URUGUAY

Buenos Aires **X**
(1st)   ◉   ■ Montevideo

R. Plate Estuary

⊠ Mar del Plata

Bahia Blanca (5th) **X** ⊠ ◉
Puerto Belgrano

FR *Guerrico* to
South Georgia

Trelew ◉

900 miles

Comodoro Rivadavia ○

Puerto Deseado ○

600 miles

San Julian ○

Santa Cruz ○

Rio Gallegos ○   500 miles   ⊠ ● Stanley
FALKLAND IS

440 miles

Rio Grande ○   HMS *Endurance*

Ushuaia
Cape Horn ○

CHILE

Drake Passage

TASK FORCE 20 — DISTANT COVER AND SUPPORT
(Vice-Adm Juan Lombardo in command)
CV — *25 de Mayo* (flagship)
DDs — *Comodoro Py, Hipolito Bouchard,
    Piedra Buena, Segui* (all ex-US)
Tanker — *Punta Medanos*

TASK FORCE 40 — AMPHIBIOUS
(Rear-Adm Jorge Gualter Allara)
DDs — *Santisima Trinidad* (flagship)
    Hercules (both British Type 42s)
FRs — *Drummond, Granville*
SS — *Santa Fe*

TASK GROUP 40.1 — LANDING FORCES
(Rear-Adm of Marines Carlos Busser)
LST — *Cabo San Antonio*
Icebreaker — *Almirante Irizar*
Transport — *Isla de los Estados*

Icebreaker *Bahia Paraiso*,
becomes Task Force 60 with
arrival of *Guerrico*

South Georgia

○ ○ South Orkney Is

○ ○ South Shetland Is

KEY

⊠ Naval Bases

◉ Naval Airfields

X Army Corps HQ (Corps No.)

○ Southern Airfields

Ships at sea on Thursday 1 April

MAP 3

The Armed Forces of Argentina

As Argentina goes to war for the first time since the Paraguayan War of 1865-70, the Navy and Marines will spearhead the invasion on Friday 2 April 1982, the Army will garrison and finally lose the Falklands, and the Air Force, which could possibly have won the coming Anglo-Argentine war, gets ready to establish a presence there.

Navy (*Armada Republica Argentina*)

With a strength of 30,000 officers and men, including 12,000 conscripts, the Navy is a mix of World War 2 and modern ships. Main units in commission are four patrol submarines (*Santa Fe* lost), one light fleet carrier and the old cruiser *General Belgrano* (sunk), six destroyers and three frigates (all Exocet-armed), amphibious warfare craft, eight fleet tankers and transports, and two icebreakers or polar vessels, a large proportion of which are at sea on the eve of invasion. Under the overall command of Vice-Adm Juan Lombardo, most have sailed by Friday 26 March from the main base of Puerto Belgrano. Distant support and cover is provided by Task Force (TF) 20, while the landings will take place from the ships of amphibious Task Force 40. Before being recalled to join TF40, frigates *Drummond* and *Granville* had earlier left for South Georgia, while fleet transport *Bahia Buen Suceso* has already returned to Argentina from there.

Marine Corps (*Infanteria de Marina*)

The Navy also includes a 6,000 strong Marine Corps organised into two Fleet Marine forces, each with two infantry battalions and supporting arms. It is from these, that the assault commandos or *Buzos Tactico* and the landing force of some 800 men of the 2nd Marine Infantry Battalion are drawn. Another battalion is later deployed near Stanley.

Naval Aviation Command (*Comando Aviacion Naval Argentina*) (CANA)

Assets at the disposal of this force include four operational Super Etendard strike fighters and their air-launched version of Exocet, 10 Skyhawk A-4Q attack bombers, 10 Aermacchi MB-339s and 15 Mentor T-34Cs in the light attack role, Tracker anti-submarine aircraft and Lynx, Alouette and Sea King helicopters. The aircraft carrier *25 de Mayo* first sails with Skyhawks and Trackers embarked, but these are later landed, and together with the Super Etendards, moved to southern airfields. Flying from there, three of the Skyhawks will be lost in combat, and of the six MB-339s and four Mentors flown to the Falklands and operated from Stanley or Pebble Island, only one MB-339 survives.

Argentine Coastguard (*Prefectura Naval Argentina*) (PNA)

The Argentinian Coastguard operates its own aircraft and over 40 patrol vessels. The one Puma helicopter, two Skyvan light aircraft and two patrol craft transferred to the Falklands are also lost.

Army (*Ejercito*)

Although a professional army in South American terms, a weakness in comparison with the British land forces is the predominence of one-year conscripts in the ranks. Total strength is 60,000 including 20,000 regular officers and NCOs. Apparently organised into five corps, the main operational unit is the brigade of which there are around two armoured, one mechanised, four infantry, three mountain, one jungle and one airmobile — each consisting of three battalions plus one artillery and one engineer battalion. In addition there are five anti-aircraft battalions and one aviation battalion. On the Falklands the Army (with the Marines) will employ Panhard armoured cars, 105mm and 155mm artillery, 20mm, 30mm and 35mm AA guns, and Roland, Tigercat and Blowpipe SAMs.

With the islands secured by the Marines, a relatively small Army garrison will be air-lifted into Stanley, but once the British Task Force is on its way, army strength will build-up to over 10,000 troops. Of these, a reinforced brigade of 8,000 men from five regiments together with artillery, AA, armoured car and engineer units will stay in the Stanley area. Nearly 1,000 infantry with AA and some artillery will go to Goose Green. Over on West Falkland, Port Howard and Fox Bay will each receive 800 men of an infantry regiment plus engineer support. Many will be killed or wounded and the rest captured with all their surviving equipment.

Army Aviation Command (*Comando de Aviacion del Ejercito*)

The Army Aviation Command is equipped with aircraft and a large variety of helicopters, many of which are deployed to the Falklands and all lost — two Chinook CH-47s, five Puma SA330Ls, three Agusta A-109As and nine Iroquois UH-1Hs.

Argentine Air Force (*Fuerza Aerea Argentina*) (FAA)

According to best estimates, the FAA starts the war with 45 Skyhawk A-4B and A-4C attack bombers, 37 Dagger and 17 Mirage fighter and attack aircraft, 10 Canberra light bombers, more than 35 Argentine-designed and built Pucara close support aircraft, nine Hercules C-130 transports and tankers, Learjets, Boeing 707s and a number of other aircraft and helicopters. Not all are operational.

As soon as the assault forces land, the Hercules start a job they continue to the very end — flying into Stanley the men and material vital to the Argentine defence of the Falklands. Eventually transferred to the islands are 24 Pucaras at Stanley, Goose Green or Pebble Island, and two Bell 212 and two Chinook helicopters. All but the Chinooks will be lost. As the British Task Force heads south, the FAA transfers many of its aircraft to southern bases and by the time the war is over has lost 32 Daggers, Mirages and Skyhawks, two Canberras, a Hercules, a Learjet and one more Pucara. Added to the Navy, Coast Guard and Army casualties, Argentina will lose a total of 100 aircraft and helicopters.

MAP 4

South Georgia — Incident and Invasion

Argentina has long claimed South Georgia not so much in its own right, but as a dependency of the Falklands. The opportunity to exercise this claim is provided by Argentine businessman Constantino Davidoff, who contracts with the Scottish company of Christian Salvesen to clear away scrap whaling material littering parts of the island. Having agreed arrangements with the British Embassy in Buenos Aires, Davidoff charters the fleet transport *Bahia Buen Suceso* to carry him and his workmen to South Georgia, and although there is no conclusive evidence the Argentine Government has deliberately planned what follows, the ship's illegal entry leads to invasion. She arrives at Leith on Friday 19 March and starts operations without observing the usual formalities of reporting first to the island's Magistrate, the Base Commander of the British Antarctic Survey (BAS) located at King Edward Point near Grytviken.

When a BAS team reaches Leith that Friday to find *Bahia Buen Suceso* in the harbour and workmen ashore with the Argentine flag flying, the incident is reported to Governor Hunt in Stanley, 900 miles away, who gives orders to the Magistrate that the Argentines must obtain proper authorisation. This they refuse to do. Meanwhile ice patrol ship HMS *Endurance* sails into Stanley on passage back to Britain and at the end of what is supposed to be her last season in the Antarctic.

Two days later, early on Sunday 21 March and at the start of nearly two week's diplomatic efforts to resolve the incursion, HMS *Endurance*, on orders from Fleet HQ at Northwood, near London, sails for South Georgia. In addition to her own complement of 13 Royal Marines she takes on board nine more from the small Falklands garrison of Naval Party 8901. That same day, BAS men set up an observation post overlooking Leith and see the Argentine transport sail away leaving behind

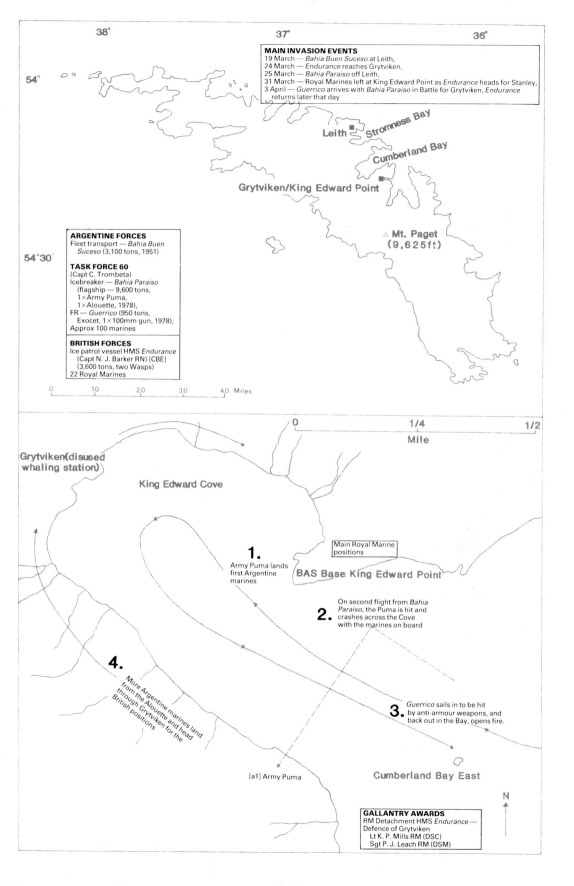

38°   37°   36°

54°

MAIN INVASION EVENTS
19 March — *Bahia Buen Suceso* at Leith,
24 March — *Endurance* reaches Grytviken,
25 March — *Bahia Paraiso* off Leith,
31 March — Royal Marines left at King Edward Point as *Endurance* heads for Stanley,
3 April — *Guerrico* arrives with *Bahia Paraiso* in Battle for Grytviken, *Endurance* returns later that day

Leith ■ Stromness Bay
Cumberland Bay
Grytviken/King Edward Point

△ Mt. Paget
(9,625ft)

54°30'

ARGENTINE FORCES
Fleet transport — *Bahia Buen Suceso* (3,100 tons, 1951)

TASK FORCE 60
(Capt C. Trombeta)
Icebreaker — *Bahia Paraiso* (flagship — 9,600 tons, 1×Army Puma, 1×Alouette, 1978),
FR — *Guerrico* (950 tons, Exocet, 1×100mm gun, 1978),
Approx 100 marines

BRITISH FORCES
Ice patrol vessel HMS *Endurance* (Capt N. J. Barker RN) [CBE] (3,600 tons, two Wasps)
22 Royal Marines

0   10   20   30   40 Miles

0   1/4   1/2
Mile

Grytviken(disused whaling station)

King Edward Cove

1.
Army Puma lands first Argentine marines

Main Royal Marine positions

BAS Base King Edward Point

2.
On second flight from *Bahia Paraiso*, the Puma is hit and crashes across the Cove with the marines on board

4.
More Argentine marines land from the Alouette and head through Grytviken for the British positions

3.
Guerrico sails in to be hit by anti-armour weapons, and back out in the Bay, opens fire.

[a1] Army Puma

Cumberland Bay East

N

GALLANTRY AWARDS
RM Detachment HMS *Endurance* — Defence of Grytviken
Lt K. P. Mills RM (DSC)
Sgt P. J. Leach RM (DSM)

some of the civilian workers. HMS *Endurance* reaches Grytviken on Wednesday 23 March at the start of a week of coastal patrols and replaces the BAS men above Leith with Marines flown in by Wasp helicopter.

As negotiations continue between London and Buenos Aires HMS *Endurance* takes no steps to remove the scrap men, but the Argentines have already ordered icebreaker *Bahia Paraiso* to sail to protect them, and by Thursday 25 March, she has arrived at Leith. Approximately 100 marines go ashore under the command of Lt-Cdr Alfredo Astiz and the icebreaker uses her Alouette helicopter to shadow HMS *Endurance* for the next few days.

Almost a week later, on Wednesday 31 March, as the Falkland's invasion threatens, HMS *Endurance* lands her heavily-armed Royal Marine detachment at King Edward Point to prepare defences and then, unnoticed by *Bahia Paraiso*, slips out of Cumberland Bay that evening and heads for Stanley. Two days later, on news of the town's capture, HMS *Endurance* reverses course, by which time the Argentinian frigate *Guerrico* has sailed from Argentina to join *Bahia Paraiso* as the hastily assembled TF60. The other two Argentinian frigates — *Drummond* and *Granville* — previously on their way to support *Bahia Paraiso* — play no part in the events that follow.

The Battle for Grytviken, Saturday 3 April

That morning the Argentinian frigate *Guerrico* and the icebreaker *Bahia Paraiso*, under the command of Capt Trombeta and by now carrying many of the marines re-embarked from Leith, arrive off Grytviken. The Magistrate is called upon to surrender by radio, but he passes authority for the island to Lt Mills of the Royal Marines, and at mid-day, with the Alouette going ahead to reconnoitre, *Guerrico* lying out in the Bay and the Puma about to land the first 20 troops near King Edward Point, battle commences.

As the troop-carrying Puma makes her second trip in from *Bahia Paraiso* she is hit by small arms fire and badly damaged just off the Point with two marines killed. Barely managing to lift off, she makes it to the other side of King Edward Cove before crashing [a1]. The Alouette is also hit, but only lightly damaged and continues to bring more marines across from the base. Now *Guerrico* sails in to support the landings and opens fire on the British positions, but it is her turn to be hit by hundreds of rounds of small arms fire as well as 66mm LAW and 84mm Carl Gustav anti-tank weapons before heading back out into the Bay.

From there, she uses her 100mm gun against Lt Mills' men as the Argentine marines move around the Cove, through the whaling station at Grytviken and close in. Trapped, with one man wounded and having convincingly defended British sovereignty, he decides to surrender. All 22 Royal Marines as well as the 13 civilians at Grytviken are taken prisoner. HMS *Endurance* arrives too late the same day to take part in the action, but from extreme range flies in a Wasp helicopter. Landing across Cumberland Bay from Grytviken, its crew can only observe the Argentines in possession of the scientific base. HMS *Endurance* stays on station for two more days, before sailing north early on Monday 5 April to replenish and meet the first ships of the British Task Force.

The Royal Marines return in triumph to Britain on 20 April by way of Montevideo, and just six days later, the Argentine forces at Grytviken and Leith are themselves in British hands.

MAP 5

Invasion of the Falklands, Operation 'Rosario'

2 April 1982

The build-up to invasion starts when Britain protests about the landing on South Georgia. With talks on the future of the Falklands stalled, Argentina reacts strongly and by 26 March, two frigates are on their way south and more ships have put to sea — ostensibly for exercises with the Uruguayan Navy. But it seems that only now is the final decision taken to invade and they head for Stanley although bad weather delays their arrival. By Wednesday 31 March, British intelligence has to assume landings are imminent. Governor Hunt is warned, and the following evening he announces over the radio that an invasion is expected early on Friday 2 April.

Before the broadcast takes place, the defence of Stanley is already being put in hand by the small Falklands garrison of Naval Party 8901. Usually consisting of just 40 Royal Marines, the remaining members of the 1981/82 Detachment (others have left with HMS *Endurance*), have only been relieved that day by Maj M. J. Norman (MID) RM and his 1982/83 Detachment. Assuming that the main landing will be made near the airfield and followed by an advance on Stanley, he deploys his 70 men accordingly and positions four delaying sections on the Stanley road ready to fall back on the main HQ at Government House. By the early hours of Friday, they are mostly in position and the small coaster *Forrest* is out in Port William on radar watch.

Landings around Stanley, Friday 2 April

The plan appears to be for the *Buzo Tactico* to attack both the Royal Marine barracks at Moody Brook and Government House to force a surrender, supported if necessary by men of the 2nd Marine Infantry Battalion landed from ships of Task Group 40.1. Once the airfield is in Argentine hands, the Army garrison will then fly in. The first landings may have been before midnight with a *Buzo Tactico* party going ashore from the destroyer *Santisima Trinidad* to secure Mullet Creek, followed early on Friday morning by a smaller group from the

submarine *Santa Fe* to check out the main landing beach north of Stanley.

Reports now start reaching the defenders about the presence of Argentine ships, and at 04.30hrs, more *Buzo Tactico* land at Mullet Creek — apparently from Sea King helicopters embarked on the icebreaker *Almirante Irizar*. Most of them head for the by now empty barracks at Moody Brook while the rest pass quietly below Sapper Hill on their way to Government House. As they approach their objectives the destroyers and frigates of TF40 take up support and escort positions and the LST heads in for the unguarded beach at York Bay.

From 06.00hrs the main attacks and supporting landings get underway. The larger body of *Buzo Tactico* hit Moody Brook and then head east for Government House which by then is under fire from the smaller group. Around 06.30hrs, the first of some 20 LVTP-7 Amtraks with 20 marines each inside are landing from *Cabo San Antonio* and by 06.45hrs more troops are coming into the airfield by helicopter. As the off-balanced Royal Marine defenders fall back on Government House, one of the sections on the Stanley road stops an Amtrak with anti-armour weapons.

At daybreak, with Government House surrounded, under sniper fire and the Amtraks approaching, Governor Hunt attempts to negotiate. Faced with the overwhelming forces at Adm Busser's disposal, he orders the Marines to lay down their arms, which they do at 09.30hrs without having suffered any casualties. The Argentines only admit to one dead and others wounded. That evening, Governor and Mrs Hunt and most of the Royal Marines and the few men from HMS *Endurance* are flown out. Maj Norman and his men are back in Stanley 76 days later with J Coy, 42 Cdo RM.

Before the surrender, the Army garrison, mainly from the 25th Infantry Regt is flying in. Another early arrival by Hercules is an AN/TPS-43F surveillance radar which becomes the centre of Argentina's command, control

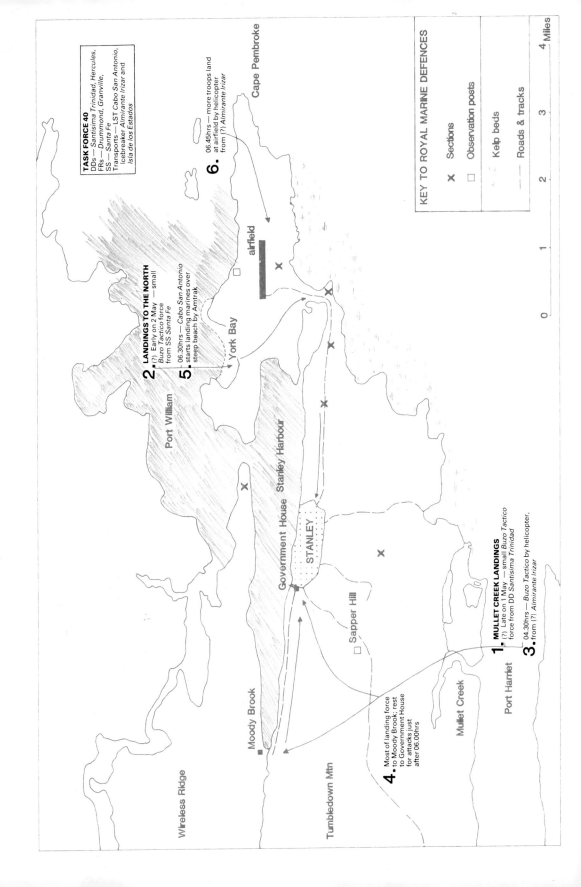

TASK FORCE 40
DDs — *Santisima Trinidad, Hercules,*
FRs — *Drummond, Granville,*
SS — *Santa Fe*
Transports — LST *Cabo San Antonio,*
Icebreaker *Almirante Irizar* and
Isla de los Estados

2. LANDINGS TO THE NORTH
(?) Early on 2 May — small
Buzo Tactico force
from SS *Santa Fe*

5. 06.30hrs — *Cabo San Antonio*
starts landing marines over
steep beach by Amtrak

6. 06.45hrs — more troops land
at airfield by helicopter
from (?) *Almirante Irizar*

airfield

Cape Pembroke

York Bay

Port William

Stanley Harbour

Government House

STANLEY

Sapper Hill

Moody Brook

Wireless Ridge

Tumbledown Mtn

Mullet Creek

Port Harriet

1. MULLET CREEK LANDINGS
(?) Late on 1 May — small *Buzo Tactico*
force from DD *Santisima Trinidad*

3. 04.30hrs — *Buzo Tactico* by helicopter,
from (?) *Almirante Irizar*

4. Most of landing force
to Moody Brook; rest
to Government House
for attacks just
after 06.00hrs

KEY TO ROYAL MARINE DEFENCES

✕   Sections
☐   Observation posts
     Kelp beds
- - - Roads & tracks

0   1   2   3   4 Miles

and communications structure at Stanley right through until the end of the war. Now, Lt-Gen Osvaldo Garcia takes over as Commander, Malvinas Operational Theatre, but as Britain's military response becomes clearer, the command is relocated to Argentina to cover the South Atlantic as a whole. Then on Wednesday 7 April, Maj-Gen Mario Menendez is appointed Commander-in-Chief as well as Military Governor, the same day Britain announces a 200 nautical mile maritime exclusion zone (MEZ) around the Falklands to take effect from 12 April.

By Monday 5 April following the landings, the invading warships are returning to port, although some of the naval transports are used in the build-up, and after the MEZ comes into force the blockade is run by fleet transport *Bahia Buen Suceso* and merchantmen *Formosa* (12,800grt) and *Rio Carcarana* (8,500grt). Most of the aircraft destined to be lost on the islands fly over although some of the helicopters are air-lifted, and Coast Guard patrol craft *Islas Malvinas* and *Rio Iguaza* reach Stanley for local duties. The occupying forces are soon imposing their rules and regulations on the Islanders, many of whom get out of Stanley to the 'camp'. Coasters *Forrest* (144grt) and *Monsunen* (230grt) are requisitioned together with a number of civil aircraft, some of which are lost in the subsequent bombardments. By the end of the month, as the Task Force draws near, air raid precautions are introduced and a curfew and black-out is in force. A number of people are rounded up, some deported, and others confined, sometimes, as at Goose Green, in poor conditions.

MAP 6

Diplomatic Events to Early May

In London, Mrs Thatcher directs Britain's diplomatic and economic response to events. Across the Atlantic, President Reagan tries to stay neutral and agrees to Secretary Haig starting his shuttle diplomacy. The United Nations is soon brought into the act by the British ambassador there, and very much to Britain's advantage, whilst equally unsuccessful in their attempts to gain support is the junta in Buenos Aires. Amongst the main politicians and diplomats taking part are:

London

Prime Minister Margaret Thatcher and inner cabinet, including Foreign Secretary Francis Pym (successor to Lord Carrington), Secretary of State for Defence John Nott, Home Secretary William Whitelaw and Conservative Party Chairman Cecil Parkinson.

Washington D.C.

President Ronald Reagan, Secretary of State Alexander Haig, British Ambassador Sir Nicholas Henderson, Argentine Ambassador Snr Esteban Takacs.

Buenos Aires

Gen Galtieri, Brig-Gen Lami Dozo, Adm Anaya and Foreign Minister Snr Nicanor Costa Mendez.

United Nations, New York

Secretary General Snr Javier Perez de Cuellar, British Ambassador Sir Anthony Parsons, Argentine Ambassadors Senors Eduardo Roca and (later) Enrique Ros.

Britain has reacted to developments in South Georgia through talks in London and Buenos Aires, but as the invasion looms, her international diplomacy moves into top gear. Within days, a highly successful campaign gains the support of the United Nations, the EEC, NATO and the Commonwealth. In contrast Argentina fails even to win over the Organisation of American States (OAS). The first steps are taken on Wednesday 31 March when Sir Nicholas Henderson briefs Secretary Haig in Washington and President Reagan is called on by Mrs Thatcher to warn off President Galtieri, but in this he is unsuccessful. Over the

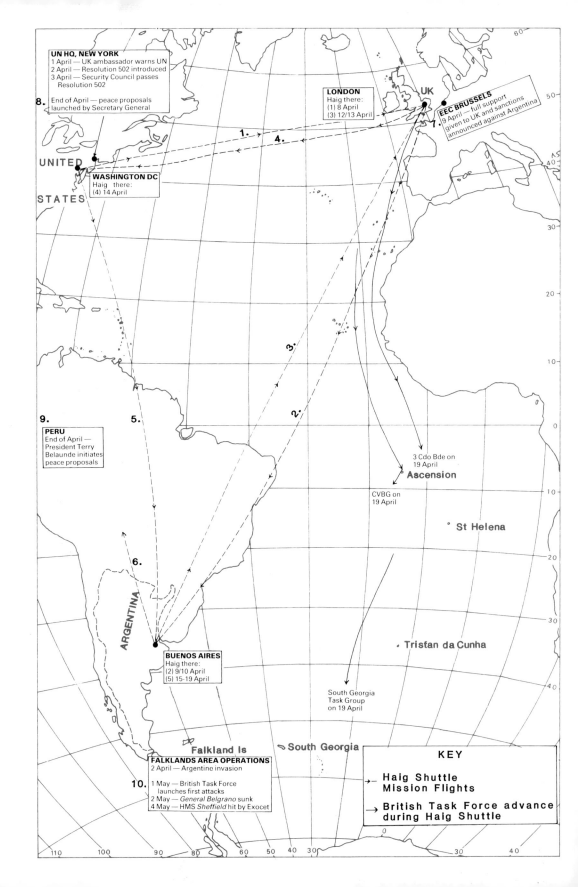

UN HQ, NEW YORK
1 April — UK ambassador warns UN
2 April — Resolution 502 introduced
3 April — Security Council passes
Resolution 502

8. End of April — peace proposals
launched by Secretary General

LONDON
Haig there:
(1) 8 April
(3) 12/13 April

EEC BRUSSELS
9 April — full support
given to UK and sanctions
announced against Argentina

7.

1.

4.

UNITED

STATES

WASHINGTON DC
Haig there:
(4) 14 April

UK

3.

2.

3 Cdo Bde on
19 April
↘ Ascension

CVBG on
19 April

° St Helena

9.

PERU
End of April —
President Terry
Belaunde initiates
peace proposals

5.

6.

ARGENTINA

• Tristan da Cunha

South Georgia
Task Group
on 19 April

BUENOS AIRES
Haig there:
(2) 9/10 April
(5) 15-19 April

Falkland Is

⬲ South Georgia

FALKLANDS AREA OPERATIONS
2 April — Argentine invasion

10. 1 May — British Task Force
launches first attacks
2 May — *General Belgrano* sunk
4 May — HMS *Sheffield* hit by Exocet

KEY

⇢ **Haig Shuttle
Mission Flights**

→ **British Task Force advance
during Haig Shuttle**

next four weeks, America's attempts to be even-handed are not appreciated by Mrs Thatcher, although in US terms, having to choose between Latin American friend and main European ally is no easy matter.

On the evening of Thursday 1 April, before the invasion, Sir Anthony Parsons alerts the United Nations and addresses the 15-member Security Council. With confirmation next day that the invaders are ashore, Resolution 502 is formally introduced. Drafted by Britain, it calls for an end to hostilities, the immediate withdrawal of Argentine forces and for both sides to seek a diplomatic solution. Voting is delayed until Saturday to allow Snr Costa Mendez to reach New York, but to no avail. That evening the vote takes place in Britain's favour with only Panama voting against and Russia abstaining along with Poland, China and Spain. Sir Anthony Parsons has laid the main plank of Britain's diplomatic position over the coming weeks.

Concerned about the prospect of war, Secretary Haig and his team fly to London late on Wednesday 7 April at the start of their two-week, 30,000-mile shuttle mission. The basis of this and all later peace plans are threefold — both sides' forces to withdraw from the Falklands, an interim administration to be set up, and a long-term settlement to be negotiated. In all that follows, Argentina will not move far from its demand for total sovereignty, and Britain, with Resolution 502 behind her, will insist on Argentine withdrawal and (implicitly) a return to the status quo. Mr Haig visits both London and Buenos Aires twice in his attempt to bring about a peaceful settlement, but by 19 April has to accept there is little chance of success.

Before then, on Good Friday 9 April, and after lobbying both by diplomats in Brussels and directly by Mrs Thatcher, the EEC gives full support to Britain and announces economic sanctions against Argentina at least until 17 May. These include a total ban on imports and arms sales.

Thus, only a week after invasion, Britain has wide support, the lead elements of the Task Force are on their way and Gen Galtieri must realise he has totally misjudged both Britain's resolve and world opinion, including that of the Americas. On Monday 26 April, some days after Argentina's request, foreign ministers of the OAS meet in Washington DC. In a vote two days later, they accept Argentine sovereignty over the Falklands and call on Britain to cease hostilities. But in what amounts to a diplomatic defeat for the junta, they endorse Resolution 502.

By the last day of April, President Reagan has come to accept there is little chance of a settlement and declares American support for Britain. He offers military aid and announces sanctions against Argentina. Mr Pym now returns to Washington as an ally, but still committed to the search for peace, and, as he does, proposals are independently launched in the UN and by Peru. Both are similar, but as events in the South Atlantic escalate from 1 May and Britain's military options reduce in number with the onset of winter, neither have much chance of success. The torpedoing of the cruiser *General Belgrano* loses Britain much of her support, especially in the EEC, and as the Task Force is by now bombarding the Falklands, the last chances for peace have realistically gone.

But this is a long month in the making and follows Britain's rapid military response. On Monday 29 March orders are given for a fleet auxiliary to head south to support HMS *Endurance* and for three nuclear submarines to be prepared to follow. Two days later, British intelligence confirms the likelihood of invasion and next day, on Thursday 1 April, the decision is taken to send a Task Force and the first submarine leaves.

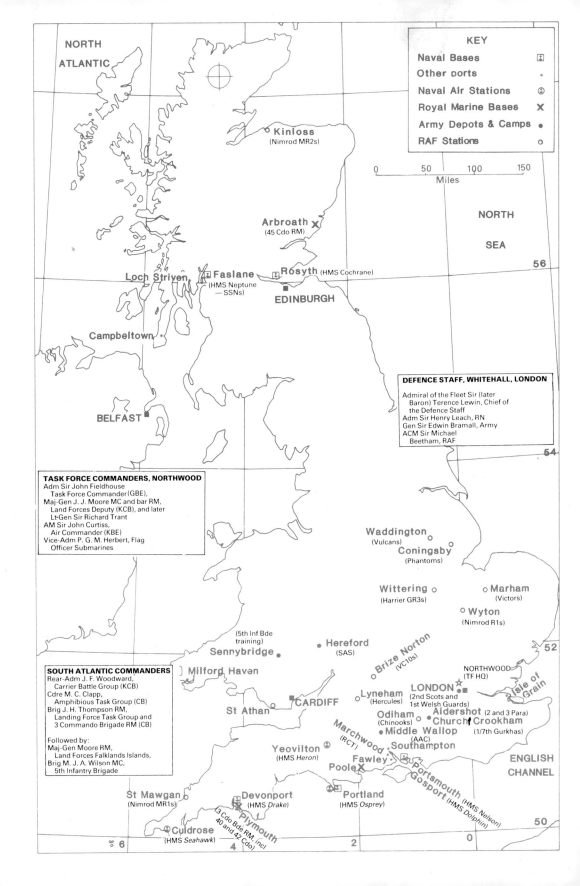

NORTH
ATLANTIC

NORTH

SEA

KEY

Naval Bases	⬇
Other ports	•
Naval Air Stations	☺
Royal Marine Bases	X
Army Depots & Camps	▪
RAF Stations	○

0   50   100   150
Miles

Kinloss
(Nimrod MR2s)

Arbroath X
(45 Cdo RM)

56

Loch Striven   Faslane   Rosyth (HMS Cochrane)
(HMS Neptune
— SSNs)
EDINBURGH

Campbeltown

BELFAST

DEFENCE STAFF, WHITEHALL, LONDON

Admiral of the Fleet Sir (later
 Baron) Terence Lewin, Chief of
 the Defence Staff
Adm Sir Henry Leach, RN
Gen Sir Edwin Bramall, Army
ACM Sir Michael
 Beetham, RAF

54

TASK FORCE COMMANDERS, NORTHWOOD
Adm Sir John Fieldhouse
 Task Force Commander (GBE),
Maj-Gen J. J. Moore MC and bar RM,
 Land Forces Deputy (KCB), and later
 Lt-Gen Sir Richard Trant
AM Sir John Curtiss,
 Air Commander (KBE)
Vice-Adm P. G. M. Herbert, Flag
 Officer Submarines

Waddington
(Vulcans)
Coningsby
(Phantoms)

Wittering ○   ○ Marham
(Harrier GR3s)   (Victors)
○ Wyton
(Nimrod R1s)

(5th Inf Bde
training)
Sennybridge •   Hereford
(SAS)

52

Milford Haven

Brize Norton
(VC10s)

NORTHWOOD
(TF HQ)

SOUTH ATLANTIC COMMANDERS
Rear-Adm J. F. Woodward,
 Carrier Battle Group (KCB)
Cdre M. C. Clapp,
 Amphibious Task Group (CB)
Brig J. H. Thompson RM,
 Landing Force Task Group and
 3 Commando Brigade RM (CB)

Followed by:
Maj-Gen Moore RM,
 Land Forces Falklands Islands,
Brig M. J. A. Wilson MC,
 5th Infantry Brigade

CARDIFF

St Athan

Lyneham ○   LONDON ☆
(Hercules)   (2nd Scots and
 1st Welsh Guards)

Odiham   Aldershot (2 and 3 Para)
(Chinooks) ○ Church Crookham
 Middle Wallop (1/7th Gurkhas)
 (AAC)

Isle of Grain

Yeovilton ☺
(HMS *Heron*)

Marchwood
(RCT)
Southampton

Fawley •
Poole X

Portsmouth (HMS *Nelson*)
Gosport (HMS *Dolphin*)

ENGLISH

CHANNEL

St Mawgan ○
(Nimrod MR1s)

Devonport
(HMS *Drake*)

Portland
(HMS *Osprey*)

50

Plymouth
(3 Cdo Bde RM, incl
40 and 42 Cdo)

Culdrose ☺
(HMS *Seahawk*)

6   4   2   0

MAP 7

The Build-Up of the British Task Force

Once the decision is taken to launch Operation 'Corporate' and dispute the Argentine invasion by force if necessary, Britain's military power is rapidly mobilised. Commanders are nominated and from bases throughout the country, ships and aircraft are readied and despatched to transport and support a limited number of professional marines, paras and guardsmen. Fighting as infantrymen, they will retake the Falklands the hard way, and at the end of an 8,000-mile-long logistical nightmare and lengthy chain of command. Directly responsible to the British Cabinet for all military aspects is the Defence Staff at Whitehall not far from Downing Street with its Chief, Admiral of the Fleet Sir Terence Lewin and the other service heads. Working out of Northwood, Middlesex, are the Task Force Commanders led by the Commander-in-Chief Fleet, Admiral Sir John Fieldhouse, who in turn must control events in the South Atlantic through the commanders on the spot.

Taking part in this vast undertaking are nearly 30,000 men and a few women, a large proportion of Britain's Royal Navy and Marines, fleet auxiliaries and merchantmen, aircraft and helicopter squadrons, plus five Army battalions and supporting arms. Up to the final Argentine surrender, each of the ships, aircraft squadrons and main military units, as they enter the South Atlantic for the **first** time in the campaign, can now be introduced.

Submarines reaching the Falklands Area, early April to May:

Nuclear submarines *Spartan, Splendid, Conqueror, Courageous* (?), *Valiant* and conventionally powered *Onyx*, possibly with some SBS.

RAF Squadrons reaching or deploying to Ascension, early April to May:

VC10 transports of No 10 Sqn, Hercules transports of Nos 24, 30, 47 and 70 Sqns, Nimrod maritime reconnaissance aircraft of Nos 42(TB), 51(?), 120, 201 and 206 Sqns, Victor tankers of Nos 55 and 57 Sqns, Vulcan bombers of Nos 44, 50 and 101 Sqns, Harrier GR3 attack aircraft of No 1(F) Sqn, Chinook helicopters of No 18 Sqn and a Sea King of No 202 Sqn, Phantom fighters of No 29(F) Sqn, and units of the RAF Regiment.

South Georgia recaptured on 25 April in Operation 'Paraquet':

Naval forces — HM destroyer *Antrim*, frigates *Brilliant, Plymouth*, ice patrol ship *Endurance*, RFA's *Tidespring* and (earlier) *Brambleleaf* and *Fort Austin*.

Land forces — M Coy 42 Cdo RM, SBS RM and D Sqn 22 SAS.

Carrier Battle Group starts attacks on Falklands, 1 May:

Naval forces — HM carriers *Hermes, Invincible*, destroyers *Glamorgan, Coventry, Glasgow, Sheffield*, frigates *Broadsword, Alacrity, Arrow, Yarmouth* and RFAs *Olmeda* and *Resource*. Joined later in May by destroyer *Exeter*, frigate *Ambuscade* and RFA *Regent*.

Carrier aircraft — Sea Harriers of Nos 800 and 801 NAS, anti-submarine and assault Sea King helicopters of Nos 820, 826 and 846 NAS, and later, Sea Harriers of No 809 NAS and RAF Harrier GR3s of No 1(F) Sqn.

Land forces — SBS RM, D and G Sqns 22 SAS.

Amphibious Group reaches the TEZ, followed by landings in San Carlos Water on 21 May in Operation 'Sutton':

Naval forces — including HM assault ships *Fearless, Intrepid*, frigates *Ardent, Argonaut* and later *Antelope*, RFAs *Stromness, Tidepool*, LSLs *Sir Galahad, Sir Geraint, Sir Lancelot, Sir Percivale, Sir Tristram* and (later) *Sir Bedivere*, transports *Canberra, Elk, Europic Ferry, Norland*, and aircraft and helicopter support ship *Atlantic Conveyor*.

Land forces — 3 Commando Brigade RM including 40, 42 and 45 Cdos RM, 2 and 3 Para, and No 3 CBAS Gazelle and Scout helicopters.

Other Ships and Helicopter Squadrons supporting the Task Force up to the End of May:

At Ascension — RMAS mooring vessel *Goosander* and tanker *Alvega*; also detached despatch vessel *Dumbarton Castle*.

At Tanker Holding Areas in the South Atlantic and in Tug, Repair and Logistics Area (TRALA) — RFA tankers *Appleleaf*, *Pearleaf* and *Plumleaf* plus tankers *Anco Charger*, *Eburna*, eight British Petroleum ships and water tanker *Fort Toronto*.

Operating in Falklands area — hospital ship *Uganda* and ambulance ships *Hecla*, *Herald* and *Hydra* in Red Cross Box (RCB), repair ship *Stena Seaspread* and tugs *Irishman*, *Salvageman*, *Yorkshireman* in TRALA.

Reaching South Georgia — requisitioned minesweepers *Cordella*, *Farnella*, *Junella*, *Northella* and *Pict*, RFA tanker *Blue Rover*, RMAS tug *Typhoon*, detached despatch vessels *Iris* and *Leeds Castle*, ammo ship *Lycaon* and stores ship *Saxonia*.

Other Helicopters — Sea Kings of Nos 824 and 846 NAS, Wessex of Nos 737, 845 and 848 NAS, Lynx of No 815 and Wasps of No 829 NAS on warships, RFAs and merchantmen, together with one RAF Chinook of No 18 Sqn.

Bristol Group arrives in TEZ, late May:

HM destroyers *Bristol*, *Cardiff*, frigates *Active*, *Avenger*, *Andromeda*, *Minerva*, *Penelope*, RFAs *Bayleaf* and *Olna*.

5th Infantry Brigade reaches South Atlantic late May to join in Advance on Stanley, early June:

Land forces — 5th Infantry Brigade including 2nd Scots and 1st Welsh Guards, 1/7th Gurkha Rifles and Gazelle and Scout helicopters of No 656 Sqn AAC.

Transports — *Queen Elizabeth 2*, *Baltic Ferry* and *Nordic Ferry*.

Other Ships and Helicopter Squadrons arriving to support Task Force up to the Surrender:

RFAs *Engadine* and *Fort Grange*, merchantmen *Atlantic Causeway*, *Balder London*, *Contender Bezant*, *Geestport*, *St Edmund*, *Tor Caledonia* and *Wimpey Seahorse*, Sea Kings of No 825 and Wessex of No 847 NAS.

Losses in major equipment amount to four warships and a landing craft, one fleet auxiliary and one merchantman, and 23 Royal Navy, seven RAF, three Marine and one Army helicopters and aircraft. One thousand of the men taking part are killed or wounded.

MAP 8 — WEEK ONE

Royal Navy Warships and Task Force Departures

29 March-4 April

Before the end of hostilities many of the major warships of the Royal Navy reach the Falkland's area, there to operate in the storms, heavy seas and fogs of the far South Atlantic as winter approaches. Their tasks are numerous and include denying the surrounding seas to the Argentine Navy, providing the only air cover available, landing special forces and carrying out shore bombardment before and after the San Carlos landings, escorting the troop and supply ships and protecting them from attack by aircraft, submarine and surface ship and acting as command, control and communications centres.

Soon in operation are the only four big surface ships left to the Navy — the old carrier HMS *Hermes* (28,700 tons full load), the new but smaller HMS *Invincible* (19,800 tons) and HM assault ships *Fearless* and *Intrepid* (12,100 tons) — and half the force of nuclear fleet

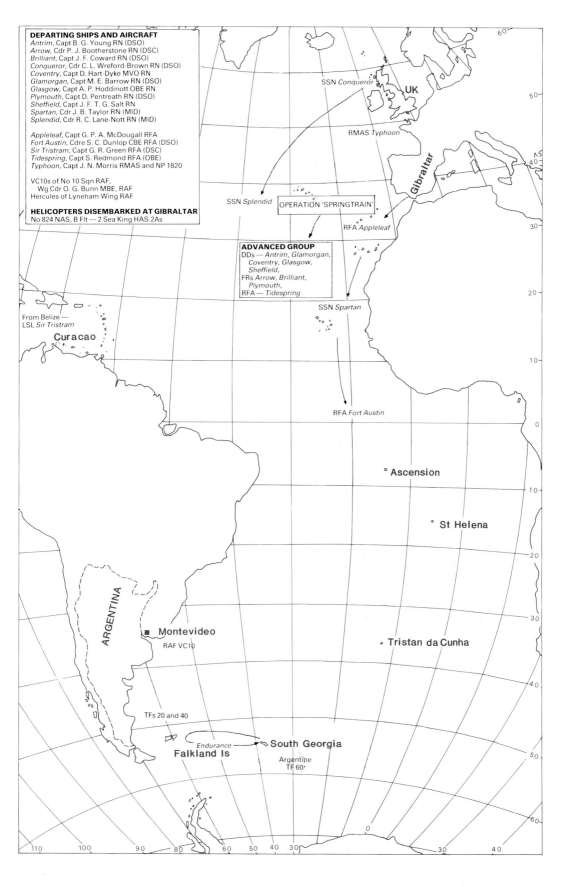

DEPARTING SHIPS AND AIRCRAFT
Antrim, Capt B. G. Young RN (DSO)
Arrow, Cdr P. J. Bootherstone RN (DSC)
Brilliant, Capt J. F. Coward RN (DSO)
Conqueror, Cdr C. L. Wreford-Brown RN (DSO)
Coventry, Capt D. Hart-Dyke MVO RN
Glamorgan, Capt M. E. Barrow RN (DSO)
Glasgow, Capt A. P. Hoddinott OBE RN
Plymouth, Capt D. Pentreath RN (DSO)
Sheffield, Capt J. F. T. G. Salt RN
Spartan, Cdr J. B. Taylor RN (MID)
Splendid, Cdr R. C. Lane-Nott RN (MID)

Appleleaf, Capt G. P. A. McDougall RFA
Fort Austin, Cdre S. C. Dunlop CBE RFA (DSO)
Sir Tristram, Capt G. R. Green RFA (DSC)
Tidespring, Capt S. Redmond RFA (OBE)
Typhoon, Capt J. N. Morris RMAS and NP 1820

VC10s of No 10 Sqn RAF,
 Wg Cdr O. G. Bunn MBE, RAF
Hercules of Lyneham Wing RAF

HELICOPTERS DISEMBARKED AT GIBRALTAR
No 824 NAS, B Flt — 2 Sea King HAS.2As

SSN *Conqueror*

UK

RMAS *Typhoon*

Gibraltar

SSN *Splendid*   OPERATION 'SPRINGTRAIN'

RFA *Appleleaf*

ADVANCED GROUP
DDs — *Antrim, Glamorgan,*
  Coventry, Glasgow,
  Sheffield,
FRs *Arrow, Brilliant,*
  Plymouth,
RFA — *Tidespring*

SSN *Spartan*

From Belize —
LSL *Sir Tristram*

Curacao

RFA *Fort Austin*

° **Ascension**

° **St Helena**

ARGENTINA

■ **Montevideo**
RAF VC10

· **Tristan da Cunha**

TFs 20 and 40

Endurance ——→ **South Georgia**
Falkland Is   Argentine
                    TF 60·

submarines, HMS *Conqueror, Courageous (?), Spartan, Splendid* and *Valiant*, plus the diesel-engined HMS *Onyx*. Even more significantly, most of the modern destroyers and frigates also take part. As they carry a confusing diversity of weapons and suffer heavily (nine out of 23 being sunk or seriously damaged, and others less so by enemy action) their main characteristics are summarised below:

and before the week is out, many are heading south. But even before the question of a Task Force arises, the lone HMS *Endurance* will need replenishment, so on Monday, RFA *Fort Austin* under the command of the Fleet Commodore sails from Gibraltar. She leaves behind her two assigned Sea Kings of No 824 NAS which play an important part supplying other ships passing by.

Once the go ahead is given, the next vessel

Destroyers

	Type 82	'County'	Type 42
Tons (full load):	7,100	6,200	4,100
SSM:	—	Exocet	—
SAM:	Sea Dart	Seaslug/Sea Cat	Sea Dart
ASW:	Ikara	—	STWS
Main guns:	1×4.5in	2×4.5in	1×4.5in
Helicopters:	Can carry Wasp	1×Wessex	1×Lynx
	Bristol	*Antrim* (UXB damage)	*Cardiff*
		Glamorgan (Exocet damage)	*Coventry* (sunk by bombs)
			Exeter
			Glasgow (UXB damage)
			Sheffield (sunk by Exocet)

Frigates

	Type 22	Type 21	'Leander'	'Rothesay'
Tons:	4,000	3,200	3,200	2,800
SSM:	Exocet	Exocet	Exocet	—
SAM:	Sea Wolf	Sea Cat	Sea Wolf* or Sea Cat	Sea Cat
ASW:	STWS	STWS	STWS	Limbo
Main guns:	—	1×4.5in	—	2×4.5in
Helicopters:	2×Lynx	1×Wasp* or Lynx	1×Lynx	1×Wasp
	Brilliant	*Active**	*Andromeda**	*Plymouth* (bomb
	Broadsword	*Alacrity*	*Argonaut* (UXB	damage)
		Ambuscade	damage)	*Yarmouth*
		Antelope (sunk by	*Minerva*	
		bombs)	*Penelope*	
		Ardent (sunk by		
		bombs)		
		Arrow		
		Avenger		

Apart from HMS *Endurance*, other warships taking part up to the surrender are survey ships *Hecla, Herald* and *Hydra* (2,700 tons, Wasp helicopter) as ambulance ships, and fishery protection vessels *Dumbarton Castle* and *Leeds Castle* (1,450 tons) in the role of despatch vessels.

Task Force departures from Monday 29 March

Quite fortuitously, warships of the First Flotilla commanded by Rear-Adm Woodward are in the Gibraltar area for Operation 'Springtrain',

to leave on Thursday 1 April, after loading live torpedoes at Gibraltar, is HM nuclear submarine *Spartan*, tasked to help establish a credible maritime exclusion zone. The following day (Friday) an Advanced Group of ships starts to head for Ascension. Included with Adm Woodward's flagship, the 'County' class destroyer HMS *Antrim* is sister ship HMS *Glamorgan*, Type 42 destroyers HMS *Coventry, Glasgow* and *Sheffield*, HM frigates *Arrow, Brilliant* and *Plymouth* and RFA fleet tanker *Tidespring*. Previously on passage from Curacao to the UK, the RFA support tanker *Appleleaf* also sails from Gibraltar to refuel Task Force ships on the way south.

Two more nuclear submarines follow HMS *Spartan* to the South Atlantic, but this time from Faslane in Scotland. First to go on Thursday 1 April is HMS *Splendid* and within three weeks she is on patrol off the Argentine coast to shadow the carrier *25 de Mayo*. Then on Sunday 4 April HMS *Conqueror* leaves, later to sink the *General Belgrano*. Some sources also show HMS *Courageous* leaving at this time, but if she went, she is more likely to have sailed a month later. Also departing on Sunday is the first of many support ships — RMAS ocean tug *Typhoon* which sails from Portland for Ascension Island before later heading on to South Georgia.

Far to the west of the 'Advanced Group' as it starts south, the RFA LSL *Sir Tristram* sails from Belize in Central America for Ascension Island as the first of the many ships that will later merge as the Amphibious Task Group. The RAF also begins building the vital air-bridge to Ascension Island and beyond when the first C130 Hercules transports fly from Lyneham to Gibraltar. However, beating them to the South Atlantic is a VC10 of No 10 Sqn which leaves on Saturday for Montevideo to pick up Rex Hunt and the men of NP 8901. They arrive back at Brize Norton on Monday.

By the end of the week, the first special forces units must be on their way south or about to leave. Some SBS may have sailed with HMS *Conqueror* from Faslane, but most appear to have flown direct to Ascension Island.

MAP 9 — WEEK TWO

Fleet Air Arm and Task Force Movements

5-11 April

Without fleet carriers and with the Falklands lying less than 500 miles from Argentina, the Royal Navy has to provide the only possible air cover with its few Sea Harrier FRS1 jump-jets, armed with 30mm Aden cannon and the lethal AIM-9L Sidewinder AAM for combat air patrols and cluster bombs for ground attack. Including those transferred from No 899 HQ Training Sqn, 12 are scraped together for No 800 NAS on HMS *Hermes* and eight for No 801 NAS on HMS *Invincible*. Thus 20 aircraft, some piloted by RAF aircrew, will have to defend the Task Force against more than 100 Argentine attackers. Only in mid-May are they reinforced by eight more Sea Harriers of No 809 NAS (plus six RAF GR3s). Just six Royal Navy Harriers are lost by accident or ground fire, and not one in air-to-air combat.

The rest of the Royal Navy's airpower comes from its numerous helicopters, although three

Helicopter	NAS	Embarked from UK/main role
Sea King	No 820	11 HAS5s on HMS *Invincible* for ASW
	No 824	5 HAS2As on RFAs, 2 at Gibraltar
	No 825	Reformed squadron of 10 HAS2As reaching Falklands late May in support role
	No 826	9 HAS5s on HMS *Hermes* for ASW
	No 846	15 HC4 Assault, including 9 initially on HMS *Hermes*, 3 on HMS *Fearless* and 1 on HMS *Intrepid*
Wessex	No 737	2 HAS3s on 'County' class destroyers
	No 845 ⎱	30 HU5s before end of war on RFAs, HMS *Intrepid*,
	No 848 ⎰	carried on *Atlantic Conveyor* (6) and at Ascension (2). No 848 is reformed NAS
	No 847	Reformed Sqn of 24 HU5s reaching Falklands early June in support role
Lynx	No 815	HAS2s on destroyers and frigates
Wasp	No 829	HAS1s on 'Rothesay' class frigates and small ships

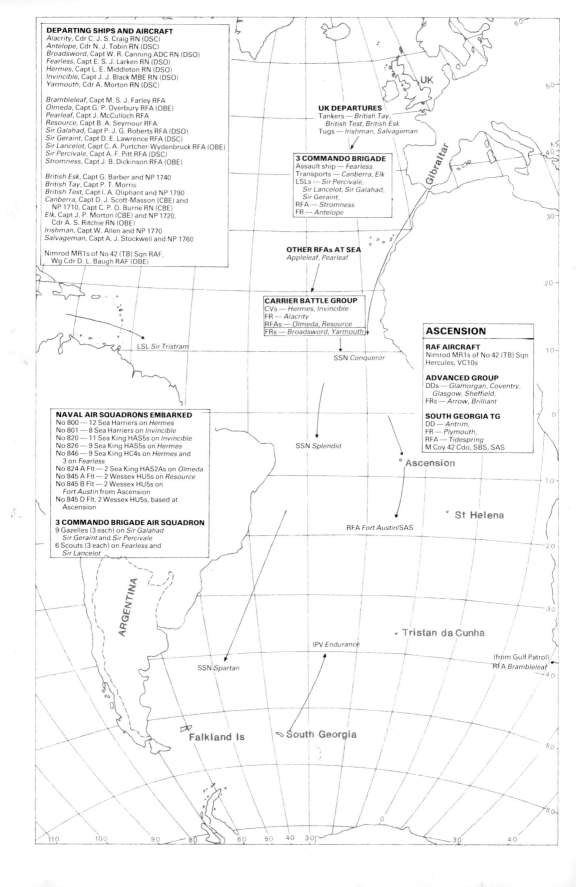

DEPARTING SHIPS AND AIRCRAFT
Alacrity, Cdr C. J. S. Craig RN (DSC)
Antelope, Cdr N. J. Tobin RN (DSC)
Broadsword, Capt W. R. Canning ADC RN (DSO)
Fearless, Capt E. S. J. Larken RN (DSO)
Hermes, Capt L. E. Middleton RN (DSO)
Invincible, Capt J. J. Black MBE RN (DSO)
Yarmouth, Cdr A. Morton RN (DSC)

Brambleleaf, Capt M. S. J. Farley RFA
Olmeda, Capt G. P. Overbury RFA (OBE)
Pearleaf, Capt J. McCulloch RFA
Resource, Capt B. A. Seymour RFA
Sir Galahad, Capt P. J. G. Roberts RFA (DSO)
Sir Geraint, Capt D. E. Lawrence RFA (DSC)
Sir Lancelot, Capt C. A. Purtcher-Wydenbruck RFA (OBE)
Sir Percivale, Capt A. F. Pitt RFA (DSC)
Stromness, Capt J. B. Dickinson RFA (OBE)

British Esk, Capt G. Barber and NP 1740
British Tay, Capt P. T. Morris
British Test, Capt I. A. Oliphant and NP 1790
Canberra, Capt D. J. Scott-Masson (CBE) and
    NP 1710, Capt C. P. O. Burne RN (CBE)
Elk, Capt J. P. Morton (CBE) and NP 1720,
    Cdr A. S. Ritchie RN (OBE)
Irishman, Capt W. Allen and NP 1770
Salvageman, Capt A. J. Stockwell and NP 1760

Nimrod MR1s of No 42 (TB) Sqn RAF,
    Wg Cdr D. L. Baugh RAF (OBE)

UK DEPARTURES
Tankers — *British Tay,
    British Test, British Esk*
Tugs — *Irishman, Salvageman*

3 COMMANDO BRIGADE
Assault ship — *Fearless*
Transports — *Canberra, Elk*
LSLs — *Sir Percivale,
    Sir Lancelot, Sir Galahad,
    Sir Geraint*
RFA — *Stromness*
FR — *Antelope*

OTHER RFAs AT SEA
Appleleaf, Pearleaf

CARRIER BATTLE GROUP
CVs — *Hermes, Invincible*
FR — *Alacrity*
RFAs — *Olmeda, Resource*
FRs — *Broadsword, Yarmouth*

ASCENSION

RAF AIRCRAFT
Nimrod MR1s of No 42 (TB) Sqn
Hercules, VC10s

ADVANCED GROUP
DDs — *Glamorgan, Coventry,
    Glasgow, Sheffield,*
FRs — *Arrow, Brilliant*

SOUTH GEORGIA TG
DD — *Antrim,*
FR — *Plymouth,*
RFA — *Tidespring*
M Coy 42 Cdo, SBS, SAS

NAVAL AIR SQUADRONS EMBARKED
No 800 — 12 Sea Harriers on *Hermes*
No 801 — 8 Sea Harriers on *Invincible*
No 820 — 11 Sea King HAS5s on *Invincible*
No 826 — 9 Sea King HAS5s on *Hermes*
No 846 — 9 Sea King HC4s on *Hermes* and
    3 on *Fearless*
No 824 A Flt — 2 Sea King HAS2As on *Olmeda*
No 845 A Flt — 2 Wessex HU5s on *Resource*
No 845 B Flt — 2 Wessex HU5s on
    Fort Austin from Ascension
No 845 D Flt, 2 Wessex HU5s, based at
    Ascension

3 COMMANDO BRIGADE AIR SQUADRON
9 Gazelles (3 each) on *Sir Galahad
    Sir Geraint* and *Sir Percivale*
6 Scouts (3 each) on *Fearless* and
    Sir Lancelot

UK

Gibraltar

LSL *Sir Tristram*

SSN *Conqueror*

SSN *Splendid*

RFA *Fort Austin/SAS*

SSN *Spartan*

IPV *Endurance*

° Ascension

° St Helena

· Tristan da Cunha

(from Gulf Patrol)
RFA *Brambleleaf*

ARGENTINA

Falkland Is

South Georgia

more squadrons have to be reformed to support the land forces in their later drive on Stanley. Flying mainly from the warships and RFAs, they carry out transport and vertical replenishment (vertrep) duties, special forces landings, naval gunfire support and anti-submarine and anti-ship missions — the latter by Sea Skua-equipped Lynx. But they do **not** provide airborne early warning which is sadly lacking. Some helicopters transfer from ship to ship, including the merchantmen, and many later go ashore on the Falklands. In all, 17 are lost — five Sea Kings by accident, two Wessex on South Georgia, six Wessex and a Lynx go down with *Atlantic Conveyor*, one Lynx each with HMS *Ardent* and *Coventry* and last of all a Wessex is destroyed on the Exocet-hit HMS *Glamorgan*.

Task Force departures from Monday 5 April

Through an incredible amount of effort, a Carrier Battle Group (CVBG) and most of 3 Commando Brigade (3 Cdo Bde) are on their way to Ascension by the week's end, with the carriers and some of their escort and supply ships being the first to leave. HMS *Hermes* and *Invincible* sail from Portsmouth on Monday with the RFA support tanker *Pearleaf* carrying heavy fuel oil for the older *Hermes*. On the same day, HM frigates *Alacrity* and *Antelope* leave Devonport along with the RFA fleet tanker *Olmeda*, while the RFA replenishment ship *Resource*, loaded with naval stores, leaves Rosyth to join the carriers. By the end of the week, HMS *Antelope* has joined the ships carrying 3 Commando Brigade, but after sailing from Gibraltar on Thursday, the frigates HMS *Broadsword* and HMS *Yarmouth* have taken her place.

By Good Friday, 9 April, most of the 3 Commando Brigade units and their equipment have left on a variety of ships, although some fly to Ascension. Apart from one Royal Marine Commando company on HMS *Hermes* and part of one on *Resource*, the rest sail in ships of the Amphibious Task Group. On Tuesday 6 April, assault ship HMS *Fearless* heads out from Portsmouth as Brigade HQ with Cdre Clapp, and off Portland takes on board Brig Thompson and three of No 846 NAS Sea Kings. Of the four LSLs sailing at this time, *Sir*

Percivale and *Sir Lancelot* leave from Marchwood, and *Sir Galahad* and *Sir Geraint* from Devonport. Next day, RFA stores support ship *Stromness* leaves Portsmouth after being converted to carry 45 Cdo RM.

The first merchantmen also sail. Taking just two days to convert from cruise ship to troop ship, *Canberra* leaves Southampton on Friday 9 April with nearly 3,000 men including most of 40 and 42 Cdo RM and 3 Para, and accompanied by RO-RO ship *Elk* loaded with ammunition and vehicles. Over the weekend, the first tankers head for the South Atlantic, mainly to top-up the RFAs in the tanker holding areas — these are *British Esk* from Portland, *British Tay* after loading at Milford Haven and Cambeltown, and *British Test* from Portsmouth. Also from Portsmouth on Saturday, tugs *Irishman* and *Salvageman* loaded with towing and salvage gear leave first for Ascension. Apart from the SBS, the other units destined to take part in recapturing South Georgia fly to Ascension during the week — D Sqn 22 SAS apparently earlier on, followed by M Coy 42 Cdo from Brize Norton on Friday.

Ascension and South Atlantic

On Tuesday 6 April the first RAF aircraft move to Wideawake airfield on Ascension Island. Two Nimrod MR1s of No 42 (TB) Sqn arrive from St Mawgan via the Azores and next day start patrolling the seas around Ascension and supporting the nuclear submarines on their passage south. They are replaced in mid-month by more modern MR2s, but from the UK, later fly SAR for the Harriers that stage to Ascension.

Also on Tuesday, RFA *Fort Austin* reaches the island and three days later continues on with D Sqn SAS, two newly-embarked Wessex from No 845 NAS as well as three Sea Skua-equipped Lynx for ships of the Advanced Group. It is from these that the South Georgia Task Group is detached. After Adm Woodward has transferred his flag to HMS *Glamorgan*, and under the command of Capt Young in HMS *Antrim* they go ahead and reach Ascension on Saturday, but neither they, nor the rest of the Advanced Group which get in next day spend much time there. Earlier in the week, RFA support tanker *Brambleleaf*, having left her Gulf Patrol heads via the Cape of Good Hope to refuel the South Georgia ships.

Right:
Rear-Adm J. F. Woodward KCB, RN, Commander, Carrier Battle Group.
Courtesy — MOD (Navy)

Above:
Sea Harriers of (from top) Nos 899, 801 and 800 NAS. *Courtesy — RNAS Yeovilton*

Left:
RFA *Olmeda* replenishing HMS *Invincible*.
Courtesy — RFA Service

Above:
Maj-Gen J. J. Moore KCB, MC, RM, Commander, Land Forces Falkland Islands.
Courtesy — Royal Marines Museum

Below:
Capt J. J. Black DSO, MBE, RN, Commanding Officer, HMS *Invincible*.
Courtesy — RNAS Yeovilton

Top:
Soldiers of the 1/7th Gurkha Rifles on north side of Tumbledown Mountain.
Courtesy — Capt Narain prasad Rai

Above centre:
Tug *Salvageman* at South Georgia.
Courtesy — United Towing Ltd

Above:
Marines of K. Coy, 42 Cdo RM move off Mount Kent towards Mount Harriet.
Courtesy — Royal Marines Museum

35

Left:
Capt G. R. Green DSC, RFA, CO, RFA *Sir Tristram*. *Courtesy — RFA Service*

Below:
Crew of tug *Yorkshireman* at South Georgia. *Courtesy — United Towing Ltd*

Above:
RAF Hercules at Wideawake Airfield, Ascension Island. *Courtesy — MOD (RAF)*

Left:
Adm Sir John Fieldhouse GBE, RN, Task Force Commander. *Courtesy — MOD (Navy)*

Right:
Lt-Col H. Jones VC, OBE, CO, 2 Para. *Courtesy — Airborne Forces Museum*

Far right:
RAF Victor crew briefing at Ascension for maritime radar reconnaissance mission to South Georgia. *Courtesy — MOD (RAF)*

Right:
David Norris of the *Daily Mail*, Brig J. H. Thompson RM, 3 Commando Brigade, Clr Sgt Cotton, 2 Para, Maj A. Rice RA and Lt-Col H. W. R. Pike, 3 Para waiting to fly to 2 Para memorial service at Goose Green.
Courtesy — Airborne Forces Museum

Below:
Frigate HMS *Plymouth*. *Courtesy — MOD (Navy)*

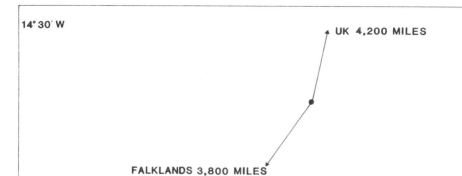

14° 30′ W

UK 4,200 MILES

FALKLANDS 3,800 MILES

ENGLISH BAY
The only location where
conventional landing
craft can beach.

CLARENCE BAY
Main anchorage for
arriving ships with
only one small jetty
at Georgetown,
3 miles from Wideawake.

•Georgetown

Green Mtn(2,800ft)

WIDEAWAKE AIRFIELD
Single 10,000ft
runway

0 1 2 3 4 5 6
MILES

8° 00′ S

BRITISH FORCES SUPPORT UNIT ASCENSION ISLAND

RAF DEFENCES
Surrounding area — Nimrod maritime reconnaissance aircraft
from early April,

Local air defence — three Harrier GR3s of No 1 (F) Sqn
from early May until relieved later in the month by three
Phantom FGR2s of No 29 (F) Sqn. RAF-manned mobile early warning radar on Green
Mountain.

Ground defence — HQ Unit, No 3 Wing and No 15 Field Sqn
RAF Regiment

Other RAF Units — one No 202 Sqn Sea King and one No 18 Sqn
Chinook helicopter for vertrep duties from early May.
Also air movements, mobile servicing, tactical
communications and meteorological units.

ARMY UNITS INCLUDE
Royal Corps of Signals — to establish rear link
Communications Centres for the Task Force.

Royal Engineers — to construct 3½-mile fuel pipeline system
to the airfield along with 180,000gal bulk fuel
storage, and a desalination plant.

Royal Army Ordnance Corps — to operate the pipeline system
capable of delivering up to 300,000gal each day.

Royal Corps of Transport, No 47 Air Despatch Sqn — to
prepare stores for air dropping

ROYAL NAVY
Naval Party 1222 — arrives in early April to receive men,
stores, equipment and helicopters flown out from Britain
and to arrange for transhipment south.

Fleet Air Arm — maintenance personnel prepare the arriving helicopters.

D Flt, No 845 NAS provides two Wessex HU5s for
vertrep and crossdeck delivery services, together with the
two RAF helicopters which arrive later.

MAP 10

Ascension — Stepping Stone to Victory

Located at position 7.56° south, 14.22° west, 4,200 miles (3,700 nautical) from Britain and 3,800 (3,300 nautical) from the Falklands, Ascension Island is vital to the success of the Task Force. Close to the equator, but not unbearably hot, the 38sq mile island is a product of the mid-Atlantic ridge and completely volcanic in origin. In effect a mountain peak rising out of the sea, it is covered by sharp rock and extinct cones of dust and clinker. The highest point of Green Mountain is covered by the only tropical vegetation and trees in a largely barren landscape devoid of water and shelter. Surrounded by the almost continual swell of the South Atlantic, there are no natural harbours and only a single jetty at Clarence Bay and a small landing cove at English Bay. Amongst the abundant wildlife around the island can be found the Sooty Tern or Wideawake.

Discovered in 1501, presumably on Ascension Day, the island remained uninhabited until the early 19th century, when with Napoleon exiled to nearby St Helena, a small Royal Navy garrison was established. Until 1922, the Admiralty was in control but then Ascension became a dependency of St Helena with the Administrator appointed by Britain. Wideawake airfield was built in World War 2 as a staging post between Brazil and Africa and has since been developed by the Americans and the single runway extended to over 10,000ft to take heavy transport aircraft. With only a few movements each week, it mainly serves the US satellite and missile tracking facilities and British submarine cable and satellite relay stations. American-controlled and operated by Pan American Airways, British aircraft must normally give 24hr notice of use, but during the war this requirement is waived. The population consists solely of contracted employees and their families from St Helena, Britain and the United States, and at the last census totalled 1,051. The capital is Georgetown.

By 1982 the associated islands of St Helena, Ascension and Tristan da Cunha are one of the few colonies remaining to Britain. With the use of Simonstown in South Africa ruled out for obvious political reasons, Ascension Island with its airfield is the only possible forward base. But one nearly 4,000 miles from the scene of action.

Even then it is invaluable. The Task Force cannot be completely self-contained and a lot of men and supplies have to be ferried out to the South Atlantic by a constant stream of RAF Hercules and VC10s, chartered freighters and mainly undisclosed American aircraft bringing in such stores as the latest Sidewinder AAMs. These are either delivered to the ships as they call in or pass by or, in urgent cases, air-dropped to them on the way to the Falklands or South Georgia. Few ships spend much time there although most of the Amphibious Task Group with 3 Cdo Bde does stay to prepare for the coming landings.

In the case of the troops, only limited preparation is possible as there is no room for large scale manoeuvres other than marching, although they are able to train on the rapidly constructed firing ranges and practice disembarking from the troopships by helicopters and landing craft. More importantly, the opportunity is taken for the hastily-loaded ships to redistribute some of their stores to other ships, to receive much needed supplies from the UK, and where possible to 'combat load' for an amphibious landing. Much of the necessary 'cross-decking' is carried out by the helicopters with their vertical replenishment capabilities, but also taking part are the Navy landing craft, Royal Corps of Transport Mexeflotes, and locally hired lighters. In all this movement there are major logistical problems. Wideawake has one runway and limited dispersal areas and helicopters can only land there because of the volcanic dust, there is no port, and the one jetty is three miles away and not always usable because of the Atlantic swell.

Ascension is also the main base for RAF operations in support of the Task Force. Usually refuelled in the air by a great number of Victor tanker sorties, air attacks on Stanley, reconnaissance, airdrops, and SAR are carried out by the resident Vulcans, Nimrods and Hercules. Added to all the helicopter and transport movements, these will make Wideawake one of the busiest airfields in the world with up to 400 movements of all types each day.

Responsible for this array of activities is the British Forces Support Unit Ascension Island commanded by Capt R. McQueen, RN (CBE). Involving all three services, some 1,000 men, occasionally rising to 1,500 do everything needed to support the Task Force, work the airfield in co-operation with the resident Americans and defend the island against possible attack by Argentine forces. In general the RAF is responsible for airfield operations and both air and ground defence, the Army builds and mans the necessary additional facilities, and the Navy in the shape of NP 1222, commanded by Cdr G. A. C. Woods, RN (OBE) operates a forward logistical base for the Task Force ships.

So important to the morale of the men taking part as well as the operation of the Task Force is the efficient handling of the vast amounts of private and official mail passing through the island. Although involving all services, the Royal Engineers Postal and Courier Service (WO1 R. G. Randall, RE [MBE]) handles up to 2 tons of airmail daily and 1,000 bags of parcels each week.

PRELIMINARY OPERATIONS AND THE ARRIVAL OF 3 COMMANDO BRIGADE

MAP 11 — WEEK THREE

3 Commando Brigade Royal Marines and Task Force Movements

12-18 April

The Brigade's job is to establish a bridgehead before the Army's 5th Infantry Brigade (5th Inf Bde) arrives to help complete the recapture of the Falklands. Its 'teeth' are three Royal Marine Commandos each with three rifle companies of 120 men, one HQ and one support company, all backed up by a number of other Marine and commando-trained Army units. The Army also provides strong reinforcements including the 3rd Battalion The Parachute Regt, and later the 2nd Battalion, both from 5th Inf Bde. Main infantry weapons are the 7.62mm SLR rifle and 7.62mm general purpose machine gun (GPMG), 66mm light (LAW) and 84mm Carl Gustav medium (MAW) anti-armour weapons and in support companies, 81mm mortars and Milan anti-tank wire-guided missiles.

3 Commando Brigade Royal Marines

Infantry — Nos 40, 42 and 45 Cdos RM (M Coy 42 Cdo to South Georgia, replaced later by newly formed J Coy 42 Cdo).

Artillery — 29 Cdo Regt RA with Nos 7, 8 and 79 Btys each of 6×105mm artillery and 148 Cdo Forward Observation Bty RA for naval gunfire observation.

Combat engineers — 59 Independent Cdo Sqn RE.

Logistics — Commando Logistics Regt RM.

Helicopters — 3 Cdo Bde Air Squadron RM with nine Gazelle AH1s and six Scout AH1s (two RM Gazelles and one Scout are lost).

HQ and Communications — Brigade HQ and Signal Sqn including No 1 Raiding Sqn equipped with rigid raiders and Gemini assault craft and an Air Defence Troop with 12×Blowpipe SAMs.

In medium range reconnaissance role — Mountain & Arctic Warfare (Training) Cadre.

Raiding and reconnaissance — 3 Sections, Special Boat Squadron (No 2 Section to South Georgia).

Other units — include Tactical Air Control Parties RM for directing air strikes, Y Signals Troop RM, Commando Forces Band RM for medical duties, and two Royal Navy Surgical Support Teams.

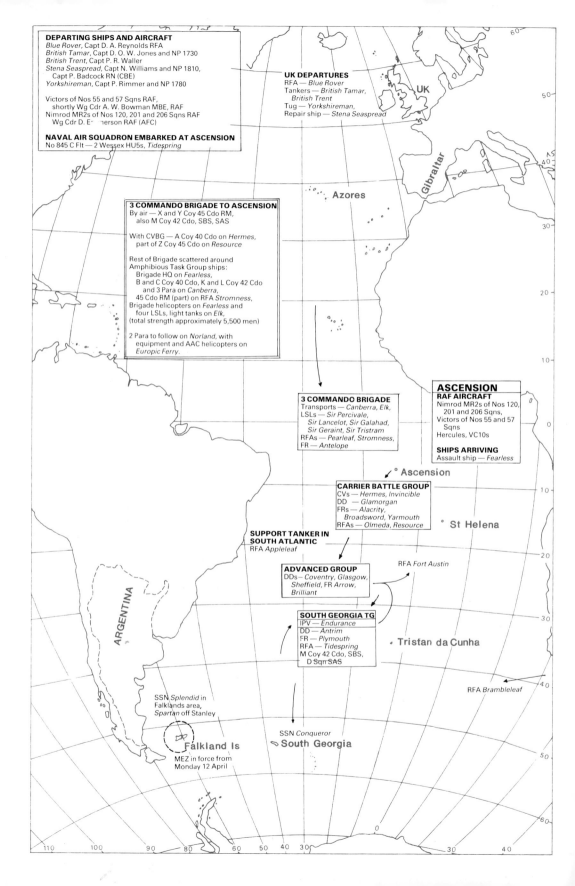

DEPARTING SHIPS AND AIRCRAFT
Blue Rover, Capt D. A. Reynolds RFA
British Tamar, Capt D. O. W. Jones and NP 1730
British Trent, Capt P. R. Waller
Stena Seaspread, Capt N. Williams and NP 1810,
    Capt P. Badcock RN (CBE)
Yorkshireman, Capt P. Rimmer and NP 1780

Victors of Nos 55 and 57 Sqns RAF,
    shortly Wg Cdr A. W. Bowman MBE, RAF
Nimrod MR2s of Nos 120, 201 and 206 Sqns RAF
    Wg Cdr D. E. merson RAF (AFC)

NAVAL AIR SQUADRON EMBARKED AT ASCENSION
No 845 C Flt — 2 Wessex HU5s, *Tidespring*

UK DEPARTURES
RFA — *Blue Rover*
Tankers — *British Tamar*,
    British Trent
Tug — *Yorkshireman*,
Repair ship — *Stena Seaspread*

3 COMMANDO BRIGADE TO ASCENSION
By air — X and Y Coy 45 Cdo RM,
    also M Coy 42 Cdo, SBS, SAS

With CVBG — A Coy 40 Cdo on *Hermes*,
    part of Z Coy 45 Cdo on *Resource*

Rest of Brigade scattered around
Amphibious Task Group ships:
    Brigade HQ on *Fearless*,
    B and C Coy 40 Cdo, K and L Coy 42 Cdo
    and 3 Para on *Canberra*,
    45 Cdo RM (part) on RFA *Stromness*,
    Brigade helicopters on *Fearless* and
    four LSLs, light tanks on *Elk*,
    (total strength approximately 5,500 men)

2 Para to follow on *Norland*, with
    equipment and AAC helicopters on
    Europic Ferry.

3 COMMANDO BRIGADE
Transports — *Canberra*, *Elk*,
LSLs — *Sir Percivale*,
    Sir Lancelot, *Sir Galahad*,
    Sir Geraint, *Sir Tristram*
RFAs — *Pearleaf*, *Stromness*,
FR — *Antelope*

ASCENSION
RAF AIRCRAFT
Nimrod MR2s of Nos 120,
    201 and 206 Sqns,
Victors of Nos 55 and 57
    Sqns
Hercules, VC10s

SHIPS ARRIVING
Assault ship — *Fearless*

° Ascension

CARRIER BATTLE GROUP
CVs — *Hermes*, *Invincible*
DD — *Glamorgan*
FRs — *Alacrity*,
    Broadsword, *Yarmouth*
RFAs — *Olmeda*, *Resource*

° St Helena

**SUPPORT TANKER IN
SOUTH ATLANTIC**
RFA *Appleleaf*

RFA *Fort Austin*

ADVANCED GROUP
DDs — *Coventry*, *Glasgow*,
    Sheffield, FR *Arrow*,
    Brilliant

SOUTH GEORGIA TG
IPV — *Endurance*
DD — *Antrim*
FR — *Plymouth*
RFA — *Tidespring*
M Coy 42 Cdo, SBS,
    D Sqn SAS

· Tristan da Cunha

RFA *Brambleleaf*

ARGENTINA

SSN *Splendid* in
Falklands area,
Spartan off Stanley

Falkland Is

MEZ in force from
Monday 12 April

SSN *Conqueror*
⊷ South Georgia

UK

Gibraltar

Azores

Army reinforcements

Infantry — 2nd and 3rd Battalions The Parachute Regiment each with one HQ, three rifle, one patrol and one support company.

Light armour — B Sqn, The Blues and Royals with four Scorpion and four Scimitar light tanks and one Samson recovery vehicle.

Air defence — T Bty, 12 Air Defence Regt with 12×Rapier SAMs.

Helicopters — No 656 Sqn AAC with a flight of three Scout AH1s.

Raiding and reconnaissance — D and G Sqns, 22 SAS Regt (D Sqn initially to South Georgia).

Attached to 2 Para — 29 Bty, 4 Field Regt RA with 6×105mm guns, and a troop each from 43 Air Defence Bty, 32 Guided Weapons Regt RA with Blowpipe, 9 Para Sqn RE, and 16 Field Ambulance RAMC.

Explosive ordnance disposal — from 49 EOD Sqn RE (and EOD Team RAF).

Other units — Forward Observation Officer parties from 4 Field Regt RA, Tactical Air Control parties, and units from Postal and Courier Regt RE, Rear Link Detachments Royal Signals, 81 Ordnance Coy RAOC, and Mexeflote detachment 17 Port Regt RCT.

Task Force departures from Monday 12 April

The few ships leaving all head for Ascension. Tug *Yorkshireman* sails from Portsmouth on Tuesday, followed on Friday by RFA small fleet tanker *Blue Rover* and off-shore support vessel *Stena Seaspread* with a heavy machine shop in her role as repair ship. More chartered tankers also sail — *British Tamar* from Milford Haven and *British Trent* after loading at Fawley, Isle of Grain and Gosport.

Ascension

With M Coy 42 Cdo and two No 845 NAS Wessex now on board RFA *Tidespring*, the South Georgia ships are on their way by Monday. Two days later the Advanced Group follows them south with the exception of HMS *Glamorgan* which returns north to transfer Adm Woodward to HMS *Hermes* as Commander, Carrier Battle Group. Reaching Ascension on Friday, the carriers continue working up their air wings as the CVBG helicopters and especially the No 846 NAS Sea Kings take part in a massive vertrep. Next day, they are followed in by RFA *Resource*, and

ahead of the other amphibious ships by HMS *Fearless* to allow Brig Thompson and Cdre Clapp to join Adm Woodwood on HMS *Hermes* for a council of war chaired by Adm Fieldhouse who has flown in from Northwood with the other commanders. The basic plan is to blockade the Falklands with the nuclear submarines, recapture South Georgia, establish air and sea control with the Advanced and Carrier Battle Groups, carry out a landing from the Amphibious Group ships, and then retake the islands.

On their way south, Thompson, Clapp and their staffs, including Maj S. E. Southby-Tailyour RM (OBE), who as a yachtsman and previous commander of NP 8901 has surveyed much of the Falklands coast, have been planning how and where to land. With so little intelligence on Argentine forces and positions, a major task will be to put ashore SBS and G Sqn SAS teams to gather this information. On Sunday 18 April the Carrier Group presses on, leaving HMS *Fearless* and other arriving ships of the Amphibious Group including LSL *Sir Tristram* to stay for up to three weeks preparing for the coming landings. To assist them, HMS *Hermes* leaves behind four of her nine No 846 NAS Sea Kings. Other arrivals over the next two days are nine Victor tankers of Nos 55 and 57 Sqns whose first job is to fly reconnaissance for the South Georgia Task Group.

South Atlantic and Falklands

On Monday 12 April HMS *Endurance* meets *Fort Austin* to embark D Sqn SAS and replenish, and two days later joins up with the South Georgia ships. Next day, and only two days after arriving at Ascension, the first Nimrod MR2 of the Kinloss Wing flies on to drop secret orders to HMS *Antrim*. Meanwhile *Fort Austin* heads back to Ascension transfering her Lynx to ships of the Advanced Group, whilst way off to the southwest, nuclear submarine HMS *Spartan* has been on patrol off Port Stanley since Monday.

Argentine warships now go to sea as TF79 to prepare for battle. Carrier *25 de Mayo* exercises her air group with land-based aircraft, further south three frigates sortie, and submarines *Salta* and *San Luis* probably start patrols to the north of the Falklands around this time, although reportedly *Salta* returns to port with mechanical problems. Over the next two weeks the Exocet-carrying Super Etendards practice attacks on their own Type 42 destroyers.

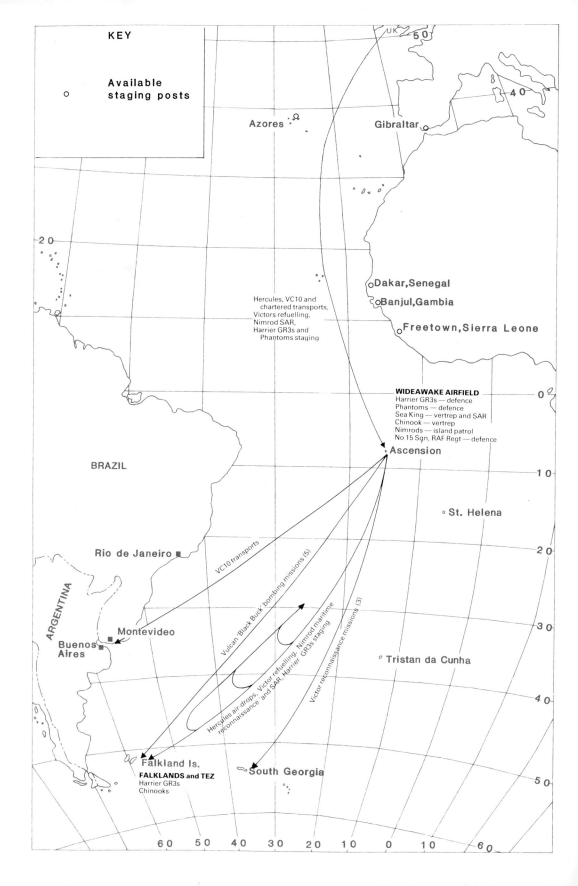

KEY

○ Available staging posts

UK 50

40

Azores ⟋Ω

Gibraltar ○

—20

Hercules, VC10 and
  chartered transports,
Victors refuelling,
Nimrod SAR,
Harrier GR3s and
  Phantoms staging

○Dakar, Senegal

○Banjul, Gambia

○Freetown, Sierra Leone

WIDEAWAKE AIRFIELD
Harrier GR3s — defence
Phantoms — defence
Sea King — vertrep and SAR
Chinook — vertrep
Nimrods — island patrol
No 15 Sqn, RAF Regt — defence

0

• Ascension

BRAZIL

10

○ St. Helena

20

Rio de Janeiro ■

VC10 transports

Vulcan 'Black Buck' bombing missions (5)

Hercules air-drops, Victor refuelling, Nimrod maritime
  reconnaissance and SAR, Harrier GR3s staging

Victor reconnaissance missions (3)

ARGENTINA

Montevideo

Buenos
Aires

○ Tristan da Cunha

30

40

Falkland Is.
FALKLANDS and TEZ
Harrier GR3s
Chinooks

⌒ South Georgia

50

60   50   40   30   20   10   0   10   60

MAP 12

The Role of the Royal Air Force

With the Navy flying just about all the operations around South Georgia and then the Falklands, although with a number of RAF Sea Harrier pilots, the RAF's role could be easily overlooked. Yet its ability to rapidly transport men, supplies and aircraft, first to Ascension and then later further south is so important to success.

Between the UK and Ascension

Hercules and VC10 transports fly over 500 sorties to Ascension by the end of the war to bring in more than 5,000 people and 6,000 tons of freight. The Hercules, some the lengthened C3s, but mostly C1s, are from the pool of over 50 aircraft of Nos 24, 30, 47 and 70 Sqns of the Lyneham Transport Wing. The first two squadrons concentrate on the UK — Ascension airbridge and the other two on missions south; by the end of the war, six aircraft have been fitted for in-flight refuelling to extend their range.

Apart from flying to Ascension, the 13 VC10 passenger aircraft of No 10 Sqn from Brize Norton later return with ship's survivors, and from Montevideo, bring back prisoners and deportees from the Falklands and South Georgia and wounded men from battle. They also continue to fly the Atlantic to the United States. Extra transport capacity is provided by chartered Boeing 707s and five ex-RAF Belfast freighters.

Ascension-based Aircraft and Units

On their way south in early May, three Harrier GR3s of No 1 (Fighter) Sqn are retained at Wideawake for air defence, but are later relieved by three supersonic Phantom FGR2s of No 29(F) Sqn from RAF Coningsby. By then, and with the shortage of helicopters on the island, a Sea King HAR3 of No 202 Air-Sea Rescue Sqn has joined a Chinook of No 18 Sqn on vertrep duties. Apart from units responsible for air movements, communications and supply, the RAF also takes on ground defence with the arrival of HQ Unit, 3 Wing and Field Flight, No 15 Sqn of the RAF Regt.

Missions Flown from Ascension

First to deploy are two Nimrod MR1 maritime patrol aircraft of No 42(TB) Sqn from St Mawgan to patrol Ascension waters and act as links with the nuclear submarines. Later in April, they are replaced by some of the 13 plus and more modern MR2s of Nos 120, 201 and 206 Sqns from Kinloss. In over 100 sorties from Wideawake, they fly ahead of the Task Force, reach as far as Argentine waters, provide SAR and radio links and co-ordinate air refuelling for Victor and Vulcan missions and Harrier staging flights. By the surrender, some MR2s are fitted for air-refuelling and some with Sidewinder AAMs for self defence, but no aircraft equipped with the Harpoon anti-shipping missile are ready in time. In addition, R1 reconnaissance aircraft of Wyton's No 51 Sqn may have taken part.

At least south from Ascension, few missions will be possible without the Victor K2 tankers of Nos 55 and 57 Sqns from Marham, some 20 of which reach Ascension. Apart from refuelling each other as needed, they first fly three maritime radar reconnaissance missions leading up to the recapture of South Georgia. Then in nearly 600 sorties they support other aircraft in often complicated logistics patterns. These include (with outline numbers of tanker sorties) fighters staging to Ascension and some Harrier GR3s on from there, Hercules long range drops (6), extended Nimrod patrols (12) and the Vulcan raids on Stanley (15). They also provide cover as *Atlantic Conveyor* goes south with her Harriers and helicopters.

Although the Waddington-based Vulcan B2 bombers of Nos 44, 50 and 101 Sqns are due to retire from service, a number are fitted with extra ECM and readied for action. Four aircraft in total reach Ascension, the first two at the end of April to start a planned series of seven, single-aircraft 'Black Buck' missions against Stanley through to mid-June. Conventional bombs are used on three occasions and Shrike anti-radar missiles on two, with one mission of each type being called off.

The Hercules of Nos 47 and 70 Sqns are trained in tactical support and based at

Ascension to air drop men and urgent supplies to the Task Force further south. As No 47 Sqn includes a Special Forces Flight, it may have been used for undisclosed covert operations.

Based in the Falklands

To reinforce the Navy's Sea Harriers, Harrier GR3s of No 1(F) Sqn, RAF Wittering are prepared for carrier service. Although fitted with Sidewinder and ECM and with the pilots receiving limited 'ski-jump' training at Yeovilton, they are mainly used in their normal ground attack role. Nine out of 10 aircraft setting out in early May reach Ascension, and apart from the three that temporarily stay on, the other six sail with *Atlantic Conveyor* and later fly off to HMS *Hermes*. Six more arrive at the end of May to add to the three already there. Of this nine, four fly direct to HMS *Hermes*, four sail with merchantman *Contender Bezant* too late to join the fighting and one returns to the UK with fuel leaks. Thus a total of 10 GR3s fly with the Navy, with three shot down by ground fire and one damaged beyond repair in landing.

With the boggy terrain and an almost total lack of roads, heavy lift helicopters are a must. Hence the importance of the first five Chinook HC1s of No 18 Sqn, RAF Odiham carried by *Atlantic Conveyor*. One stays on Ascension, but three of the remaining four are lost in the Exocet attack. The one survivor works wonders, and not until the surrender do three more plus the Ascension Chinook arrive on *Contender Bezant*.

MAP 13 — WEEK FOUR

The Royal Fleet Auxiliary and Task Force Movements

19-25 April

Away from its few shore bases, the Navy simply cannot operate without the Royal Fleet Auxiliary, which like its parent service sends a large proportion of its strength to the South Atlantic before the end of the war — no less than 22 of the 27 ships in commission. Civilian-manned and flying the Blue Ensign, the RFAs usually supply warships underway by Replenishment-at-Sea (RAS) techniques. Heavy furnace fuel oil for older ships, diesel and aviation fuels and fresh water are supplied through hoses, dry goods by jackstay and most ships are equipped to handle helicopters for vertrep, and if needed to provide the RFAs own ASW screen. The types of ships, displacement tons, and helicopters embarked are:

Fleet replenishment ships supply ammunition, food and dry stores:
   Regent, Resource (22,800 tons/Wessex)
   Fort Austin, Fort Grange (17,200 tons/ Wessex/Sea Kings)
   Stores support ship *Stromness* (14,000 tons/helicopter deck)

Fleet tankers carry all three types of fuel as well as fresh water, and can replenish three ships at a time, including one astern:
   Olmeda, Olna (36,000 tons/Sea Kings/ Wessex) also *Olwen*.
   Tidepool, Tidespring (27,400 tons/Wessex), *Blue Rover* (one of five small fleet tankers, 11,500 tons/helicopter deck) also carries dry cargo.

Support tankers normally transport ship and aviation fuel between terminals and depots, but can replenish the fleet tankers and directly refuel other ships. The two classes, both of 26,000 tons and without flight deck, and considerably supplemented by civilian tankers are:
   Appleleaf, Brambleleaf and *Bayleaf*, older *Pearleaf* and *Plumleaf*.

Landing ship logistics (LSLs) are 5,500 ton, RO-RO vessels with a helicopter deck, bow and stern doors and ramps for loading and unloading troops and tanks:

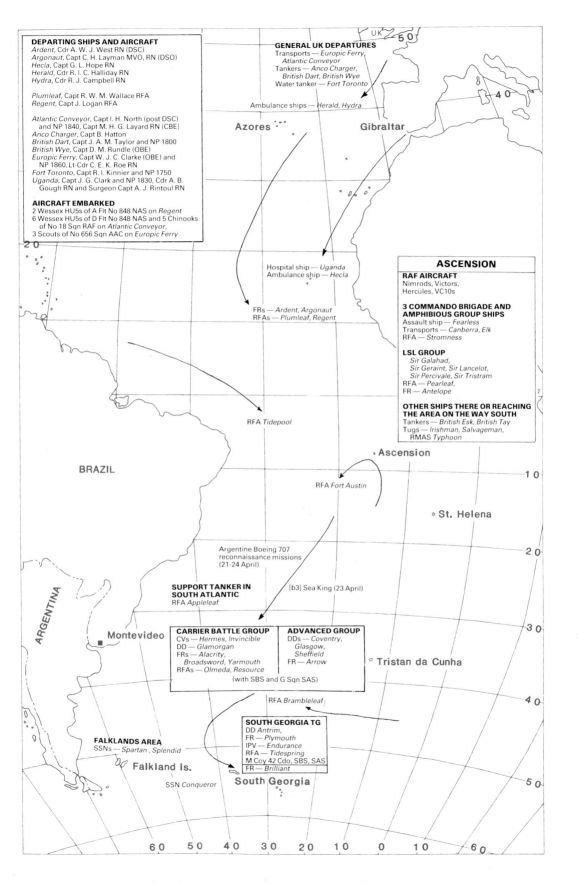

DEPARTING SHIPS AND AIRCRAFT
Ardent, Cdr A. W. J. West RN (DSC)
Argonaut, Capt C. H. Layman MVO, RN (DSO)
Hecla, Capt G. L. Hope RN
Herald, Cdr R. I. C. Halliday RN
Hydra, Cdr R. J. Campbell RN

Plumleaf, Capt R. W. M. Wallace RFA
Regent, Capt J. Logan RFA

Atlantic Conveyor, Capt I. H. North (post DSC)
 and NP 1840, Capt M. H. G. Layard RN (CBE)
Anco Charger, Capt B. Hatton
British Dart, Capt J. A. M. Taylor and NP 1800
British Wye, Capt D. M. Rundle (OBE)
Europic Ferry, Capt W. J. C. Clarke (OBE) and
 NP 1860, Lt-Cdr C. E. K. Roe RN
Fort Toronto, Capt R. I. Kinnier and NP 1750
Uganda, Capt J. G. Clark and NP 1830, Cdr A. B.
 Gough RN and Surgeon Capt A. J. Rintoul RN

AIRCRAFT EMBARKED
2 Wessex HU5s of A Flt No 848 NAS on *Regent*
6 Wessex HU5s of D Flt No 848 NAS and 5 Chinooks
 of No 18 Sqn RAF on *Atlantic Conveyor,*
3 Scouts of No 656 Sqn AAC on *Europic Ferry*

GENERAL UK DEPARTURES
Transports — *Europic Ferry,*
 Atlantic Conveyor
Tankers — *Anco Charger,*
 British Dart, British Wye
Water tanker — *Fort Toronto*

Ambulance ships — *Herald, Hydra*

UK 50

Azores

Gibraltar

40

20

Hospital ship — *Uganda*
Ambulance ship — *Hecla*

FRs — *Ardent, Argonaut*
RFAs — *Plumleaf, Regent*

ASCENSION

RAF AIRCRAFT
Nimrods, Victors,
Hercules, VC10s

**3 COMMANDO BRIGADE AND
AMPHIBIOUS GROUP SHIPS**
Assault ship — *Fearless*
Transports — *Canberra, Elk*
RFA — *Stromness*

LSL GROUP
 Sir Galahad,
 Sir Geraint, Sir Lancelot,
 Sir Percivale, Sir Tristram
RFA — *Pearleaf,*
FR — *Antelope*

**OTHER SHIPS THERE OR REACHING
THE AREA ON THE WAY SOUTH**
Tankers — *British Esk, British Tay*
Tugs — *Irishman, Salvageman,*
 RMAS Typhoon

RFA *Tidepool*

BRAZIL

• Ascension

10

RFA *Fort Austin*

○ St. Helena

Argentine Boeing 707
reconnaissance missions
(21-24 April)

20

**SUPPORT TANKER IN
SOUTH ATLANTIC**
RFA *Appleleaf*

(b3) Sea King (23 April)

30

ARGENTINA

■ Montevideo

CARRIER BATTLE GROUP
CVs — *Hermes, Invincible*
DD — *Glamorgan*
FRs — *Alacrity,*
 Broadsword, Yarmouth
RFAs — *Olmeda, Resource*

ADVANCED GROUP
DDs — *Coventry,*
 Glasgow,
 Sheffield
FR — *Arrow*

(with SBS and G Sqn SAS)

° Tristan da Cunha

RFA *Brambleleaf*

40

SOUTH GEORGIA TG
DD *Antrim,*
FR — *Plymouth*
IPV — *Endurance*
RFA — *Tidespring*
M Coy 42 Cdo, SBS, SAS
FR — *Brilliant*

FALKLANDS AREA
SSNs — *Spartan, Splendid*

Falkland Is.

SSN *Conqueror*

South Georgia

50

60   50   40   30   20   10   0   10   60

Sir Bedivere, Sir Galahad (lost by air attack), *Sir Geraint, Sir Lancelot* (UXB damage), *Sir Percivale* and *Sir Tristram* (UXB damage).

Helicopter support ship *Engadine* (8,000 tons) is equipped for naval training in the handling and maintenance of helicopters.

Separate from the RFA is the **Royal Maritime Auxiliary Service** with 400 civilian-manned ships providing marine services in and around naval bases. Two ships sail south — ocean tug *Typhoon* (1,030grt) and mooring, salvage and boom vessel *Goosander* (900grt).

Task Force Departures from Monday 19 April

Only now are two more frigates ready to leave for Ascension. On Monday, Type 21 HMS *Ardent* and 'Leander' class HMS *Argonaut* sail from Devonport along with two RFAs from Portland — support tanker *Plumleaf* and replenishment ship *Regent*. That same day, the first of four white-painted and Red Cross-marked hospital ships depart. Liner *Uganda* cuts short a children's Mediterranean cruise and arriving at Gibraltar spends the weekend having full medical facilities installed before heading south. She is followed from Gibraltar on Tuesday by survey ship *Hecla*, and from Portsmouth on Saturday by *Herald* and *Hydra* all in the role of ambulance ships. One of their main tasks will be to ferry casualties between *Uganda* in the Red Cross Box and Montevideo.

Monday 19 April also sees the departure from Southampton of *Fort Toronto* as the only fresh water tanker with the Task Force through to the end of the war. And by the end of the week, three more tankers are on their way as fleet refuellers — *British Dart* after delayed loading at Loch Striven, *Anco Charger* from Fawley, and *British Wye* from Devonport. Finally on Sunday, another two RO-RO transports set out as part of the build-up of 3 Cdo Bde. After conversion at Southampton, ferry *Europic Ferry* leaves Portland with much of 2 Para's equipment and three Scout helicopters. And joining her from Devonport is container ship *Atlantic Conveyor* in an aircraft and helicopter support role, complete with flight deck, fuelling and maintenance facilities, and carrying six Royal Navy Wessex and five RAF Chinook helicopters.

Ascension

Now the ships of the Amphibious Group start arriving to spend their time storing and restowing, replenishing by helicopter, landing craft and Mexeflote, and sending their troops ashore for limited exercises and weapons training. The slower LSL group will only stay until the end of the following week, but the others remain a week longer. Meanwhile, and typical of the enterprise shown, *Elk* has the sides of her upper deck cut away for helicopter operations and adds two 40mm Bofors guns. Two civilian tugs also arrive to join RMAS *Typhoon*, with *Irishman* staying into early May, but *Salvageman* soon heading for Tristan da Cunha and on to South Georgia. During the week, RFA *Fort Austin* gets back from her rendezvous with HMS *Endurance*, reloads with stores and returns south to join the CVBG.

South Atlantic

On Wednesday 21 May, as the South Georgia Group arrives off this forbidding island, far to the north, one of HMS *Hermes* Sea Harriers intercepts an Argentine Boeing 707 of Grupo 1 approaching the carriers. This happens each time one of them comes near over the next three days, when in response to warnings through diplomatic channels, they stay away. On Friday evening, the first Task Force aircraft is lost at sea when one of HMS *Hermes* five remaining No 846 NAS Sea King HC4s crashes in poor weather with the loss of her crewman while undertaking vertrep duties [b3].

That Sunday, 25 April, and less than seven days from combat, the carriers rendezvous with the Advanced Group ships. By then in the South Georgia area, two helicopters have been lost on Fortuna Glacier [b1, b2] (see Map 14), detached frigate HMS *Brilliant* has joined other ships there in the helicopter attacks on submarine *Santa Fe*, and by Sunday the Argentine garrison is surrendering.

MAP 14

The Retaking of South Georgia, Operation 'Paraquet'

21-26 April

Before the Task Group arrives off South Georgia on the morning of Wednesday 21 April HM submarine *Conqueror* has already been on patrol for two days and on Tuesday, an RAF Victor from Ascension has made the first radar reconnaissance flight off the coast. Two more of these 7,000-mile, 14hr missions follow over Thursday and Saturday nights, but neither they nor HMS *Conqueror* spot any Argentine ships.

The first task is for observation posts to be set up by the SAS near Leith and the SBS south of Grytviken. Although there are doubts about the SAS plans, Mountain Troop is put down safely on Fortuna Glacier at mid-day that Wednesday by the three available Wessex helicopters. Forced to camp overnight in blizzard conditions, attempts are made to pick up the men next morning, but as the helicopters fly up the glacier in atrocious weather, they have to return to refuel. Next time in, the men are lifted off, but in the blinding snow both of *Tidespring's* Wessex crash [b1, b2]. Then HMS *Antrim's* Wessex, skilfully piloted by Lt-Cdr Stanley, first unloads its passengers and eventually manages to rescue the stranded men in one over-loaded lift later that afternoon. To make up the losses, HMS *Brilliant* is detached from the Task Force with her two Lynx helicopters.

Late that Thursday night (22 April) from HMS *Antrim* out in Stromness Bay, SAS Boat Troop now heads in for Grass Island, but again with near fatal results. Five Gemini assault craft set out in the dark, but two break down and are reported missing next morning. HMS *Antrim's* Wessex is once again to the rescue and soon finds one of the crews, but the other is not located until after the surrender when their rescue beacon is activated. But at least by Friday morning the SAS men are in position near Leith.

All this time the SBS are no more fortunate in their first attempts to approach Grytviken.

Accounts somewhat differ, but apparently they land at Hound Bay from HMS *Endurance* early on Thursday morning, and make their way across Sorling Valley before trying to cross Cumberland Bay East by Gemini. Stopped by glacier ice, they lay up, are later picked up and reportedly landed at Moraine Fiord by Wasp on Saturday.

Before then RFA tanker *Brambleleaf* arrives and starts to refuel *Tidespring*, but in a submarine alert on Friday 23 April, breaks away damaging some of her gear. (The transfer is completed on Saturday and the tanker heads for England.) Then the Task Group is warned that the *Santa Fe* (Lt-Cdr Bicain) is on her way into Grytviken with men and supplies. Apart from HMS *Endurance* which stays close to the coast amongst the ice, the ships head away taking with them the main landing force of M Coy 42 Cdo on *Tidespring*. A Boeing 707 of Grupo 1 now overflies HMS *Endurance* on Saturday, and HMS *Antrim*, *Plymouth* and the newly arrived *Brilliant* are ordered to close on South Georgia to deal with the submarine threat leaving *Tidespring* some 200 miles away in comparative safety. Armed with a variety of weapons, the ship's helicopters prepare to hunt down the submarine which gets into Grytviken that evening.

On the Sunday morning (25 April) as *Santa Fe* heads out on the surface, she is spotted off Cumberland Bay by Lt-Cdr Stanley's Wessex. Near-missed by two Mk 11 depth charges and with some damage, the submarine limps back towards Grytviken. As she does, one of HMS *Brilliant's* Lynx helicopters attacks with a Mk 46 torpedo, the two Wasps (Flight Commander, Lt-Cdr Ellerbeck) from HMS *Endurance* fire AS12 missiles hitting her fin, HMS *Plymouth's* Wasp fires another AS12 and both of HMS *Endurance's* Wasps strafe with machine guns. Meanwhile the warships head for the action at high speed. Although the attacks only slightly

49

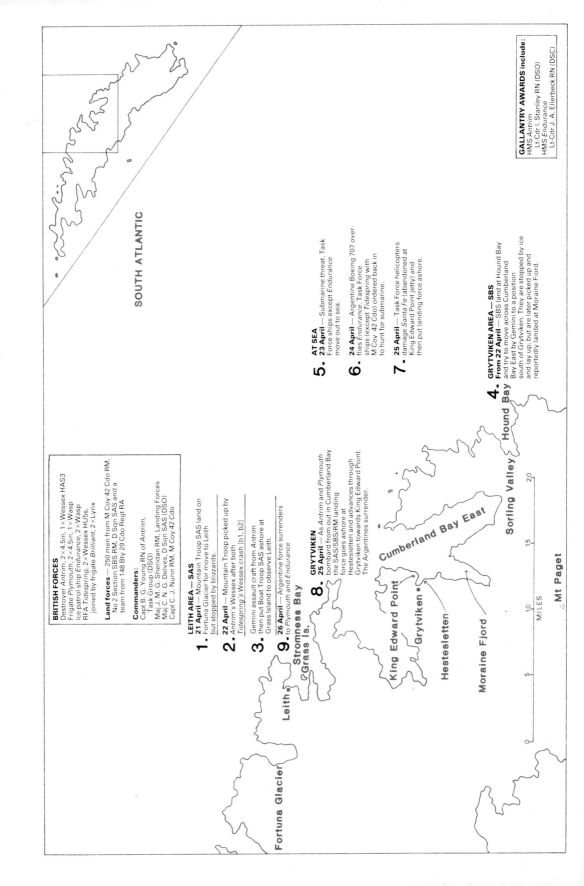

SOUTH ATLANTIC

BRITISH FORCES

Destroyer *Antrim*, 2 × 4.5in, 1 × Wessex HAS3
Frigate *Plymouth*, 2 × 4.5in, 1 × Wasp
Ice patrol ship *Endurance*, 2 × Wasp
RFA *Tidespring*, 2 × Wessex HU5s,
joined by frigate *Brilliant*, 2 × Lynx

Land forces — 250 men from M Coy 42 Cdo RM,
No 2 Section SBS RM, D Sqn SAS and a
team from 148 Bty 29 Cdo Regt RA

Commanders:
Capt B. G. Young RN of *Antrim*,
   Task Group (DSO)
Maj J. M. G. Sheridan RM, Landing Forces
Maj C. N. G. Delves, D Sqn SAS (DSO)
Capt C. J. Nunn RM, M Coy 42 Cdo

1. **LEITH AREA — SAS**
21 April — Mountain Troop SAS land on
Fortuna Glacier for move to Leith
but stopped by blizzards.

2. **22 April** — Mountain Troop picked up by
Antrim's Wessex after both
Tidespring's Wessex crash [b1, b2]

3. Gemini assault craft from *Antrim*
then put Boat Troop SAS ashore at
Grass Island to observe Leith.

9. **26 April** — Argentine force surrenders
to *Plymouth* and *Endurance*

8. **GRYTVIKEN**
25 April — As *Antrim* and *Plymouth*
bombard from out in Cumberland Bay
the SAS/SBS/RM landing
force goes ashore at
Hesteslotten and advances through
Grytviken towards King Edward Point.
The Argentines surrender.

5. **AT SEA**
23 April — Submarine threat. Task
Force ships except *Endurance*
move out to sea.

6. **24 April** — Argentine Boeing 707 overflies *Endurance*. Task Force
ships (except *Tidespring* with
M Coy 42 Cdo) ordered back in
to hunt for submarine.

7. **25 April** — Task Force helicopters
damage *Santa Fe* (abandoned at
King Edward Point jetty) and
then put landing force ashore.

4. **GRYTVIKEN AREA — SBS**
From 22 April — SBS land at Hound Bay
and try to move across Cumberland
Bay East by Gemini to a position
south of Grytviken. They are stopped by ice
and lay up, but are later picked up and
reportedly landed at Moraine Fiord.

GALLANTRY AWARDS include:
HMS *Antrim*
   Lt-Cdr I. Stanley RN (DSO)
HMS *Endurance*
   Lt-Cdr J. A. Ellerbeck RN (DSC)

Fortuna Glacier

Stromness Bay
Grass Is.
Leith.

King Edward Point
Grytviken ■
Hesteslotten

Cumberland Bay East

Moraine Fiord

Sorling Valley Hound Bay

△ Mt Paget

MILES
0   5   10   15   20

damage the *Sante Fe* and wound one crewman, by noon she is abandoned alongside the jetty at King Edward Point, (Later, on being moved to Grytviken, one of her crew is shot and killed in the mistaken belief he is trying to scuttle the boat.)

With the submarine's return and the potential defenders now numbering some 140, the decision is made to land whatever force can be mustered under covering naval gunfire and without waiting for the bulk of M Coy to arrive on *Tidespring*. Under the command of Maj Sheriden RM, a company of 75 men is assembled from the SAS, SBS and other Royal Marines with Maj Delves and Capt Nunn RM as troop commanders. In the early afternoon, from out in Cumberland Bay and under the control of a naval gunfire observer landed by HMS *Endurance's* Wasp, HMS *Antrim* and *Plymouth* lay down a barrage of 4.5in gunfire all around the Argentine positions at King Edward Point. Landed by HMS *Antrim's*

Wessex and HMS *Brilliant's* two Lynx at Hestesletten, the first wave of the *ad hoc* force advances through the whaling station at Grytviken and across an unsuspected minefield towards the BAS base. As they approach, white flags are hoisted and at around 17.00hrs local time, the Argentines surrender without a shot being fired. When contacted by radio, the small detachment of marines at Leith under the command of Lt-Cdr Astiz refuse to surrender.

Next morning (Monday 26 April) HMS *Endurance* and *Plymouth* sail along to Leith and the marines give in. HMS *Plymouth* and *Brilliant* leave on Wednesday to join the CVBG, but *Tidespring*, now with nearly 150 Argentine POWs and the 40 civilian workers from Leith embarked, and escorted by HMS *Antrim* does not head north for Ascension until Sunday 2 May. A disappointed M Coy 42 Cdo stays on to garrison South Georgia, and HMS *Endurance* remains as guard ship.

MAP 15 — WEEK FIVE

Ships of the Merchant Navy and Task Force Movements

26 April-2 May

Up to the surrender in mid-June, 40 merchantmen totalling over 500,000grt reach the South Atlantic. Without them, the war will not be won as the RFA lacks the ships to transport the land forces and then support them and the warships 8,000 miles from home. Chartered (Ch) when available, requisitioned (Req) when under contract, the Ships Taken Up From Trade (STUFT) from Britain's dwindling merchant fleet are rapidly converted to their military role in naval and civilian dockyards — mainly Devonport and Portsmouth. All receive minimum naval communications and some Satnav (SN) and Satcom (SC) equipment, most are fitted for RAS, many with one or two helipads (H or 2H) and some with extra accommodation and light AA weapons. Soon loaded, most sail with Naval Parties embarked for ciphering, RAS, vertrep and other duties. Taking only those ships which arrive on station before the end of the war, their main military roles,

starting with the troop and equipment transports are:

Transports reaching TEZ mid-May with 3 Cdo Bde and more aircraft

Canberra (44,800grt, Req/2H), *Elk* (5,500grt, Req), *Europic Ferry* (4,200grt, Req/SN/SC), *Norland* (13,000grt, Req/2H/SN/SC), and aircraft and helicopter support ship *Atlantic Conveyor* (15,000grt, Req/flight deck/SC — sunk by Exocet).

Transports arriving end of May with 5th Inf Bde and military stores

Queen Elizabeth 2 (67,100grt, Req/2H), *Baltic Ferry* and *Nordic Ferry* (both 6,500grt, Req/2H/SN/SC), ammunition ship *Lycaon* (11,800grt, Ch/SC) and helicopter support ship *Atlantic Causeway* (15,000grt, Req/flight deck and hangar/SC).

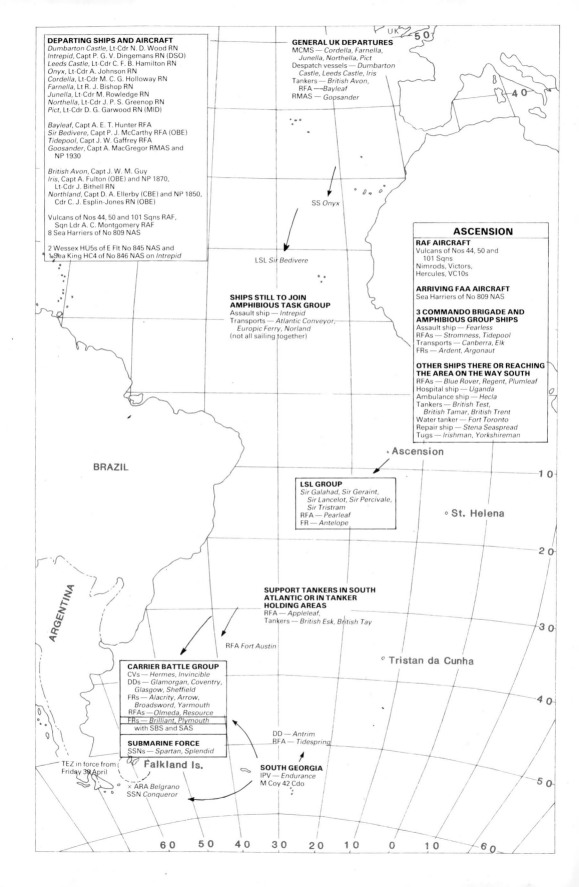

DEPARTING SHIPS AND AIRCRAFT
Dumbarton Castle, Lt-Cdr N. D. Wood RN
Intrepid, Capt P. G. V. Dingemans RN (DSO)
Leeds Castle, Lt-Cdr C. F. B. Hamilton RN
Onyx, Lt-Cdr A. Johnson RN
Cordella, Lt-Cdr M. C. G. Holloway RN
Farnella, Lt R. J. Bishop RN
Junella, Lt-Cdr M. Rowledge RN
Northella, Lt-Cdr J. P. S. Greenop RN
Pict, Lt-Cdr D. G. Garwood RN (MID)

Bayleaf, Capt A. E. T. Hunter RFA
Sir Bedivere, Capt P. J. McCarthy RFA (OBE)
Tidepool, Capt J. W. Gaffrey RFA
Goosander, Capt A. MacGregor RMAS and
    NP 1930

British Avon, Capt J. W. M. Guy
Iris, Capt A. Fulton (OBE) and NP 1870,
    Lt-Cdr J. Bithell RN
Northland, Capt D. A. Ellerby (CBE) and NP 1850,
    Cdr C. J. Esplin-Jones RN (OBE)

Vulcans of Nos 44, 50 and 101 Sqns RAF,
    Sqn Ldr A. C. Montgomery RAF
8 Sea Harriers of No 809 NAS

2 Wessex HU5s of E Flt No 845 NAS and
1 Sea King HC4 of No 846 NAS on *Intrepid*

GENERAL UK DEPARTURES
MCMS — *Cordella, Farnella,*
    Junella, Northella, Pict
Despatch vessels — *Dumbarton*
    Castle, Leeds Castle, Iris
Tankers — *British Avon,*
    RFA —*Bayleaf*
RMAS — *Goosander*

UK

50

40

SS *Onyx*

LSL *Sir Bedivere*

**SHIPS STILL TO JOIN
AMPHIBIOUS TASK GROUP**
Assault ship — *Intrepid*
Transports — *Atlantic Conveyor;*
    Europic Ferry, Norland
(not all sailing together)

ASCENSION

RAF AIRCRAFT
Vulcans of Nos 44, 50 and
    101 Sqns
Nimrods, Victors,
Hercules, VC10s

ARRIVING FAA AIRCRAFT
Sea Harriers of No 809 NAS

**3 COMMANDO BRIGADE AND
AMPHIBIOUS GROUP SHIPS**
Assault ship — *Fearless*
RFAs — *Stromness, Tidepool*
Transports — *Canberra, Elk*
FRs — *Ardent, Argonaut*

**OTHER SHIPS THERE OR REACHING
THE AREA ON THE WAY SOUTH**
RFAs — *Blue Rover, Regent, Plumleaf*
Hospital ship — *Uganda*
Ambulance ship — *Hecla*
Tankers — *British Test,*
    British Tamar, British Trent
Water tanker — *Fort Toronto*
Repair ship — *Stena Seaspread*
Tugs — *Irishman, Yorkshireman*

· Ascension

10

BRAZIL

LSL GROUP
Sir Galahad, Sir Geraint,
    Sir Lancelot, Sir Percivale,
    Sir Tristram
RFA — *Pearleaf*
FR — *Antelope*

º St. Helena

20

ARGENTINA

**SUPPORT TANKERS IN SOUTH
ATLANTIC OR IN TANKER
HOLDING AREAS**
RFA — *Appleleaf,*
Tankers — *British Esk, British Tay*

º Tristan da Cunha

30

RFA *Fort Austin*

CARRIER BATTLE GROUP
CVs — *Hermes, Invincible*
DDs — *Glamorgan, Coventry,*
    Glasgow, Sheffield
FRs — *Alacrity, Arrow,*
    Broadsword, Yarmouth
RFAs —*Olmeda, Resource*
FRs — *Brilliant, Plymouth*
    with SBS and SAS

SUBMARINE FORCE
SSNs — *Spartan, Splendid*

40

DD — *Antrim*
BFA — *Tidespring*

TEZ in force from
Friday 30 April

Falkland Is.

SOUTH GEORGIA
IPV — *Endurance*
M Coy 42 Cdo

50

× ARA *Belgrano*
SSN *Conqueror*

60   50   40   30   20   10   0   10   60

Transports arriving in June

Troopship *St Edmund* (9,000grt, Req/2H/SN/SC), transport *Tor Caledonia* (5,100grt, Req) and aircraft and helicopter carrier *Contender Bezant* (11,400grt, Ch/flight deck and hangar).

Oil Tankers

All chartered, and mostly used to replenish RFAs in the tanker holding areas set out in the order *British Esk*, *British Tay*, *British Test*, *British Tamar*, *British Trent*, *Anco Charger*, *British Dart*, *British Wye*, *British Avon*, (all 15,600grt), *Alvega* (33,300grt), *Eburna* (19,800grt) and *Balder London* (20,000grt).

Other vessels and their outlined order of departure are:

Ocean tugs *Irishman* and *Yorkshireman* (both 700grt, Req), *Salvageman* (1,600grt, Req),
Mooring vessel *Wimpey Seahorse* (1,600grt, Req/SC)
Repair ship *Stena Seaspread* (6,100grt, Req/SN/SC),
Water tanker *Fort Toronto* (20,000grt, Ch)
Hospital ship *Uganda* (16,900grt, Req/H/SC)
Minesweepers *Cordella*, *Farnella*, *Junella*, *Northella*, *Pict* (1,200 to 1,600grt, Req), Despatch vessel *Iris* (3,900grt, Req/H/SC), Refrigerated stores ships *Saxonia* (12,000grt, Ch/H/SN/SC) and *Geestport* (7,700grt, Req/H).

Task Force Departures from Monday 26 April

Diesel patrol submarine HMS *Onyx* sails from Gosport on Monday at the same time as the last of the Amphibious Group head for Ascension. Assault ship HMS *Intrepid*, not long after being readied for disposal, leaves from Portland, RO-RO ferry *Norland* from Portsmouth with the men of 2 Para, followed by the sixth LSL *Sir Bedivere* from Marchwood after returning from Vancouver, Canada. The early part of the week also sees the departure from Devonport of RFA support tanker *Bayleaf* on her maiden voyage and tanker *British Avon* from Portsmouth. Quite separately, RFA fleet tanker *Tidepool* arrives at Ascension from Curacoa with a full British crew after being borrowed back from Chile to where she was being delivered.

During the week a variety of small ships also head for Ascension. Converted for minesweeping duties at Rosyth, the five trawlers *Cordella*, *Farnella*, *Junella*, *Northella* and *Pict* leave Portland on Tuesday 27 April with Royal Navy crews after working-up as the 11th Mine Countermeasures Sqn. Next to go are three despatch ships, two of them Royal Navy fishery protection vessels from Portland after being modified at Portsmouth — *Leeds Castle* on Thursday and *Dumbarton Castle* on Saturday, and from Devonport on Thursday cable ship *Iris*. By the end of the week RMAS mooring, salvage and boom vessel *Goosander* is on her way from Rosyth to lay out and maintain the moorings at Ascension.

Ascension

As 3 Cdo bde prepares to move south and *Canberra* practises offloading her troops by LCU and helicopter, various ships reach the island and, usually in a matter of days or less, continue south. By the weekend, this includes the slower LSL component of the Amphibious Task Group which is on its way escorted by frigate HMS *Antelope*. By then, Maj-Gen Moore has flown down to meet Thompson and Clapp to review the landing options now reduced to three sites on East Falkland. With two around Stanley and thus close to the main Argentine defences, San Carlos Water becomes the preferred option.

Important air movements also take place. On Thursday 29 April the first two Vulcan B2 bombers arrive from Waddington to prepare for 'Black Buck 1', the opening raid on Stanley on Saturday. And over Saturday and Sunday, eight Sea Harriers of No 809 NAS reach Wideawake after making the 9hr flight from Yeovilton refuelled by Victor tankers. There they await the arrival of RAF Harrier GR3s and their transport south, the doomed *Atlantic Conveyor*.

South Atlantic

As the carriers approach the eastern edge of the TEZ, frigates HMS *Brilliant* and HMS *Plymouth* join up on Thursday from South Georgia carrying No 2 SBS and D Sqn SAS. Next day the TEZ comes into force, and on Saturday 1 May, the Royal Navy sails in to start the softening-up attacks designed to establish air and sea superiority. Earlier in the week, the Argentine trawler *Narwhal* is warned to keep clear of the Task Force and on Sunday, off to the southwest, the cruiser *General Belgrano* is torpedoed and sunk by HMS *Conqueror*. That same Sunday, *Tidespring* and HMS *Antrim* leave South Georgia for Ascension carrying the Argentine POWs.

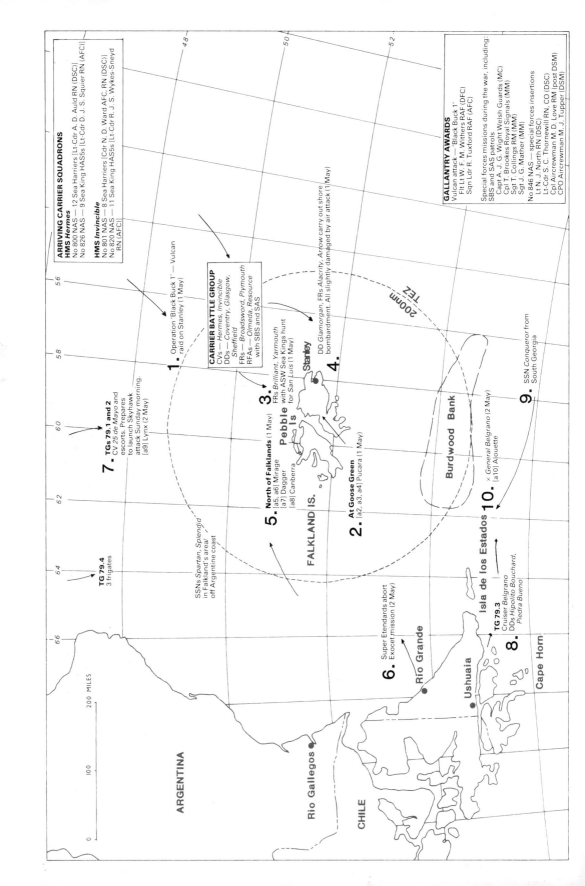

ARRIVING CARRIER SQUADRONS
HMS *Hermes*
No 800 NAS — 12 Sea Harriers [Lt-Cdr A. D. Auld RN (DSC)]
No 826 NAS — 9 Sea King HAS5s [Lt-Cdr D. J. S. Squier RN (AFC)]

HMS *Invincible*
No 801 NAS — 8 Sea Harriers [Cdr N. D. Ward RN (DSC)]
No 820 NAS — 11 Sea King HAS5s [Lt-Cdr R. J. S. Wykes-Sneyd RN (AFC)]

GALLANTRY AWARDS
Vulcan attack — 'Black Buck 1'
Flt Lt W. F. M. Withers RAF (DFC)
Sqn Ldr R. Tuxford RAF (AFC)

Special forces missions during the war, including:
SBS and SAS patrols
Capt A. J. G. Wight Welsh Guards (MC)
Cpl T. Brookes Royal Signals (MM)
Sgt T. Collings RM (MM)
Sgt J. G. Mather (MM)

No 846 NAS — special forces insertions
Lt-Cdr S. C. Thornewill RN, CO (DSC)
Cpl Aircrewman M. D. Love RM (post DSM)
CPO Aircrewman M. J. Tupper (DSM)

1. Operation 'Black Buck 1' — Vulcan raid on Stanley (1 May)

CARRIER BATTLE GROUP
CVs — *Hermes*, *Invincible*
DDs — *Coventry*, *Glasgow*, *Sheffield*
FRs — *Broadsword*, *Plymouth*
RFAs — *Olmeda*, *Resource*
with SBS and SAS

4. DD *Glamorgan*, FRs *Alacrity*, *Arrow* carry out shore bombardment. All slightly damaged by air attack (1/May)

3. FRs *Brilliant*, *Yarmouth* with ASW Sea Kings hunt for *San Luis* (1 May)

7. TGs 79.1 and 2 CV 25 de Mayo and escorts. Prepares to launch Skyhawk attack Sunday morning. [a9] Lynx (2 May)

5. North of Falklands (1 May) [a5, a6] Mirage [a7] Dagger [a8] Canberra

2. At Goose Green [a2, a3, a4] Pucara (1 May)

9. SSN *Conqueror* from South Georgia

TG 79.4 3 frigates

SSNs *Spartan*, *Splendid* in Falkland's area/ off Argentine coast

Stanley

Pebble Is

Burdwood Bank

FALKLAND IS.

200nm TEZ

10. × *General Belgrano* (2 May) [a10] Alouette

Isla de los Estados

6. Super Etendards abort Exocet mission (2 May)

TG 79.3 Cruiser *Belgrano* DDs *Hipolito Bouchard*, *Piedra Bueno*

8.

ARGENTINA

Rio Gallegos

CHILE

Rio Grande

Ushuaia

Cape Horn

200 MILES

0   100   200

MAP 16 — WEEK FIVE

Falkland Area Operations

1-2 May

As Adm Woodward's carriers enter the TEZ on Saturday 1 May, a lone Vulcan bomber piloted by Flt Lt Withers approaches the Falklands on Operation 'Black Buck 1'. Leaving Ascension late on Friday with a second Vulcan and 11 Victor tankers, some of which refuel each other, the first air raid on Stanley is about to be made. Intended to deny the airfield to fast jets, 21×1,000lb bombs are dropped from an altitude of 10,000ft early that morning. Only one hits the runway, but the attack signals the RAF's ability to strike in the South Atlantic and against mainland targets. The Vulcan returns safely from its almost 16hr, 8,000-mile round trip, and one of the Victor captains — Sqn Ldr Tuxford, is decorated for his part in the action. Operation 'Black Buck 2' on Tuesday morning is carried out from 16,000ft but fails to hit the runway.

As the raid takes place, the carriers, with just 20 Sea Harriers between them, prepare to go into action. Keeping to the east of the Falklands to reduce the chance of air attack, and screened by ASW-equipped Sea King helicopters, HMS *Invincible* launches her Sea Harriers for combat air patrols while those from HMS *Hermes* follow up the Vulcan raid with ground strikes. Soon after 08.00hrs, nine of them hit Stanley airfield, destroying installations and stores and damaging a civilian Islander aircraft with CBUs. The other three go in at Goose Green, wrecking one Pucara [a2] and badly damaging two more [a3, a4].

All this time, Type 22 HMS *Brilliant* and 'Rothesay' class HMS *Yarmouth* with three ASW Sea Kings from HMS *Hermes* search all day for the suspected Argentine submarine *San Luis*, but fail to find her. Also detached are HMS *Glamorgan*, and Type 21s HMS *Alacrity* and HMS *Arrow* for the first of many bombardments of the Stanley area. HMS *Alacrity's* Lynx takes off that afternoon to provide naval gunfire observation, but discovers the Argentine patrol craft *Islas Malvinas* sheltering near Kidney Island just to the north of Stanley. Attacking with GPMG, she damages the vessel, but is hit by the return fire, and HMS *Arrow's* Lynx later takes over the spotting duties. Just before 17.00hrs, as the warships continue their bombardment, they are attacked without warning by three Grupo 6 Daggers, and all receive minor damage from cannon fire or near misses.

The Grupo 6 attack is part of Argentina's response that Saturday to what is believed to be a full scale landing. Sorties are launched from the mainland by Skyhawks, Canberras and Daggers, with some Mirages flying cover, and also by Falklands-based aircraft. Around the time of this strike, four FAA aircraft are lost towards the north of the Falklands to Sea Harriers and their Sidewinder AAMs. HMS *Glamorgan* vectors two No 801 NAS aircraft to two Grupo 8 Mirages, one of which explodes over Pebble Island in the first air-to-air kill of the war, and the other, damaged by a missile and approaching Stanley is shot down by Argentine AA [a5, a6]. Next, two Sea Harriers of No 800 NAS claim the Squadron's first victim in combat by downing one of two Grupo 6 Daggers flying escort [a7]. Then further to the north, two more No 801 NAS Harriers account for one of three Grupo 2 Canberras looking for British ships [a8]. Next day, two CANA Super Etendards fly from the mainland for an Exocet attack on the Task Force, but turn back with refuelling problems.

Earlier in the week before the British arrival, ships of the Argentine Navy sail from the north and south of the Falklands as Task Force 79. By early morning on Sunday 2 May the Argentine carrier *25 de Mayo*, lying to the north, is preparing to launch a Skyhawk attack which is aborted because of light winds. That same day, both escorting Argentinian Type 42s are involved in separate incidents. *Hercules* readies but fails to fire a Sea Dart against an approaching No 801 NAS Sea Harrier, and *Santisima Trinidad* loses her Lynx in a flying accident [a9]. By then the submarine *San Luis* may have carried out the first of a number of unsuccessful attacks before she returns to port around the end of the month. To the south, Sunday also sees one of the most controversial incidents of the war — the loss of the cruiser *General Belgrano* and over 300 men.

Not used during Operation 'Rosario', *General Belgrano* puts to sea from Ushuaia on Monday 26 April escorted by two Exocet-armed destroyers, and three days later is ordered to patrol south of the shallow Burdwood Bank. On Friday, the British nuclear

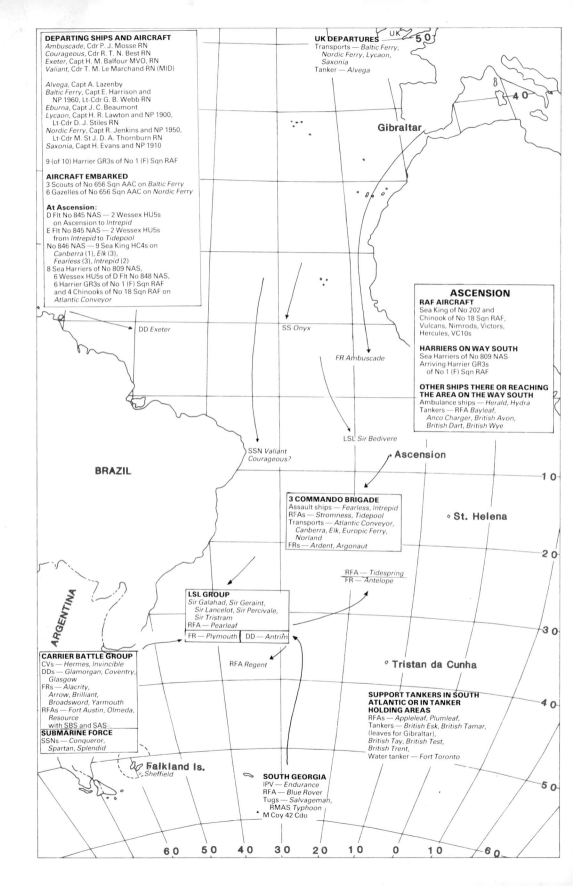

DEPARTING SHIPS AND AIRCRAFT
Ambuscade, Cdr P. J. Mosse RN
Courageous, Cdr R. T. N. Best RN
Exeter, Capt H. M. Balfour MVO, RN
Valiant, Cdr T. M. Le Marchand RN (MID)

Alvega, Capt A. Lazenby
Baltic Ferry, Capt E. Harrison and
  NP 1960, Lt-Cdr G. B. Webb RN
Eburna, Capt J. C. Beaumont
Lycaon, Capt H. R. Lawton and NP 1900,
  Lt-Cdr D. J. Stiles RN
Nordic Ferry, Capt R. Jenkins and NP 1950,
  Lt-Cdr M. St J. D. A. Thornburn RN
Saxonia, Capt H. Evans and NP 1910

9 (of 10) Harrier GR3s of No 1 (F) Sqn RAF

AIRCRAFT EMBARKED
3 Scouts of No 656 Sqn AAC on *Baltic Ferry*
6 Gazelles of No 656 Sqn AAC on *Nordic Ferry*

At Ascension:
D Flt No 845 NAS — 2 Wessex HU5s
  on Ascension to *Intrepid*
E Flt No 845 NAS — 2 Wessex HU5s
  from *Intrepid* to *Tidepool*
No 846 NAS — 9 Sea King HC4s on
  Canberra (1), *Elk* (3),
  Fearless (3), *Intrepid* (2)
8 Sea Harriers of No 809 NAS,
  6 Wessex HU5s of D Flt No 848 NAS,
  6 Harrier GR3s of No 1 (F) Sqn RAF
  and 4 Chinooks of No 18 Sqn RAF on
  Atlantic Conveyor

UK DEPARTURES
Transports — *Baltic Ferry*,
  Nordic Ferry, *Lycaon*,
  Saxonia
Tanker — *Alvega*

UK

50

40

Gibraltar

ASCENSION
RAF AIRCRAFT
Sea King of No 202 and
Chinook of No 18 Sqn RAF,
Vulcans, Nimrods, Victors,
Hercules, VC10s

HARRIERS ON WAY SOUTH
Sea Harriers of No 809 NAS
Arriving Harrier GR3s
  of No 1 (F) Sqn RAF

**OTHER SHIPS THERE OR REACHING
THE AREA ON THE WAY SOUTH**
Ambulance ships — *Herald*, *Hydra*
Tankers — RFA *Bayleaf*,
  Anco Charger, *British Avon*,
  British Dart, *British Wye*

DD *Exeter*

SS *Onyx*

FR *Ambuscade*

LSL *Sir Bedivere*

BRAZIL

SSN *Valiant*
Courageous?

• Ascension

10

○ St. Helena

3 COMMANDO BRIGADE
Assault ships — *Fearless*, *Intrepid*
RFAs — *Stromness*, *Tidepool*
Transports — *Atlantic Conveyor*,
  Canberra, *Elk*, *Europic Ferry*,
  Norland
FRs — *Ardent*, *Argonaut*

20

RFA — *Tidespring*
FR — *Antelope*

ARGENTINA

LSL GROUP
Sir Galahad, *Sir Geraint*,
Sir Lancelot, *Sir Percivale*,
Sir Tristram
RFA — *Pearleaf*

| FR — *Plymouth* | DD — *Antrim* |

30

○ **Tristan da Cunha**

CARRIER BATTLE GROUP
CVs — *Hermes*, *Invincible*
DDs — *Glamorgan*, *Coventry*,
  Glasgow
FRs — *Alacrity*,
  Arrow, *Brilliant*,
  Broadsword, *Yarmouth*
RFAs — *Fort Austin*, *Olmeda*,
  Resource
  with SBS and SAS
SUBMARINE FORCE
SSNs — *Conqueror*,
  Spartan, *Splendid*

RFA *Regent*

**SUPPORT TANKERS IN SOUTH
ATLANTIC OR IN TANKER
HOLDING AREAS**
RFAs — *Appleleaf*, *Plumleaf*,
Tankers — *British Esk*, *British Tamar*,
  (leaves for Gibraltar),
  British Tay, *British Test*,
  British Trent,
Water tanker — *Fort Toronto*

40

Falkland Is.
× *Sheffield*

SOUTH GEORGIA
IPV — *Endurance*
RFA — *Blue Rover*
Tugs — *Salvageman*,
  RMAS Typhoon
• M Coy 42 Cdo

50

60   50   40   30   20   10   0   10   60

submarine HMS *Conqueror* makes first contact at long range, and next day closes in to shadow the cruiser. Although just outside the TEZ, *General Belgrano*, as the southern arm of TF79, is a potential threat to the British carriers and her destruction is ordered. Hit at 16.00hrs by two conventional Mk 8 torpedoes, she is soon abandoned and goes down with her helicopter [a10]. A third torpedo hits *Hipolito Bouchard*, without exploding but possibly causing some damage, and HMS *Conqueror* is therefore presumably counter-attacked by *Piedra Bueno*, which later returns with other Argentine ships to search for the cruiser's survivors. Shortly after the sinking, the main units of the Argentine Navy return to port or stay in coastal waters for the rest of the war.

Although British special forces may already have landed from the nuclear submarines, the SBS and G Sqn SAS now go ashore to check out landing sites and target aircraft, troops and stores for naval bombardment and Harrier strikes. Some of the teams stay in position, close to the Argentines and in bad weather for many days at a time. Areas of operation on East Falkland are believed to include Bluff Cove, Stanley, Berkeley Sound, Cow Bay, Port Salvador, San Carlos Water, Goose Green and Lafonia and, over on West Falkland, Pebble Island, Port Howard and Fox Bay. The first patrols start flying in on the night of Saturday 1 May in the four remaining No 846 NAS Sea King HC4s from HMS *Hermes* which, equipped with PNG for night flying, play such an important role over the next six weeks.

MAP 17 — WEEK SIX

5th Infantry Brigade and Task Force Movements

3-9 May

Once 3 Cdo Bde is ashore, the Army's 5th Infantry Brigade will arrive to bring total land forces strength to approximately 10,000 men. Both brigades will then come under the divisional headquarters of Maj-Gen Jeremy Moore RM as Commander, Land Forces Falkland Islands. Even then, to retake the islands, he will be far short of the superiority of numbers needed to easily defeat the well-dug-in defenders. Brigade infantry is provided by the 1st Battalion, 7th Duke of Edinburgh's Own Gurkha Rifles, together with 1st Battalion Welsh Guards and 2nd Battalion Scots Guards transferred to 5th Infantry Brigade to replace 2nd and 3rd Battalions The Parachute Regiment. Before sailing, they train for two weeks near Sennybridge in Wales in terrain similar to the Falklands. Support will come from a variety of arms and units, some of which are already represented in 3 Cdo Bde:

Artillery — HQ and 97 Bty, 4 Field Regt RA with 6×105mm guns.
Air defence — one troop of 43 Air Defence Bty, 32 Guided Weapons Regt RA with Blowpipe SAMs.

Combat engineers — 36 Engineer Regt RE and 9 Parachute Sqn RE.
Helicopters — No 656 Sqn AAC with three Scout AH1s and six Gazelle AH1s (one Gazelle is lost).
HQ and Communications — Brigade HQ and Signal Sqn with Rear Link Detachments Royal Signals.
Other units include complete or in part — 407 Road Transport Troop RCT with Snowcats, 16 Field Ambulance RAMC, 81 and 91 Ordnance Coys and 421 Explosive Ordnance Disposal Coy RAOC, 10 Field Workshop REME, 160 Provost Coy RMP and 8 Field Cash Office RAPC.

Most of the more than 3,000 men of the Brigade sail on *Queen Elizabeth 2* and are joined from Ascension by Gen Moore as Commander (designate) who assumes full command of land forces in early June. Supporting equipment, some troops and the helicopters are carried by transports *Baltic Ferry* and *Nordic Ferry*.

Above:
Sgt I. J. McKay VC, 3 Para.
Courtesy — Airborne Forces Museum

Below:
Lt-Col J. F. Rickett OBE, CO, 1st Battalion Welsh Guards. *Courtesy — Brig J. F. Rickett*

Above:
Lt-Cdr A. D. Auld DSC, RN, CO No 800 NAS.
Courtesy — RNAS Yeovilton

Below:
Lt-Cdr I. Stanley DSO, RN, Flight Commander, No 737 NAS, HMS *Antrim*.
Courtesy — RNAS Yeovilton

Task Force departures from Monday

3 May

Monday sees the last nuclear submarines on their way to the South Atlantic when HMS *Valiant* leaves Faslane for patrol off the Argentine coast. (HMS *Courageous* also posibly leaves around this time.) Two more warships also sail from other parts of the world for Ascension and on to the TEZ after carrying out guardship duties — frigate HMS *Ambuscade* from Gibraltar on Monday and destroyer HMS *Exeter* from the West Indies on Friday to replace the lost HMS *Sheffield*.

Two merchantmen leave with much needed supplies for the Task Force, but this time via South Georgia. On Tuesday 4 May, the cargo ship *Lycaon* sails from Southampton loaded with ammunition, and on Saturday 8 May the refrigerated stores ship *Saxonia* leaves Plymouth loaded mainly with food. Additional tankers also head for the South Atlantic during the week — *Alvega* from Portsmouth for Ascension to serve out the war as a base storage tanker supplying heavy fuel oil, diesel and aviation fuel, and *Eburna* sailing from the West Indies having earlier been converted for fleet refuelling at Plymouth. Then on Sunday, part of 5th Infantry Brigade heads out from Southampton on RO-RO ferries *Baltic Ferry* and *Nordic Ferry*.

Ascension

Late on Monday 3 May, two Vulcans and their Victor tankers take off to get one of the bombers to Stanley early next morning for Operation 'Black Buck 2'. Meanwhile the build-up of aircraft continues. Starting on Monday, nine Harrier GR3s from RAF Wittering (a 10th returns) reach Wideawake over the next three days after making the 9hr flight from St Mawgan. Of these, three stay on to provide the first local air defence for Ascension and the other six prepare to embark on *Atlantic Conveyor* later in the week. During the week the two No 845 NAS Wessex based on the island are joined in their vertrep duties by one of her Chinooks and by a flown-in Sea King HAR3 which also provides SAR.

Now the bulk of 3 Cdo Bde follows in the wake of the slower LSLs. On Thursday 6 May *Canberra* leaves with 40 and 42 Cdo RM and 3 Para, and with both her and *Elk* carrying their own Sea King HC4s. Accompanying them is RFA *Tidepool* and two escorting frigates. As they leave, the rest of the Amphibious Group ships are arriving to join HMS *Fearless* and RFA *Stromness* (now with most of 45 Cdo RM on board), but only to stay for a short time.

Assault ship HMS *Intrepid* and transport *Atlantic Conveyor* reach the island on Wednesday, and the merchantman takes on board the awaiting eight Sea Harriers and six GR3s to add to her already large complement of helicopters. Finally, transports *Europic Ferry* and *Norland* get in with 2 Para after calling in at Freetown on the way. Within a matter of hours on Friday, they and the last of the amphibious ships are heading south.

South Atlantic

Later in the week, escorting warships HMS *Antelope* and HMS *Antrim* meet and exchange roles. HMS *Antelope* carries on north with *Tidespring* and her POWs bound for Ascension, while HMS *Antrim* takes over the task of escorting the LSL Group south, in which she is joined by HMS *Plymouth* from the CVBG.

Further south, but back on Tuesday 4 May, the Carrier Battle Group suffers its first, shocking casualty when the destroyer HMS *Sheffield* is hit by an air-launched Exocet, the missile which exercises such an influence on Task Force operations throughout the war. Meanwhile, HMS *Endurance*, on her own at South Georgia, sees the start of the build-up there when two tugs arrive. RMAS *Typhoon* stays through May, while *Salvageman* soon leaves to assist HMS *Sheffield* but without success, and moves on to what is later known as the Tug, Repair and Logistic Area (TRALA) to the east of the Falklands. On Sunday, RFA *Blue Rover* follows them in to Cumberland Bay to take up her duties as station tanker.

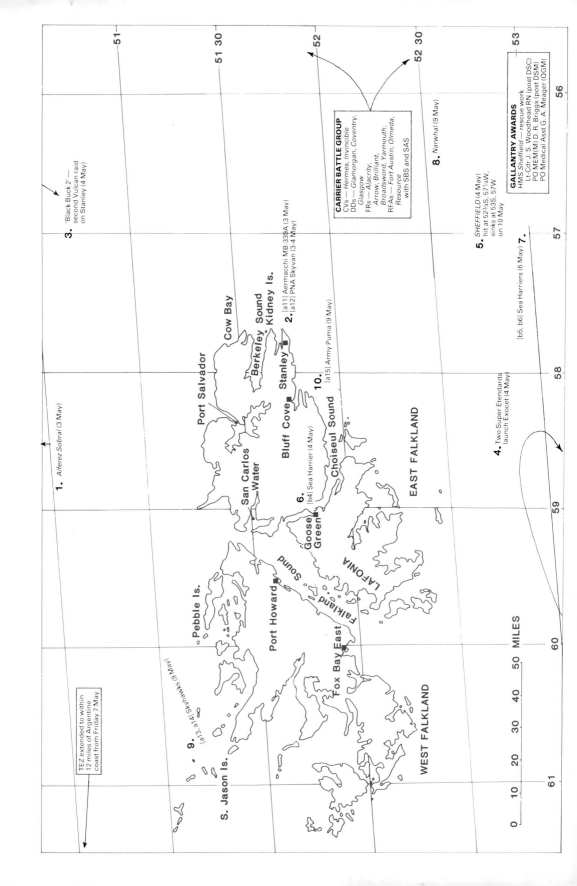

1. *Alferez Sobral* (3 May)

3. 'Black Buck 2' — second Vulcan raid on Stanley (4 May)

TEZ extended to within 12 miles of Argentine coast from Friday 7 May

Cow Bay

Port Salvador

Berkeley Sound

Kidney Is.

2. [a11] Aermacchi MB-339A (3 May)
[a12] PNA Skyvan (3-4 May)

Stanley

10. [a15] Army Puma (9 May)

Bluff Cove

San Carlos Water

Choiseul Sound

6. [b4] Sea Harrier (4 May)

Goose Green

EAST FALKLAND

LAFONIA

Falkland Sound

Port Howard

Pebble Is.

Fox Bay East

WEST FALKLAND

S. Jason Is.

9. [a13, a14] Skyhawks (9 May)

0 10 20 30 40 50 MILES 60 61

CARRIER BATTLE GROUP
CVs — *Hermes, Invincible*
DDs — *Glamorgan, Coventry,
Glasgow*
FRs — *Alacrity,
Arrow, Brilliant,
Broadsword, Yarmouth,*
RFAs — *Fort Austin, Olmeda,
Resource*
with SBS and SAS

8. *Narwhal* (9 May)

5. *SHEFFIELD* (4 May) hit at 52¾S, 57¼W, sinks at 53S, 57W on 10 May

4. Two Super Etendards launch Exocet (4 May)

[b5, b6] Sea Harriers (6 May) 7.

GALLANTRY AWARDS
HMS *Sheffield* — rescue work
Lt-Cdr J. S. Woodhead RN (post DSC)
PO MEM(M) D. R. Briggs (post DSM)
PO Medical Asst G. A. Meager (QGM)

51

51 30

52

52 30

53

56 57 58 59 60 61

MAP 18 — WEEK SIX

Falkland Area Operations

3-9 May

With the Argentine Navy's return to port, the British Task Force establishes control of the surrounding seas, but it will be weeks before air supremacy is achieved. As a foretaste of events, the first ships and aircraft are lost in combat on Tuesday 4 May. However before then it is the Argentine forces which suffer more casualties.

At midnight on Sunday 2 May, as patrol vessel *Alferez Sobral* searches for the crew of the downed Canberra [a8] to the north of the Falklands, she is detected by a No 826 NAS Sea King. Fired on, the helicopter calls for help and from a range of eight miles, HMS *Coventry's* Lynx helicopters fires two of the new Sea Skua missiles. These are followed shortly afterwards by two more from HMS *Glasgow's* Lynx. Badly damaged and with eight crew dead, the *Sobral* is escorted into Puerto Deseado two days later, but the Canberra's crew is never found. Later in the day one of two MB-339As of CANA 1 Esc, returning to Stanley from a patrol to the southeast, crashes in bad weather near the airfield killing the pilot [a11], and that night, a PNA Skyvan [a12] at the airfield is badly damaged in another bombardment by HMS *Glamorgan*, HMS *Alacrity* and HMS *Arrow*. Then early on Tuesday morning, the same Vulcan as before attacks the runway in Operation 'Black Buck 2'.

Most of the TF79 ships are returning to port by Tuesday and *25 de Mayo* disembarks her aircraft. Although the submarine *San Luis* stays out a few more days, the rest of the Navy keeps well clear of the British nuclear submarines. However, to the south of the Falklands a number of ships join the search for survivors from the *General Belgrano* with most of them returning on Wednesday. Then, to confirm control of the seas, Britain extends the TEZ on Friday and warns Argentina that any warships or military aircraft found more than 12 miles from the Argentine coast are liable to attack.

By late morning on Tuesday 4 May the CVBG is 70 miles to the southeast of Stanley. Aware of the Exocet threat, the frigates HMS *Brilliant* and HMS *Broadsword*, with their point defence Sea Wolf missiles, stay in close to the carriers. Near them is a screen of three RFAs, further out a second one of HMS *Glamorgan* and three more frigates, and then 20 miles ahead, the three Type 42s including HMS *Sheffield* with their high altitude Sea Darts. Finally towards the Falklands, Sea Harriers of No 801 NAS fly CAP and at this time investigate a number of possible air contacts.

Before then a CANA Neptune has picked up the ships by radar and two Super Etendards of 2 Esc take off from Rio Grande each armed with an Exocet AM39. Refuelled by a Grupo 1 Hercules, they go in at low altitude, climb for a radar check and release the missiles from 20 to 30 miles. One of the Exocets may just have missed HMS *Yarmouth*, but with hardly any warning the other slams into HMS *Sheffield* soon after 11.00hrs. Hitting her amidships, the warhead does not explode, but the impact and unused fuel start uncontrollable fires, leaving the ship badly damaged and with little power. The frigate HMS *Arrow* soon comes alongside to assist and HMS Yarmouth stands by. Capt Salt's crew fight gallantly to save their ship, but with 20 men dead, the order to abandon is given that afternoon. With the wounded already on board HMS *Hermes*, HMS *Arrow* takes off most of the 260 survivors. HMS *Sheffield* drifts for four days until HMS *Yarmouth* is ordered to pull her clear of the TEZ. Taken in tow by Sunday, HMS *Sheffield* finally sinks next day not too many miles from where she was hit. The survivors later return to Ascension on the tanker *British Esk*.

Shortly after HMS *Sheffield* is hit, three No 800 NAS Sea Harriers from HMS *Hermes* attack Goose Green airstrip with CBUs and retard bombs. Little damage is done, but one aircraft is hit by Skyguard-directed 35mm Oerlikon fire and crashes killing the pilot [b4]. With the threat from Exocet, the carriers now move further away from Stanley, and there is little activity over the next few days, but that does not prevent further losses. On the morning of Thursday 6 May, two No 801 NAS Sea Harriers on CAP are sent to check a radar contact and disappear without trace after presumably colliding in the poor visibility [b5, b6].

With the carriers down to 17 Harriers, their next action takes place on the morning of Sunday 9 May when two No 800 NAS aircraft take off from HMS *Hermes* to bomb Stanley.

Stopped by cloud cover, they detect the intelligence trawler *Narwhal* on the way back and are given permission to attack by the control ship HMS *Coventry*. Strafing fails to stop her and the high-altitude fuzed bombs are dropped, one of which hits without exploding. With the trawler at a standstill, Sea Kings from Nos 820 and 846 NAS fly an SBS party in some 150 miles to capture her. But before their arrival, two more No 800 NAS Sea Harriers attack and further damage *Narwhal* with cannon fire. The SBS boarding goes ahead, but next day she sinks while under tow with one crewman dead.

Returning to the Saturday evening, and with the Task Force back on the offensive, the frigate HMS *Alacrity* bombards the Stanley area as HMS *Brilliant* and her Lynx enter the north end of Falkland Sound to intercept any supply ships. Meanwhile HMS *Coventry* and HMS *Broadsword* have moved closer to Stanley with the unenviable job of tempting out Argentine aircraft. Late on Sunday morning, HMS *Coventry* fires three Sea Dart missiles at distant aircraft, including a Hercules on a supply run to Stanley, and apparently misses. However, around this time, two Grupo 4 Skyhawks are lost. They may have been hit by the Sea Darts or alternatively they may have crashed in low visibility on their way to attack the two ships. Whatever the case, one of them is later found on South Jason Island [a13, a14]. Then in the afternoon, as an Argentinian Army Puma heads out over Choiseul Sound to search for the *Narwhal*, another Sea Dart fired at extreme range brings her down with the loss of all on board [a15].

MAP 19 — WEEK SEVEN

The Attacking Argentine Aircraft and Task Force Movements

10-16 May

Aside from the land battles, most of the war is fought between Argentine aircraft and the British ships and carrier-borne Harriers. Argentine losses are heavy, but so are the Royal Navy's, and only the hit on HMS *Glamorgan* by a land-based Exocet at the end of the war is not due to aircraft. Just before the San Carlos landings, this is a useful point to summarise the main Argentine aircraft involved and the losses they sustain, as well as inflict:

Naval Aviation Command (CANA)

1st Attack Sqn (1 Esc) — 6 Aermacchi MB-339As to Falklands, two lost and three captured. Minor damage to HMS *Argonaut* by cannon (21 May).

2nd Fighter and Attack Sqn (2 Esc) — Super Etendard flying from Rio Grande with no losses. Destroyer HMS *Sheffield* (4 May) and transport *Atlantic Conveyor* (25 May) hit by Exocets and sunk.

3rd Fighter and Attack Sqn (3 Esc) — Skyhawk A-4Qs flying from Rio Grande, three lost. Frigate HMS *Ardent* sunk by bombs (21 May).

4th Attack Sqn (4 Esc) — 4 Mentor T-34Cs to Falklands, all lost.

Argentine Air Force (FAA)

1st Air Transport Group (Grupo 1) — Hercules (one lost), Boeing 707s. Also photo-reconnaissance Learjets (one lost).

2nd Light Bomber Group (Grupo 2) — Canberras flying from Trelew and Rio Gallegos, two lost.

3rd Attack Group (Grupo 3) — 24 Pucaras to

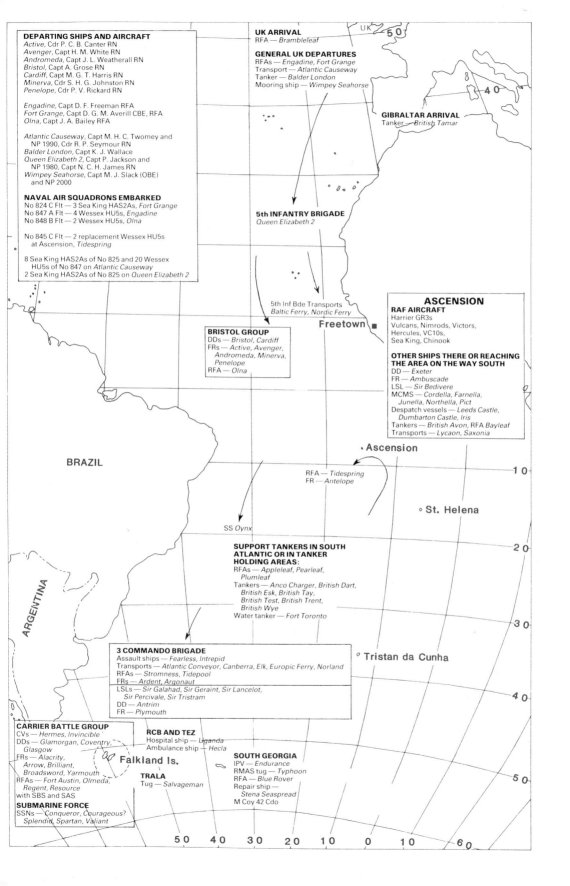

DEPARTING SHIPS AND AIRCRAFT
Active, Cdr P. C. B. Canter RN
Avenger, Capt H. M. White RN
Andromeda, Capt J. L. Weatherall RN
Bristol, Capt A. Grose RN
Cardiff, Capt M. G. T. Harris RN
Minerva, Cdr S. H. G. Johnston RN
Penelope, Cdr P. V. Rickard RN

Engadine, Capt D. F. Freeman RFA
Fort Grange, Capt D. G. M. Averill CBE, RFA
Olna, Capt J. A. Bailey RFA

Atlantic Causeway, Capt M. H. C. Twomey and
  NP 1990, Cdr R. P. Seymour RN
Balder London, Capt K. J. Wallace
Queen Elizabeth 2, Capt P. Jackson and
  NP 1980, Capt N. C. H. James RN
Wimpey Seahorse, Capt M. J. Slack (OBE)
  and NP 2000

NAVAL AIR SQUADRONS EMBARKED
No 824 C Flt — 3 Sea King HAS2As, *Fort Grange*
No 847 A Flt — 4 Wessex HU5s, *Engadine*
No 848 B Flt — 2 Wessex HU5s, *Olna*

No 845 C Flt — 2 replacement Wessex HU5s
  at Ascension, *Tidespring*

8 Sea King HAS2As of No 825 and 20 Wessex
  HU5s of No 847 on *Atlantic Causeway*
2 Sea King HAS2As of No 825 on *Queen Elizabeth 2*

UK ARRIVAL
RFA — *Brambleleaf*

GENERAL UK DEPARTURES
RFAs — *Engadine*, *Fort Grange*
Transport — *Atlantic Causeway*
Tanker — *Balder London*
Mooring ship — *Wimpey Seahorse*

GIBRALTAR ARRIVAL
Tanker — *British Tamar*

5th INFANTRY BRIGADE
Queen Elizabeth 2

5th Inf Bde Transports
Baltic Ferry, Nordic Ferry

Freetown ■

BRISTOL GROUP
DDs — *Bristol, Cardiff*
FRs — *Active, Avenger,*
  Andromeda, Minerva,
  Penelope
RFA — *Olna*

ASCENSION
RAF AIRCRAFT
Harrier GR3s
Vulcans, Nimrods, Victors,
Hercules, VC10s,
Sea King, Chinook

**OTHER SHIPS THERE OR REACHING
THE AREA ON THE WAY SOUTH**
DD — *Exeter*
FR — *Ambuscade*
LSL — *Sir Bedivere*
MCMS — *Cordella, Farnella,*
  Junella, Northella, Pict
Despatch vessels — *Leeds Castle,*
  Dumbarton Castle, Iris
Tankers — *British Avon, RFA Bayleaf*
Transports — *Lycaon, Saxonia*

BRAZIL

• Ascension

RFA — *Tidespring*
FR — *Antelope*

∘ St. Helena

SS *Oynx*

**SUPPORT TANKERS IN SOUTH
ATLANTIC OR IN TANKER
HOLDING AREAS:**
RFAs — *Appleleaf, Pearleaf,*
  Plumleaf
Tankers — *Anco Charger, British Dart,*
  British Esk, British Tay,
  British Test, British Trent,
  British Wye
Water tanker — *Fort Toronto*

∘ **Tristan da Cunha**

3 COMMANDO BRIGADE
Assault ships — *Fearless, Intrepid*
Transports — *Atlantic Conveyor, Canberra, Elk, Europic Ferry, Norland*
RFAs — *Stromness, Tidepool*
FRs — *Ardent, Argonaut*
LSLs — *Sir Galahad, Sir Geraint, Sir Lancelot,*
  Sir Percivale, Sir Tristram
DD — *Antrim*
FR — *Plymouth*

ARGENTINA

CARRIER BATTLE GROUP
CVs — *Hermes, Invincible*
DDs — *Glamorgan, Coventry,*
  Glasgow
FRs — *Alacrity,*
  Arrow, Brilliant,
  Broadsword, Yarmouth
RFAs — *Fort Austin, Olmeda,*
  Regent, Resource
with SBS and SAS
SUBMARINE FORCE
SSNs — *Conqueror, Courageous?*
  Splendid, Spartan, Valiant

Falkland Is.

TRALA
Tug — *Salvageman*

RCB AND TEZ
Hospital ship — *Uganda*
Ambulance ship — *Hecla*

SOUTH GEORGIA
IPV — *Endurance*
RMAS tug — *Typhoon*
RFA — *Blue Rover*
Repair ship —
  Stena Seaspread
M Coy 42 Cdo

Falklands, 13 lost and 11 captured, plus one mainland-based aircraft lost. Only British aircraft casualty directly due to Argentine aircraft is a Royal Marine Scout [b28] shot down by a Grupo 3 Pucara on the 28 May.

4th Fighter Bomber Group (Grupo 4) — Skyhawk A-4Cs flying from San Julian and Rio Grande, nine lost. Believed to have damaged LSLs *Sir Bedivere*, *Sir Galahad* and *Sir Lancelot* with UXBs (24 May).

5th Fighter Bomber Group (Grupo 5) — Skyhawk A-4Bs from Rio Gallegos, 10 lost:
Destroyer HMS *Glasgow* damaged by UXB (12 May),
Frigate HMS *Argonaut* damaged by UXB (21 May),
Frigate HMS *Antelope* sunk by bomb (23 May),
Destroyer HMS *Coventry* sunk by bombs and frigate HMS *Broadsword* damaged by UXB (25 May),
LSLs *Sir Galahad* (later scuttled) and *Sir Tristram* damaged, and HMS *Fearless* LCU F4 sunk by bombs (8 June).

6th Fighter Bomber Group (Grupo 6) — Daggers from Rio Grande and San Julian, 11 lost:
Destroyer HMS *Glamorgan*, frigates HMS *Alacrity* and HMS *Arrow*, minor damage by cannon fire and near misses (1 May).
Destroyer HMS *Antrim* damaged by UXB, frigate HMS *Ardent* damaged by bomb, frigates HMS *Brilliant* and HMS *Broadsword* minor damage by cannon fire (21 May).
Frigate HMS *Plymouth* damaged by UXB and cannon (8 June).

7th Group, Helicopter Sqn — including Bell 212s and Chinooks. Two Bell 212s to Falklands, both lost.

8th Fighter Group (Grupo 8) — Mirage IIIEs from Comodoro Rivadavia and Rio Callegos, two lost.

Adding the aircraft of the Argentine Coastguard (PNA) and Army Combat Aviation Battalion 601 transferred to the Falklands, all of which are destroyed or captured, plus two Navy helicopters lost at sea, brings total losses from all causes to a round 100.

Task Force Departures from Monday 10 May

The week sees the departure of the first (and the last) major sea and land reinforcements, starting on Monday with the 'Bristol' group of ships which hurry down in two weeks. Type 82 destroyer HMS *Bristol* and RFA fleet tanker *Olna* leave from Portsmouth and Type 21 frigates HMS *Active* and HMS *Avenger* and 'Leander' class HMS *Andromeda*, HMS *Minerva* and HMS

Penelope from Devonport. On Wednesday, Type 42 destroyer HMS *Cardiff* departs Gibraltar following a Persian Gulf patrol and by Friday has joined the group. RFA helicopter support ship *Engadine* also sails from Devonport at the same time as HMS *Bristol* and her companions but makes her own way via Gibraltar carrying four Wessex helicopters. The remaining 20 Wessex from reformed No 847 NAS and eight No 825 NAS Sea Kings follow on Friday in RO-RO container ship *Atlantic Causeway* after her conversion to a helicopter ship complete with flightdeck and hangar.

On Wednesday 12 May an even more important departure is the bulk of 5th Infantry Brigade on *Queen Elizabeth 2* from Southampton direct for South Georgia. Then on Friday, RFA fleet replenishment ship *Fort Grange* heads out from Devonport, followed on Sunday by offshore support vessel *Wimpey Seahorse* following earlier work on her at Rosyth. More tanker movements also take place with *Balder London* sailing from Portsmouth, RFA *Brambleleaf* getting into Portland later in the week for repairs to the damage received off South Georgia, and *British Tamar* reaching Gibraltar on Friday to reload.

Ascension

As *Leeds Castle* heads on south, *Dumbarton Castle* arrives to begin her duties as a despatch vessel. Arriving on Wednesday 12 May from the other direction with the South Georgia POWs is RFA *Tidespring* and escorting frigate HMS *Antelope*. After *Tidespring* picks up two replacement Wessex helicopters, she and HMS *Antelope* head back south over the weekend, hardly a week before the frigate's end. On Saturday 15 May in a record-breaking 8,300-mile flight lasting 19hr, an RAF Nimrod crewed by No 201 Sqn reconnoitres the Argentine coast for any warships that might threaten the approaching Task Force, but on Sunday 16 May Operation 'Black Buck 3' the Vulcan raid on Stanley is cancelled.

South Atlantic

RFA fleet replenishment ship *Regent* joins the carriers and around the end of the week, submarine HMS *Valiant* arrives to start patrolling off the Argentine coast. To the north of Stanley, the Red Cross Box comes into operation with the arrival of hospital ship *Uganda* on Tuesday 11 May followed three days later by the ambulance ship *Hecla*, the first of the three to arrive. Off to the east of the Falklands, the tug *Salvageman* arrives in the TRALA where she will shortly be joined by the repair ship *Stena Seaspeed* which just now reaches South Georgia. On the Sunday the bulk of 3 Cdo Bde catches up with the LSL Group only five days from the landings at San Carlos.

MAP 20 — WEEK SEVEN

Falkland Area Operations

10-16 May

In the build-up to the landings at San Carlos, Adm Woodward's destroyers and frigates continue to wear down the invaders and D Sqn SAS makes an important contribution with its Pebble Island raid. On Monday 10 May, as submarine *San Luis* makes her last reported and equally unsuccessful attack on ships of the Task Force and HMS *Sheffield* finally sinks, HMS *Glasgow* (Sea Dart) and HMS *Brilliant* (Sea Wolf) have taken over as Type 42/22 combination from HMS *Coventry* and HMS *Broadsword* and continue their radar picket and bombardment duties off Stanley. That night as HMS *Arrow* moves to the north end of Falkland Sound, sister ship HMS *Alacrity* prepares to sail right through from the south for the first time to flush out any supply ships.

As she passes up the Sound, HMS *Alacrity* detects a small ship apparently heading for Port Howard, and using her single 4.5in gun, illuminates her quarry with a star shell. Refusing to stop, the target is engaged in the only surface action of the war and after a number of hits, explodes and sinks with heavy casualties. Reportedly there are only two survivors from what turns out to be the naval transport *Isla de los Estados* carrying fuel and military supplies. HMS *Alacrity* carries on through to meet HMS *Arrow*, and now into Tuesday morning, both ships head back to the carriers. Later that day, HMS *Yarmouth* also returns from her attempts to tow HMS *Sheffield* out of the TEZ.

On the afternoon of Wednesday 12 May with HMS *Glasgow* and HMS *Brilliant* still off Stanley, eight A-4B Skyhawks of Grupo 5 are sent in to attack the bombarding ships. The first flight comes in low, and as HMS *Brilliant* fires her Sea Wolf automatically for the first time in anger, two aircraft explode in the air, a third crashes into the sea trying to escape and the fourth escapes having dropped its bomb without effect [a16, a17, a18]. The second flight of four comes in some minutes later, but for technical reasons Sea Wolf cannot fire, and this time HMS *Glasgow* is hit by a bomb which passes through the ship without exploding or causing any casualties. Although the damage is not severe, she has to withdraw to the CVBG for repairs that take a number of days and eventually becomes the first warship to return home. Meanwhile as these Skyhawks return home, they pass too close to Goose Green and HMS *Glasgow's* attacker is shot down by Argentine AA [a19].

Just a week before the landings, a raid is mounted by D Sqn SAS on the airstrip and facilities at Pebble Island, especially to destroy the ground attack Pucaras based there. First of all men of Boat Troop are put ashore over Tuesday night to reconnoitre the area and three days later on Friday 14 May, HMS *Hermes* and escort HMS *Broadsword* together with HMS *Glamorgan* in the fire support role leave the CVBG, and passing to the north, approach Pebble Island by night. As HMS *Glamorgan* closes in to gunfire range, HMS *Hermes* flies off the 48 SAS attackers and the NGFO team in her No 846 NAS Sea Kings to be guided in at midnight by the waiting patrol. After a forced march to the airstrip, the attack goes in led by Capt Hamilton, and all the aircraft there are put of action or destroyed by prepared charges. A fuel depot, ammo dump and radar installation is also destroyed. All this time HMS *Glamorgan* provides gunfire support, and as the raiders withdraw, a brief Argentine counter-attack is halted when the officer in charge is shot. With two men slightly wounded the SAS are safely picked up again by the helicopters.

The raid is a complete success and the Argentines not only lose six Pucaras of Grupo 3 [a20-25], four T-34C Mentors [a26-29] of CANA 4 Esc and one Coast Guard Skyvan [a30], but also the use of the airstrip at a crucial time. Now into Saturday morning, the warships return to the CVBG, but HMS *Glamorgan* soon moves on to other duties.

Although bad weather has restricted fixed wing flying earlier in the week, by Wednesday 12 May it has improved sufficiently for high-level bombing attacks to be made on Stanley. On the same day a No 826 NAS ASW Sea King from HMS *Hermes* ditches near the CVBG with engine failure [b7]. The crew are saved. The next main action takes place over the weekend as Sea Harriers continue to bomb Stanley. On Saturday night HMS *Brilliant's* Lynx fail in an attack on the transport *Bahia Buen Suceso* in Fox Bay East, but aircraft from HMS *Hermes* more than make up for this next day.

In the middle of Sunday 16 May, two No 800 NAS Sea Harriers bomb and strafe the

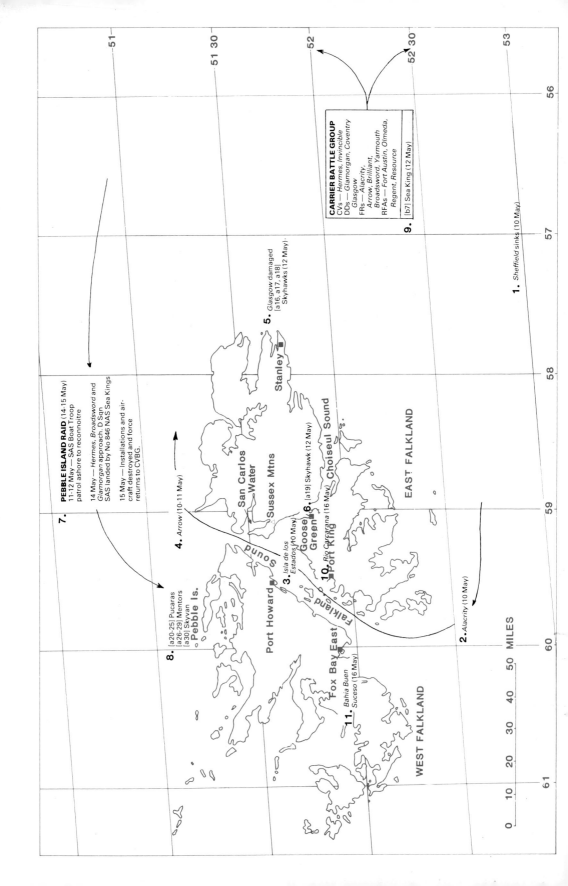

CARRIER BATTLE GROUP
CVs — Hermes, Invincible
DDs — Glamorgan, Coventry
   Glasgow
FRs — Alacrity,
   Arrow, Brilliant,
   Broadsword, Yarmouth
RFAs — Fort Austin, Olmeda,
   Regent, Resource

9. [b7] Sea King (12 May)

1. Sheffield sinks (10 May)

5. Glasgow damaged
   [a16, a17, a18]
   Skyhawks (12 May)

Stanley

7. PEBBLE ISLAND RAID (14-15 May)
   11-12 May — SAS Boat Troop
   patrol ashore to reconnoitre
   14 May — Hermes, Broadsword and
   Glamorgan approach. D Sqn
   SAS landed by No 846 NAS Sea Kings
   15 May — Installations and aircraft destroyed and force
   returns to CVBG.

4. Arrow (10-11 May)

San Carlos
Water

Sussex Mtns

Choiseul Sound

EAST FALKLAND

Sound

6. [a19] Skyhawk (12 May)

Goose
Green

Isla de los
Estados (10 May)

Port Howard

3.

10. Port King
   Rio Caracaranà (16 May)

8. [a20-25] Pucaras
   [a26-29] Mentors
   [a30] Skyvan
   Pebble Is.

Falkland
Sound

2. Alacrity (10 May)

Fox Bay East

11. Bahia Buen
   Suceso (16 May)

WEST FALKLAND

0 10 20 30 40 50 MILES

51

51 30

52

52 30

53

56

57

58

59

60

61

blockade-running cargo ship *Rio Carcarana* (8,500grt) at anchor off Port King. Although there are no casualties, she catches fire, is beached and abandoned, finally to be destroyed by HMS *Antelope's* Lynx a week later. Another two aircraft catch the *Bahia Buen Suceso* still at Fox Bay East alongside the jetty and rake her with cannon fire. Bombs are not used because of the ship's proximity to the settlement, but the damage is enough to deny her use by the Argentines, and she stays there until after the war.

Following the Pebble Island raid, HMS *Glamorgan* takes on the job of convincing the Argentines that any landings will take place on East Falkland, south of the capital. For a number of nights, she bombards Stanley and moves down the coast as far as Choiseul Sound carrying out a variety of deception activities. Other SBS and SAS operations are no doubt taking place all this time, and over Sunday night HMS *Alacrity* sails through Falkland Sound again and lands an SBS/NGFO team by Gemini near Sussex Mountains which overlooks the landing beaches around San Carlos Water.

SAN CARLOS LANDINGS AND CONSOLIDATION

MAP 21 — WEEK EIGHT

Argentine Defences and Task Force Movements

17-23 May

By the time Britain is ready to land, Argentine forces are well established on the islands. In spite of the numerous Sea Harrier attacks and naval bombardments and the Pebble Island raid, they are superior in numbers of men, artillery, attack aircraft and have a good helicopter lift capability. However on the ground, they are about to depend on well prepared defensive positions rather than aggressive counter-attack. Following is a summary of the main ground forces and supporting aircraft. On the eve of the landings most of the latter are based at Stanley although some of the FAA Pucaras and helicopters are at Goose Green. Pebble Island is of course out of action. A total of 20 attack aircraft and 23 helicopters from the four services remain available after losses to date:

Falkland Islands — commanded by Maj-Gen Menendez

Ground Forces include:
3rd Mechanised Infantry Brigade (Maj-Gen Omar Parada with 4th, 5th, 8th and 12th Regts).
10th Motorised Infantry Brigade (Maj-Gen Oscar Joffre with 3rd, 6th and 7th Regts).
The independent 25th Regt and 5th Marine Infantry Btn.

Stanley and Approaches — Commander, Maj-Gen Joffre, 10th Bde reinforced to c8,000 men from:
  3rd, 4th, 6th, 7th and 25th Regts, each of c1,000 men. All Motorised Infantry except for 4th Infantry.
  5th Marine Infantry Btn, c800 men.
  3rd Artillery Btn with 30×105mm and 3×155mm guns.
  Armoured Car Sqn with 12 Panhards.
  181st Military Police and Intelligence Coy.
  601st Anti-Aircraft Btn.

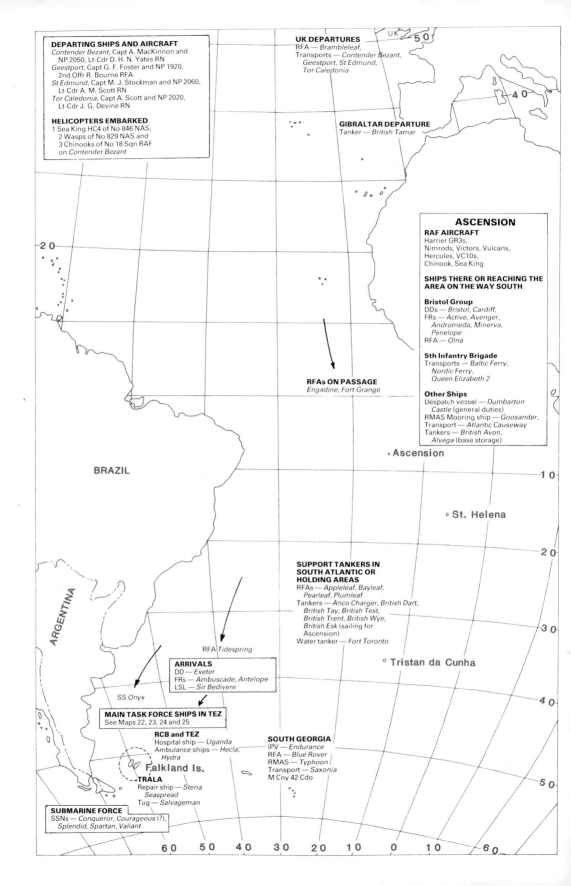

DEPARTING SHIPS AND AIRCRAFT
Contender Bezant, Capt A. MacKinnon and
  NP 2050, Lt-Cdr D. H. N. Yates RN
Geestport, Capt G. F. Foster and NP 1920,
  2nd Offr R. Bourne RFA
St Edmund, Capt M. J. Stockman and NP 2060,
  Lt-Cdr A. M. Scott RN
Tor Caledonia, Capt A. Scott and NP 2020,
  Lt-Cdr J. G. Devine RN

HELICOPTERS EMBARKED
1 Sea King HC4 of No 846 NAS,
  2 Wasps of No 829 NAS and
  3 Chinooks of No 18 Sqn RAF
  on *Contender Bezant*

UK

50

UK DEPARTURES
RFA — *Brambleleaf*,
Transports — *Contender Bezant*,
  Geestport, *St Edmund*,
  Tor Caledonia

40

GIBRALTAR DEPARTURE
Tanker — *British Tamar*

ASCENSION

RAF AIRCRAFT
Harrier GR3s,
Nimrods, Victors, Vulcans,
Hercules, VC10s,
Chinook, Sea King

**SHIPS THERE OR REACHING THE
AREA ON THE WAY SOUTH**

Bristol Group
DDs — *Bristol*, *Cardiff*,
FRs — *Active*, *Avenger*,
  Andromeda, *Minerva*,
  Penelope
RFA — *Olna*

5th Infantry Brigade
Transports — *Baltic Ferry*,
  Nordic Ferry,
  Queen Elizabeth 2

Other Ships
Despatch vessel — *Dumbarton
  Castle* (general duties)
RMAS Mooring ship — *Goosander*,
Transport — *Atlantic Causeway*
Tankers — *British Avon*,
  Alvega (base storage)

RFAs ON PASSAGE
Engadine, *Fort Grange*

20

• Ascension

10

○ St. Helena

BRAZIL

20

**SUPPORT TANKERS IN
SOUTH ATLANTIC OR
HOLDING AREAS**
RFAs — *Appleleaf*, *Bayleaf*,
  Pearleaf, *Plumleaf*
Tankers — *Anco Charger*, *British Dart*,
  British Tay, *British Test*,
  British Trent, *British Wye*,
  British Esk (sailing for
  Ascension)
Water tanker — *Fort Toronto*

30

○ Tristan da Cunha

ARGENTINA

RFA *Tidespring*

ARRIVALS
DD — *Exeter*
FRs — *Ambuscade*, *Antelope*
LSL — *Sir Bedivere*

SS *Onyx*

MAIN TASK FORCE SHIPS IN TEZ
See Maps 22, 23, 24 and 25

RCB and TEZ
Hospital ship — *Uganda*
Ambulance ships — *Hecla*,
  Hydra

SOUTH GEORGIA
IPV — *Endurance*
RFA — *Blue Rover*
RMAS — *Typhoon*
Transport — *Saxonia*
M Coy 42 Cdo

40

Falkland Is.

TRALA
Repair ship — *Stena
  Seaspread*
Tug — *Salvageman*

SUBMARINE FORCE
SSNs — *Conqueror*, *Courageous* (?),
  Splendid, *Spartan*, *Valiant*

50

60 50 40 30 20 10 0 10 60

Goose Green and West Falkland — Commander, Maj-Gen Parada, 3rd Bde who is based in Stanley:

Goose Green — c1,000 men from 12th Inf Regt, elements 601st AA Btn, FAA elements (later — half-bty of 3×105mm guns),

Port Howard — c800 men from 5th Inf Regt and elements 9th Engineer Coy,

Fox Bay — c900 men from 8th Motorised Inf Regt and elements 9th Engineer Coy.

Aircraft Strength (losses to 20 May in brackets):

Navy: 5 MB-339s (1 MB-339 and 4 Mentors lost)

Coast Guard: 1 Puma (2 Skyvan lost)

Army: 2 Chinooks, 4 Pumas, 3 Agustas, 9 Iroquois (1 Puma lost)

Air Force: 15 Pucaras, 2 Bells, 2 Chinooks (9 Pucaras lost)

Task Force Departures from Monday 17 May

From mid week, the last four merchantmen to reach the South Atlantic before the end of hostilities sail from the UK. These include three RO-RO's — from Devonport, ferry *St Edmund* in the transport role, and container ship *Contender Bezant* as an aircraft and helicopter carrier with RAF and Navy helicopters as well as her own Wasps for supply duties and self-defence, and from Southampton, cargo ship *Tor Caledonia* with vehicles and Rapier missiles. The fourth to leave is refrigerated stores ship *Geestport* from Portsmouth loaded mainly with food. The first two ships to return also head south — *British Tamar* from Gibraltar earlier in the week and RFA support tanker *Brambleleaf* from Portland at the end.

Ascension

The main reinforcements reach the island although they just pass by or barely stop for last minute stores. Over Tuesday 18 and Wednesday 19 May it is the 'Bristol' Group, and next day the 5th Inf Bde transport's *Baltic Ferry* and *Nordic Ferry*. That same day, *Queen Elizabeth 2* carrying the complete Brigade approaches Ascension taking on board Maj-Gen Moore and his staff by helicopter after they have flown down from the UK, and by Saturday they are continuing south. Helicopter support ship *Atlantic Causeway* meets *Queen Elizabeth 2* at this time, and around now RMAS mooring ship *Goosander* is assumed to arrive to lay out and maintain moorings. The RAF also makes another record-breaking flight. On Thursday, on the eve of D-day, the same Nimrod MR2 as before, but now crewed by No 206 Sqn, flies almost the length of Argentina looking for any sign that the Argentine Navy threatens the amphibious ships.

South Atlantic

Only now, on Tuesday 18 May, as the Amphibious Task Group is joining the carriers to the north east of the Falklands, are the San Carlos plans presented to the full British Cabinet. Adm Woodward is then given the go-ahead by the war cabinet and final preparations put in hand for the landing which takes place early on the Friday morning. By the end of the week, 3 Cdo Bde is safely ashore and digging in, two Type 21 frigates have been lost and other ships damaged, and the Argentine air forces are suffering heavily at the hands of the British defences.

By then more ships have arrived from the north. The sixth and last LSL, *Sir Bedivere* reaches the TEZ before moving on to San Carlos, and by the morning of Saturday 22 May the destroyer HMS *Exeter* and frigate HMS *Ambuscade* have joined the CVBG. The latter's sister ship HMS *Antelope* also gets in from escorting *Tidespring* to Ascension, but soon moves on to San Carlos to share the fate of HMS *Ardent*. Another arrival is the despatch vessel *Leeds Castle* although her duties shortly take her to South Georgia.

Other groups of ships also play their part although not involved directly in the fighting. In the Red Cross Box area *Uganda* and *Hecla* are joined in their work by the ambulance ship *Hydra*, and the TRALA opens for repair business when *Stena Seaspread* arrives from South Georgia. By mid-June this impressive vessel has carried out damage and other repairs in mid-ocean to nearly 40 ships including 11 warships and four captured vessels. Then in South Georgia, and for later delivery to *Stena Seaspread*, working parties from HMS *Endurance* take on the job of recovering scrap steel from the disused whaling stations for ship repairs, and on Sunday, cargo ship *Saxonia* gets in ready to transfer food and other supplies to the RFAs over the next three weeks.

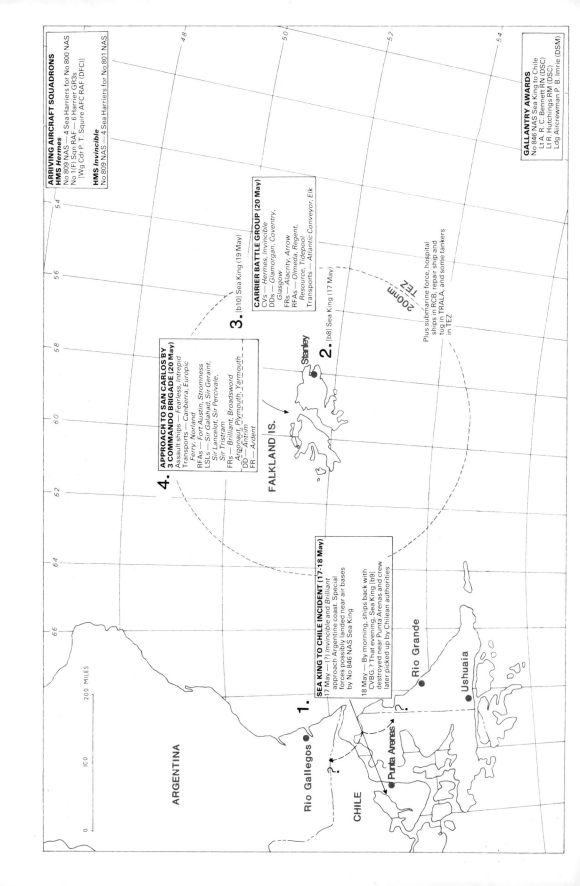

ARRIVING AIRCRAFT SQUADRONS
HMS Hermes
No 809 NAS — 4 Sea Harriers for No 800 NAS
No 1(F) Sqn RAF — 6 Harrier GR3s
[Wg Cdr P. T. Squire AFC RAF (DFC)]

HMS Invincible
No 809 NAS — 4 Sea Harriers for No 801 NAS

GALLANTRY AWARDS
No 846 NAS Sea King to Chile
Lt A. R. C. Bennett RN (DSC)
Lt R. Hutchings RM (DSC)
Ldg Aircrewman P. B. Imrie (DSM)

CARRIER BATTLE GROUP (20 May)
CVs — Hermes, Invincible
DDs — Glamorgan, Coventry,
Glasgow
FRs — Alacrity, Arrow
RFAs — Olmeda, Regent,
Resource, Tidepool
Transports — Atlantic Conveyor, Elk

3. [b10] Sea King (19 May)

2. [b8] Sea King (17 May)

Plus submarine force, hospital
ships in RCB, repair ship and
tug in TRALA, and some tankers
in TEZ

200nm TEZ

Stanley

FALKLAND IS.

**APPROACH TO SAN CARLOS BY
3 COMMANDO BRIGADE (20 May)**
Assault ships — Fearless, Intrepid
Transports — Canberra, Europic
Ferry, Norland
RFAs — Fort Austin, Stromness
LSLs — Sir Galahad, Sir Geraint,
Sir Lancelot, Sir Percivale,
Sir Tristram
FRs — Brilliant, Broadsword
Argonaut, Plymouth, Yarmouth
DD — Antrim
FR — Ardent

4.

SEA KING TO CHILE INCIDENT (17-18 May)
17 May — (?) Invincible and Brilliant
approach Argentine coast. Special
forces possibly landed near air bases
by No 846 NAS Sea King

18 May — By morning, ships back with
CVBG.? That evening, Sea King [b9]
destroyed near Punta Arenas and crew
later picked up by Chilean authorities

1.

ARGENTINA

Rio Gallegos

CHILE

Punta Arenas

Rio Grande

Ushuaia

0   100   200 MILES

MAP 22 — WEEK EIGHT

Falkland Area Operations

17-20 May

One of the strangest incidents of the war now takes place. The only certainty is that during the week the Chilean authorities find a burnt-out Sea King HC4 of No 846 NAS near the southern town of Punta Arenas, the crew of three give themselves up and are returned to the UK to later receive gallantry awards for a number of hazardous missions. Presumably, and as announced by the Ministry of Defence, these include losing their way, ending up 500 miles from the Task Force and destroying their helicopter! One possibility is that after a high speed dash to the west over the night of Monday 17 May by HMS *Invincible* and escort HMS *Brilliant*, the Sea King lands special forces near air bases in Southern Argentina either to report on aircraft as they leave to attack the Task Force or even in an attempt to destroy the Super Etendards.

Whatever happens, the carrier obviously cannot risk waiting for the helicopter to return and by the Tuesday morning is back with the CVBG. The Sea King therefore makes its way to neutral territory to be destroyed by the crew sometime over Tuesday night [b9]. Any men landed might then have been picked up later by submarine. As it happens, the diesel-engined and more manoeuvrable HMS *Onyx* arrives in the Falklands area by the end of the month and is reported to have lifted off special forces from near Rio Grande, and in doing so to have damaged herself on an uncharted rock. She also goes on to land SBS teams around the Falklands to supplement the helicopter drops.

Back on Monday 17 May, as the amphibious ships near the carrier group, the second No 826 NAS Sea King from HMS *Hermes* is lost by accident. Late that night to the east of the Falklands while on ASW patrol she hits the sea with altimeter trouble and has to be abandoned, but again fortunately with no casualties [b8]. Next day when within range, and through into Wednesday, *Atlantic Conveyor* flies off four of the embarked No 809 NAS Sea Harriers to HMS *Invincible* and the remaining four with the six RAF GR3s to HMS *Hermes*. The 25 Sea Harriers will now concentrate on air defence and the RAF GR3s on ground attack, but with a total of 31 now embarked, the carrier mainten-ance teams will be sorely stretched and yet still provide a remarkably high level of availability.

When the many ships do meet some 200 miles to the northeast of Stanley, equipment, stores, men and helicopters are redistributed ready for the landings. Eleven assault Sea Kings of No 846 NAS are moved around to four of the ships that will enter San Carlos Water, and on Wednesday evening another is lost with particularly tragic consequences. Before then, orders are received from Northwood to spread *Canberra's* major units around the other ships to avoid heavy loss of life in the event of her being hit. Through Wednesday 19 May, and in surprisingly calm weather for the South Atlantic in autumn, the larger landing craft (LCUs) carried by the assault ships transfer 40 Cdo RM to HMS *Fearless*, and Z Coy 45 Cdo and 3 Para to HMS *Intrepid*. The whole of 42 Cdo stays on *Canberra*, the rest of 45 Cdo on RFA *Stromness* and 2 Para on *Norland*.

The opportunity is also taken to transfer the special forces and three surviving night-flying No 846 NAS Sea Kings from HMS *Hermes* after their three week's covert operations. In one of the last flights that Wednesday from the carrier to HMS *Intrepid*, one of the Sea Kings loaded with SAS crashes into the sea and 21 out of the 30 men on board die [b10]. At the time a sea bird strike is thought to have brought her down, but this cause is now open to doubt. The dead include 18 men of D and G Sqns SAS — some of them so soon after their Pebble Island triumph — one member of the Royal Signals, the only RAF casualty of the war and the aircrewman, Cpl M. D. Love RM who is awarded a posthumous DSM for his special forces missions.

Carrying Brig Thompson's troops, but com-manded by Cdre Clapp, the Amphibious Task Group now heads for Falkland Sound. Leaving *Atlantic Conveyor* and *Elk* with the CVBG, it consists of command ship HMS *Fearless*, HMS *Intrepid*, the five LSLs, merchantmen *Canberra*, *Europic Ferry* and *Norland*, RFA *Stromness* as a troopship and from the carrier group, RFA *Fort Austin* for helicopter support. Apart from the original escort of HMS *Antrim*, HMS *Ardent*, HMS *Argonaut* and HMS *Ply-mouth*, Adm Woodward allocates HMS *Yarm-outh* and weakens his own defences by also sending HMS *Brilliant* and HMS *Broadsword*. Faced with sailing across the north of the Falklands through the daylight hours of Thursday 20 May, the Type 22's Sea Wolf could prove crucial in fighting off any determined aircraft attacks on the troopships.

As it happens, the convoy is hidden all day by poor weather and reaches the jumping off point for San Carlos Water without apparently being spotted. Later that Thursday, HMS *Antrim* and HMS *Ardent* go ahead on separate support missions and 3 Commando Brigade prepares to land early next morning, starting with the first assault wave of 40 Cdo and 2 Para who will go ashore at San Carlos. So much takes place in and around San Carlos Water over the next few days, three maps describe the main events.

MAP 23

Landings Around San Carlos Water, Operation 'Sutton'

21 May 1982

As the Amphibious Group sails in towards Falkland Sound, diversionary raids are mounted starting on Thursday night. Of immediate concern is a half company of infantrymen on the 800ft-high Fanning Head overlooking the entrance to San Carlos Water. To deal with these, HMS *Antrim* goes ahead with two Wessex helicopters, some 25 SBS heavily armed with machine guns, and a naval gunfire observer. The force lands by helicopter to the east of the Argentine positions under covering fire from HMS *Antrim*, and the defenders are called on to surrender. This they refuse to do and the engagement continues with a number of them killed or captured. Others escape, but Fanning Head is finally under British control and the vulnerable landing craft below saved from attack. Further south, any attempt by the Darwin garrison to move towards the beachhead is blocked by the small force of D Sqn SAS under the command of Maj Delves and supported by HMS *Ardent* out in Grantham Sound. Landed by No 846 NAS Sea Kings to the north, the attackers engage the Argentines with machine guns, anti-tank missiles and mortars to such an extent that they are reported to be in battalion strength.

While the diversions take place, the landings go ahead, admittedly with some delay and confusion, but with complete success. With the main body of the Amphibious Group anchored just outside San Carlos Water, the final plan is for 2 Para and 40 Cdo to land at San Carlos first so the paras can move south to prevent the Argentines at Darwin from occupying the Sussex Mountains. Then 45 Cdo will go ashore at Ajax Bay and 3 Para at Port San Carlos to complete the encirclement of the anchorage. With 42 Cdo remaining on *Canberra* in reserve, Rapier missiles and artillery, ammunition, fuel, rations and other stores will then be landed by the few helicopters, landing craft and Mexeflotes. The landing craft carrying the first wave are due to beach at San Carlos at 02.30hrs on Friday 21 May.

Unfortunately delays build up both in reaching the anchorage and in loading the troops, but eventually they head in below Fanning Head before turning south towards San Carlos led in by Maj Southby-Tailyour RM. The landing craft from HMS *Fearless* including the smaller LCVPs carry 40 Cdo, with two of the LCUs carrying a Scorpion and Scimitar each in the bows (four light tanks in total) ready to provide gunfire support. With them in HMS *Intrepid's* four LCUs is 2 Para from *Norland*. HMS *Plymouth* accompanies them in as close escort. Then, 3,800 miles from Ascension, the first major British landing since Suez takes place around an hour late, but completely unopposed. As soon as 2 Para lands, they move off the five miles to Sussex Mountains, and 40 Cdo digs in below the western ridge of The Verde Mountains. Now, as dawn breaks, the landing craft return to the ships still outside San Carlos Water to pick up the second wave — most of 45 Cdo from *Stromness* with Z Coy and all of 3 Para from HMS *Intrepid*. Now in daylight, the marines go ashore near the

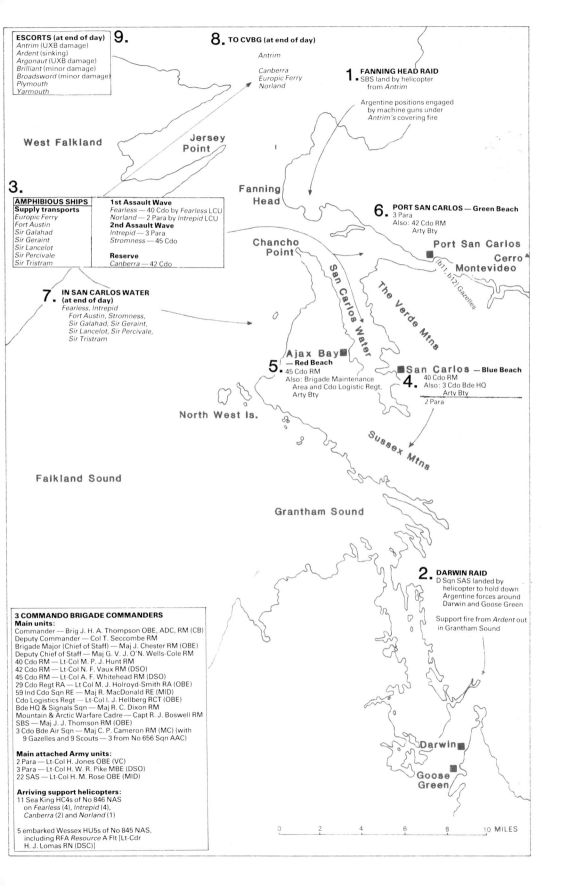

9. ESCORTS (at end of day)
Antrim (UXB damage)
Ardent (sinking)
Argonaut (UXB damage)
Brilliant (minor damage)
Broadsword (minor damage)
Plymouth
Yarmouth

8. TO CVBG (at end of day)

Antrim

Canberra
Europic Ferry
Norland

West Falkland

Jersey Point

1. FANNING HEAD RAID
• SBS land by helicopter from *Antrim*

Argentine positions engaged by machine guns under *Antrim*'s covering fire

3.

AMPHIBIOUS SHIPS	**1st Assault Wave**

Supply transports
Europic Ferry
Fort Austin
Sir Galahad
Sir Geraint
Sir Lancelot
Sir Percivale
Sir Tristram

1st Assault Wave
Fearless — 40 Cdo by *Fearless* LCU
Norland — 2 Para by *Intrepid* LCU
2nd Assault Wave
Intrepid — 3 Para
Stromness — 45 Cdo

Reserve
Canberra — 42 Cdo

Fanning Head

Chancho Point

San Carlos Water

The Verde Mtns

6. PORT SAN CARLOS — Green Beach
3 Para
Also: 42 Cdo RM
Arty Bty

Port San Carlos

Cerro Montevideo

(b.11, b'2) Gazelles

7. IN SAN CARLOS WATER
(at end of day)
*Fearless, Intrepid
Fort Austin, Stromness,
Sir Galahad, Sir Geraint,
Sir Lancelot, Sir Percivale,
Sir Tristram*

5. Ajax Bay — Red Beach
45 Cdo RM
Also: Brigade Maintenance Area and Cdo Logistic Regt, Arty Bty

4. San Carlos — Blue Beach
40 Cdo RM
Also: 3 Cdo Bde HQ
Arty Bty

2 Para

North West Is.

Falkland Sound

Grantham Sound

Sussex Mtns

2. DARWIN RAID
D Sqn SAS landed by helicopter to hold down Argentine forces around Darwin and Goose Green

Support fire from *Ardent* out in Grantham Sound

3 COMMANDO BRIGADE COMMANDERS
Main units:
Commander — Brig J. H. A. Thompson OBE, ADC, RM (CB)
Deputy Commander — Col T. Seccombe RM
Brigade Major (Chief of Staff) — Maj J. Chester RM (OBE)
Deputy Chief of Staff — Maj G. V. J. O'N. Wells-Cole RM
40 Cdo RM — Lt-Col M. P. J. Hunt RM
42 Cdo RM — Lt-Col N. F. Vaux RM (DSO)
45 Cdo RM — Lt-Col A. F. Whitehead RM (DSO)
29 Cdo Regt RA — Lt Col M. J. Holroyd-Smith RA (OBE)
59 Ind Cdo Sqn RE — Maj R. MacDonald RE (MID)
Cdo Logistics Regt — Lt-Col I. J. Hellberg RCT (OBE)
Bde HQ & Signals Sqn — Maj R. C. Dixon RM
Mountain & Arctic Warfare Cadre — Capt R. J. Boswell RM
SBS — Maj J. J. Thomson RM (OBE)
3 Cdo Bde Air Sqn — Maj C. P. Cameron RM (MC) (with 9 Gazelles and 9 Scouts — 3 from No 656 Sqn AAC)

Main attached Army units:
2 Para — Lt-Col H. Jones OBE (VC)
3 Para — Lt-Col H. W. R. Pike MBE (DSO)
22 SAS — Lt-Col H. M. Rose OBE (MID)

Arriving support helicopters:
11 Sea King HC4s of No 846 NAS on *Fearless* (4), *Intrepid* (4), *Canberra* (2) and *Norland* (1)

5 embarked Wessex HU5s of No 845 NAS, including RFA *Resource* A Flt [Lt-Cdr H. J. Lomas RN (DSC)]

Darwin

Goose Green

0   2   4   6   8   10 MILES

disused meat packing plant at Ajax Bay on the western side, and the paras a mile west of Port San Carlos on the northern side. Before 3 Para can secure the settlement, 3 Cdo Bde suffers its only fatal casualties on D-day.

With the three beachheads being secured, the 12 amphibious ships enter San Carlos Water in broad daylight — Canberra and some of the larger ones anchoring in the deeper water to the north, and the smaller LSLs nearer San Carlos. The escorts patrol nearby in Falkland Sound and take the brunt of the air attacks that follow. Using especially the No 846 NAS Sea Kings, the first priority is to get the T Bty Rapiers ashore, although it takes a number of hours to set up the 12 firing posts around the perimeter ready to join in the air defence. Early in this operation, shortly before 09.00hrs, one of the Sea Kings flies east of Port San Carlos and within gunfire range of the small Argentine garrison as it withdraws east. It escapes, but the escorting Gazelle of C Flt No 3 CBAS is hit and crashes near the shore, the pilot mortally wounded. Only minutes later a second C Flt Gazelle shares the same fate, going down on a nearby hillside, and this time both crewmen are killed [b11, b12].

Along with the tanks of The Blues and Royals, the three 105mm batteries of 29 Cdo Regt RA and the single battery of 4 Field Regt RA also land. During this time the air attacks

start, threatening the amphibious ships and their stores, and so every effort is made to unload as much as possible, particularly the ammunition so the merchantmen can leave that night. From Canberra, reserve 42 Cdo goes ashore at Port San Carlos to support 3 Para if any threat there develops, and one of the two Surgical Support Teams lands at Ajax Bay to set up a Field Dressing Station under the command of Surgeon Cdr R. T. Jolly RN, (OBE) and in the same vicinity as the Brigade Maintenance Area. Because of the air raids, Brig Thompson in not flown ashore until late afternoon but immediately starts visiting his unit commanders.

At the end of this long and violent day, and with Canberra now carrying HMS Ardent's survivors, the merchantmen, although only partly unloaded and still carrying much of the infantry unit stores, leave for the safety of the CVBG. However, Cdre Clapp and Brig Thompson have successfully secured a beachhead on the Falklands — 3 Cdo Bde is ashore with their Rapiers and artillery together with some ammunition, a start has been made on bringing a major part of the combat stores ashore, and the marines and paras are digging in and actively patrolling. However, the crucial battle over the next four days will be for air supremacy over the islands.

MAP 24

San Carlos Landings, the Air Battles of 21 May

Only two days after arriving, three of the RAF Harrier GR3s start their ground attacks by hitting a fuel dump at Fox Bay East with CBUs. Then next morning, Friday 21 May, after G Sqn SAS reports Argentine helicopters dispersing at night from Stanley a number are caught on the ground near Mount Kent and a Chinook and Puma destroyed by 30mm cannon fire [a31, a32]. Later that morning, two more aircraft leave HMS Hermes but one has to return with undercarriage problems. The lone Harrier carries on and during a photo-reconnaissance run over Port Howard is hit by ground fire and crashes [b13]. The pilot, Flt Lt Glover ejects and is taken prisoner.

The first reaction to the landings is by Falklands-based aircraft. Grupo 3 Pucaras take off from Goose Green as HMS Ardent shells the airstrip, and one is shot down over Sussex Mountains by a Stinger SAM fired by D Sqn SAS pulling back from the Darwin raid [a33]. Then a single Aermacchi MB-339A of CANA 1 Esc from Stanley makes a cannon and rocket attack on HMS Argonaut at 10.00hrs causing minor damage and some casualties. Thereafter, mainland-based sorties that day lead to heavy losses on both sides with five of the ships on the defending gunline lost or hit by bombs or cannon fire and only HMS Plymouth and HMS Yarmouth escaping

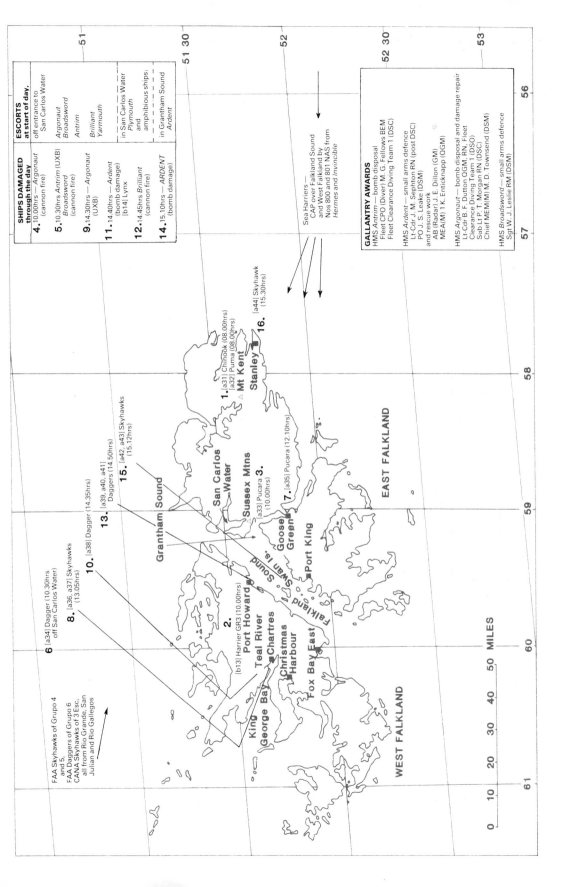

SHIPS DAMAGED
through the day

4. 10.00hrs — *Argonaut*
(cannon fire)

5. 10.30hrs *Antrim* (UXB)
Broadsword
(cannon fire)

9. 14.30hrs — *Argonaut*
(UXB)

11. 14.40hrs — *Ardent*
(bomb damage)
[b14] *Lynx*

12. 14.45hrs *Brilliant*
(cannon fire)

14. 15.10hrs — ARDENT
(bomb damage)

ESCORTS
at start of day.

off entrance to
San Carlos Water

Argonaut
Broadsword

Antrim

Brilliant
Yarmouth

in San Carlos Water
and
amphibious ships:
Plymouth

in Grantham Sound
Ardent

Sea Harriers —
CAP over Falkland Sound
and West Falkland by
Nos 800 and 801 NAS from
Hermes and *Invincible*

GALLANTRY AWARDS
HMS *Antrim* — bomb disposal
Fleet CPO (Diver) M. G. Fellows BEM
Fleet Clearance Diving Team 1 (DSC)

HMS *Ardent* — small arms defence
Lt-Cdr J. M. Sephton RN (post DSC)
PO J. S. Leake (DSM)
and rescue work
AB (Radar) J. E. Dillon (GM)
MEA(M) 1 K. Enticknapp (QGM)

HMS *Argonaut* — bomb disposal and damage repair
Lt-Cdr B. F. Dutton QGM, RN, Fleet
Clearance Diving Team 1 (DSO)
Sub Lt P. T. Morgan RN (DSC)
Chief MEM(M) M. D. Townsend (DSM)

HMS *Broadsword* — small arms defence
Sgt W. J. Leslie RM (DSM)

51

51 30

52

52 30

53

56

57

58

59

60

61

1. [a31] Chinook (08.00hrs)
[a32] Puma (08.00hrs)
△ Mt Kent
Stanley ■
16. [a44] Skyhawk
(15.30hrs)

San Carlos
Water
Sussex Mtns

15. [a42, a43] Skyhawks
(15.12hrs)

13. [a39, a40, a41]
Daggers (14.50hrs)

Grantham Sound

3. [a33] Pucara
(10.00hrs)
Goose
Green ■
■ Port King

7. [a35] Pucara (12.10hrs)

EAST FALKLAND

10. [a38] Dagger (14.35hrs)

8. [a36, a37] Skyhawks
(13.05hrs)

6 [a34] Dagger (10.30 hrs
off San Carlos Water)

FAA Skyhawks of Grupo 4
and 5.
FAA Daggers of Grupo 6
CANA Skyhawks of 3 Esc,
all from Rio Grande, San
Julian and Rio Gallegos

2. [b13] Harrier GR3 (10.00hrs)
Port Howard ■
Teal River ■
Chartres ■
Christmas
Harbour ■
King
George Bay
Fox Bay East ■
Falkland Sound
Swan Is.

WEST FALKLAND

0 10 20 30 40 50 MILES

damage. One more Pucara and nine Daggers and Skyhawks are lost to the Sea Harriers on CAP and one to a SAM fired by warships. The fierce AA fire from ship and shore makes the Argentine aircraft come in low and fast, and although many of their bombs are on target, they fail to explode. Fortunately, they also fail to hit the transports.

The main raids take place around 10.30hrs, 13.00hrs and 15.00hrs. First to arrive are a total of eight Daggers of Grupo 6. Attacking the northern end of the gunline, HMS Broadsword is hit by cannon fire and HMS Antrim is also badly damaged by a UXB with casualties on both ships, but no one killed. One of the Daggers [a34] is brought down — probably by a Sea Wolf from HMS Broadsword. HMS Antrim then moves towards San Carlos Water where the bomb is removed, before heading that night for the CVBG. Shortly after midday, the Sea Harriers on CAP have their first success of the day. Two Grupo 3 Pucaras from Goose Green attack a nearby naval gunfire observer directing HMS Ardent's fire from out in Grantham Sound. Three No 801 NAS aircraft close in, and shoot one of them down with cannon fire [a35].

The next mainland attacks are due an hour later at 13.00hrs by eight Skyhawks. Only two of the four Grupo 5 aircraft reach West Falkland because of fuelling problems, and one of these wastes its bombs on the abandoned Rio Carcarana in Port King. The fourth however carries on north up Falkland Sound and just misses HMS Ardent with two bombs. On instructions from HMS Brilliant two No 800 NAS Sea Harriers chase the returning aircraft without success, but instead spot the next four incoming Skyhawks from Grupo 4 over Chartres in West Falkland. They try to escape, but two are downed by Sidewinder missiles near Christmas Harbour [a36, a37].

Then the afternoon sorties follow, starting at 14.30hrs with six Skyhawks of Grupo 5 which nearly put paid to HMS Argonaut (some sources put this raid in the morning). Deluged by near misses, two bombs hit without exploding but two men are killed in the Sea Cat magazine. Steaming at high speed and with engine and steering controls damaged, she is anchored by the action of Sub-Lt Morgan, but has to stay in the area for a week until the UXBs are removed and the damage temporarily repaired.

Next, 12 Daggers of Grupo 6 are due to arrive. Out of the first group of six from Rio Grande, two abort and as the remaining four come in over West Falkland, HMS Brilliant vectors two No 800 NAS Sea Harriers and one of the Daggers [a38] is shot down near Teal River Inlet by yet another Sidewinder missile. The three surviving aircraft press on and catch HMS Ardent still in Grantham Sound. Coming in from astern, they blanket her with hits and near-misses destroying her Lynx [b14] and Sea Cat installation and killing a number of men. With only small arms fire left for defence, she heads for the protection of the other escorts off San Carlos Water. As these three Daggers get away, six more from San Julian arrive in two flights of three. The first hits HMS Brilliant with cannon fire causing slight damage and some casualties before they safely head back, but the second flight is wiped out before even reaching the target area. Picked up over West Falkland by HMS Brilliant again, two No 801-NAS Sea Harriers shoot them down with Sidewinder missiles to the north of Port Howard [a39, a40, a41].

The last attacks are started some 30min later by two flights of A-4Q Skyhawks of 3 Esc in the only Navy sorties to reach the Falklands that day. The first three aircraft catch HMS Ardent off North West Island and, again attacking from the stern, bracket her with hits and near misses. She is badly damaged, on fire aft and flooding, with 22 men killed and some 30 injured. Cdr West gives the order to abandon ship and HMS Yarmouth comes alongside to pick up the survivors. HMS Ardent finally sinks the following evening. One of the CANA Skyhawks is damaged by the return small arms fire, and all three are caught by two No 800 NAS Sea Harriers near Swan Island. One is shot down by Sidewinder [a42], and cannon fire destroys a second [a43] and hits the already damaged third. Unable to land at Stanley with undercarriage problems, the pilot of this one ejects [a44]. The second CANA flight runs in 15min later, but fails to hit any of the ships. The Sea Harriers continue to fly CAP, but there are no more raids that day and the transports continue unloading.

MAP 25 — WEEK EIGHT

Falkland Area Operations

22-23 May

On Saturday 22 May, the two assault ships, five LSLs, and RFAs *Fort Austin* and *Stromness* are still in San Carlos Water. Of the original escorts, only HMS *Brilliant*, HMS *Plymouth*, HMS *Yarmouth* and the damaged HMS *Argonaut* remain in direct support, and HMS *Broadsword* spends some of the time north of Pebble Island with HMS *Coventry* as a missile trap for incoming aircraft. HMS *Antrim* has gone, but HMS *Ardent* is replaced by the newly arrived HMS *Antelope,* although sadly not for long. Next day, they are joined by LSL *Sir Bedivere* and frigate HMS *Arrow* which has structural damage but can still share in the air defence. Of the merchantmen that left on Friday, *Norland* is back in to disembark her remaining troops and later take on board HMS *Antelope's* survivors, and *Canberra* out in the holding area transfers stores to RFA *Resource* for delivery on Monday.

From now on, only the more important ship movements can be followed. As air supremacy is slowly won, the carriers continue to provide the only fixed-wing airpower. The destroyers and frigates escort the transports into and out of San Carlos Water and protect them there, and also carry out bombardment, special forces insertions and other patrol duties. Meanwhile, the merchantmen and RFAs keep the Task Force supplied with fuel, ammunition, food, water and other stores, and play their part in moving the troops towards Stanley. All this takes the ships to various parts of the TEZ and around the Falklands, to South Georgia, and when in need of repair, to the TRALA.

At the northern end of the beachhead, 3 Para patrols to the west and north of Port San Carlos, while 42 Cdo follows up the retreating Argentine troops, but only as far as Cerro Montevideo to stay within artillery range. To the west, 45 Cdo is dug in above Ajax Bay and on the east, 40 Cdo likewise above San Carlos — the latter destined to spend a frustrating war mainly defending the area. In the south, 2 Para on Sussex Mountains is about to be the first unit to prepare for action. At his mobile HQ at San Carlos, while waiting for more supplies to be unloaded and for Gen Moore to arrive, Brig Thompson makes plans to push forward. Apart from the special forces patrols scattered about the Falklands, marines of the Mountain and

Arctic Warfare Cadre have been flown to Bull Hill and Evelyn Hill on the way to Stanley. Brig Thompson also decides to launch a battalion raid against the enemy forces at Goose Green, and on Sunday 23 May orders Lt-Col Jones to prepare 2 Para for this task. On the same day, 42 Cdo is ordered back from its exposed position to join in the defence of Port San Carlos, and just to the north, 3 Para suffers wounded casualties when two patrols accidentally clash.

Meanwhile as Gen Menendez attempts to supply his outlying forces, more ships and helicopters are lost. Late on Friday 21 May, the patrol craft *Rio Iguaza* leaves Stanley with Pucara spares and 105mm guns for Goose Green, and next morning is found and strafed in Choiseul Sound by two No 800 NAS Sea Harriers on CAP. She runs ashore, but two of the guns are recovered and reach their destination. Then on Saturday evening HMS *Brilliant* and HMS *Yarmouth* search for the captured coaster *Monsunen* known to be heading for Stanley from Darwin, and early on Sunday, HMS *Brilliant's* Lynx locates her off the east coast. A small SBS boarding party tries to capture the ship by helicopter, but gunfire drives them away. The frigates then run *Monsunen* aground in Lively Sound, but next day she is towed into Darwin by *Forrest*. Now into Sunday, HMS *Yarmouth* returns to San Carlos Water, but HMS *Brilliant* heads for the carriers. Finally, the damaged cargo ship *Rio Carcarana* is finished off in Port King at midday by Sea Skuas fired by the Lynx from HMS *Antelope..*

Still on Sunday morning, 23 May, three Army Pumas carrying ammunition and stores for Port Howard, and escorted by an Agusta, are on the last leg of their dangerous flight from Stanley when they are sighted near Shag Cove House by two No 800 NAS Sea Harriers. One Puma flies into the ground trying to escape [a45], the crew getting clear before it explodes, and cannon fire destroys the Agusta [a46] and disables a second Puma. Two No 801 NAS Sea Harriers shortly arrive and finish this one off by strafing [a47]. Just one Puma survives to fly the three crews to Port Howard.

Over the weekend, RAF Harrier GR3s mount

a number of denial attacks against airstrips, and the Sea Harriers continue to fly CAP although bad weather over southern Argentina means they are hardly needed on Saturday 22 May. The next heavy raids are mounted on the Sunday when the FAA also starts using Grupo 1 Learjets as pathfinders and decoys. First to arrive in the early afternoon are four A-4B Skyhawks of Grupo 5 which find HMS *Antelope* in San Carlos Water. In a confused action which puts two UXBs in her and kills one man, an attacker clips her mast and another is shot down — possibly by a Sea Wolf from HMS *Broadsword* or a Rapier [a48]. That evening, as the bombs are being defused, one explodes killing Sgt Prescott RE. Catching fire, HMS *Antelope* explodes and sinks next day with a broken back.

Minutes after the Grupo 5 attack, three Skyhawks of CANA 3 Esc come in but fail to hit any ships. One crashes on landing back at Rio Grande. Two hours later, two incoming Grupo 6 Daggers are sighted by two No 800 NAS Sea Harriers and, as they try to escape, one is destroyed over Pebble Island by a Sidewinder missile [a49]. That same afternoon, two CANA Super Etendards fly from Rio Grande on a third Exocet mission, but return to base without finding any targets. However, that evening does see the loss of a fourth Sea Harrier. As four No 800 NAS aircraft take off from HMS *Hermes* to bomb Stanley airfield, one hits the sea and explodes killing Lt-Cdr Batt [b15].

MAP 26 — WEEK NINE (page 81)

More Merchant Ships and Task Force Movements

24-30 May

With 40 merchantmen already in the South Atlantic or on their way, more are needed. Before the surrender a further eight set out, including during the week, tanker *Scottish Eagle* from Milford Haven and offshore ship *British Enterprise III* from Rosyth.

Tankers *Scottish Eagle* (33,000grt, Ch/SC) and G. A. *Walker* (18,700grt, Ch).
Despatch vessel *British Enterprise III* (1,600grt, Req).
Repair ship *Stena Inspector* (6,100grt, Ch/SN/SC).
Helicopter carrier and repair ship *Astronomer* (27,900grt, Req/flight deck and hangar).
Ammunition ship *Laertes* (11,800grt, Req).
Refrigerated stores ship *Avelona Star* (9,800-grt, Ch/H).
Minesweeper support ship *St Helena* (3,100grt, Req/H/SN/SC).

Ascension

More ships pass by or call in on their way south including RFAs *Engadine* and *Fort Grange* and mooring vessel *Wimpey Sea-*horse, but now two tankers head back for the UK to reload. On Monday 24 May it is *British Avon* after picking up Lt-Cdr Astiz, and then on Wednesday, over-crowded *British Esk* which first gets in with more than 260 survivors from HMS *Sheffield* who fly on home. Apart from all the usual RAF activity, two Phantom fighters of No 29 (F) Sqn fly down on Monday from Coningsby, followed on Wednesday by a third to take over air defence from the three Harriers. These in turn are joined over the weekend by six more GR3s from RAF Wittering before later continuing south. Then late on Friday in Operation 'Black Buck 4', and with the usual Victor support, a Vulcan armed with Shrike anti-radar missiles takes off to attack the Stanley command and control radars. Refuelling problems stop the mission, but late on Sunday Operation 'Black Buck 5' goes ahead successfully.

South Atlantic

By Wednesday morning (26 May), the 'Bristol' Group has joined the Task Force to more than make up for the ships lost. With HMS *Bristol* herself are Type 42 destroyer HMS Cardiff,

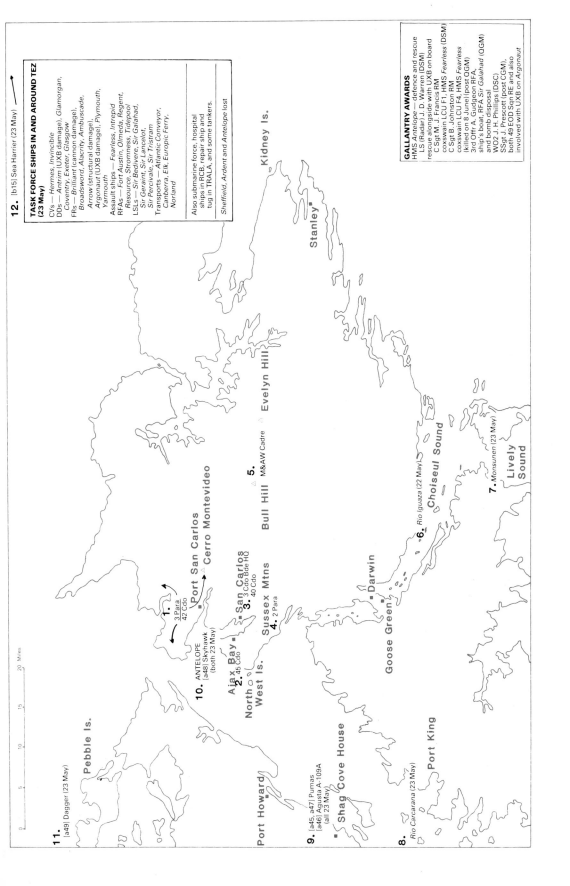

12. [b15] Sea Harrier (23 May) →

TASK FORCE SHIPS IN AND AROUND TEZ (23 May)

CVs — *Hermes, Invincible*
DDs — *Antrim* (UXB damage), *Glamorgan, Coventry, Exeter, Glasgow*
FRs — *Brilliant* (cannon damage), *Broadsword, Alacrity, Ambuscade, Arrow* (structural damage), *Argonaut* (UXB damage), *Plymouth, Yarmouth*
Assault ships — *Fearless, Intrepid*
RFAs — *Fort Austin, Olmeda, Regent, Resource, Stromness, Tidepool*
LSLs — *Sir Bedivere, Sir Galahad, Sir Geraint, Sir Lancelot, Sir Percivale, Sir Tristram*
Transports — *Atlantic Conveyor, Canberra, Elk, Europic Ferry, Norland*

Also submarine force, hospital ships in RCB, repair ship and tug in TRALA, and some tankers.

Sheffield, Ardent and Antelope lost

GALLANTRY AWARDS

HMS *Antelope* — defence and rescue
LS (Radar) J. D. Warren (DSM)
rescue alongside with UXB on board
C Sgt M. J. Francis RM
coxswain LCU F1, HMS *Fearless* (DSM)
C Sgt B. Johnston RM
coxswain LCU F4, HMS *Fearless*
(killed on 8 June) (post QGM)
3rd Offr A. Gudgeon RFA,
ship's boat, RFA *Sir Galahad* (QGM)
and bomb disposal
WO2 J. H. Phillips (DSC)
SSgt J. Prescott (post CGM),
both 49 EOD Sqn RE and also
involved with UXB on *Argonaut*

0   5   10   15   20 Miles

Pebble Is.

Kidney Is.

Stanley

11.
[a49] Dagger (23 May)

Port San Carlos
△ Cerro Montevideo

1.
3 Para
42 Cdo

10.
ANTELOPE
[a48] Skyhawk
(both 23 May)

Ajax Bay
2. 45 Cdo
North
West Is.

San Carlos
3. 3 Cdo Bde HQ
40 Cdo

Sussex Mtns
4. 2 Para

Bull Hill

5. M&AW Cadre

Evelyn Hill

Choiseul Sound
6. Rio Iguaza (22 May)

Lively Sound
7. Monsunen (23 May)

Darwin
Goose Green

8.
Rio Carcarana (23 May)

Port King

9. [a45, a47] Pumas
[a46] Agusta A-109A
(all 23 May)

Shag Cove House

Port Howard

Type 21 frigates HMS *Active* and HMS *Avenger*, and 'Leander' class frigates HMS *Minerva*, HMS *Penelope* and Sea Wolf-armed HMS *Andromeda*. Some of them screen the carriers by day, and by night bombard Argentine positions or escort transports to and from San Carlos Water. RFA fleet tanker *Olna* arrives with them to start refuelling duties, and she is joined by RFA *Tidespring* at last back from her South Georgia mission. Finally, by the end of the week, support ship *Atlantic Causeway* has arrived with her much needed Sea King and Wessex helicopters.

Now the first warships return north. With the arrival of HMS *Cardiff*, the damaged HMS *Glasgow* is patched up by *Stena Seaspread* and sails on Thursday 27 May with engines under manual control. Also around this time, nuclear submarine HMS *Splendid* presumably leaves her patrol area to get home by the second week in June. On Friday, the tanker *British Tay*, with survivors from *Atlantic Conveyor*, heads first for Ascension, but all this time there is still the danger of attack. Not content with flying supplies into Stanley and refuelling air strikes, FAA Gruppo 1 Hercules make the only apparent attempt to cut British supply lines. On Saturday a single C-130 drops eight bombs on *British Wye* to the north of South Georgia. One hits, but bounces into the sea without exploding and the tanker continues her lonely refuelling duties.

The Red Cross Box is particularly active and early in the week, *Hydra* sails to the east to pick up San Carlos casualties from *Canberra* for transfer to *Uganda*, and *Herald* finally arrives after having diverted to Rio de Janeiro to land a sick crewman. Later, *Hecla* heads for Montevideo with the first British and Argentine casualties for repatriation, and *Uganda* moves closer in to pick up the wounded from the Goose Green battle. The TRALA is also in business, with both HMS *Glasgow* and HMS *Brilliant* there, and the ships in residence are joined from Tristan da Cunha by *Irishman* and *Yorkshireman*.

South Georgia

HMS *Endurance* plays host to probably the largest tonnage of shipping the island has ever seen, with most there to meet *Queen Elizabeth 2* which cannot be risked closer to the Falklands. Before her arrival, *Canberra* (with HMS *Ardent's* survivors), *Norland* (with those from HMS *Antelope*) and destroyer HMS *Antrim* leave the TEZ on Tuesday (25 May), and RFA *Stromness* (carrying survivors from HMS *Coventry*) follows them from San Carlos Water. On the same day, despatch vessel *Iris* reaches Grytviken from Ascension with Lt Mills RM and his men for HMS *Endurance*, and loads scrap steel from the whaling stations for delivery to the TRALA. Other arrivals there to help transfer the troops from *Queen Elizabeth 2* are despatch vessel *Leeds Castle* from the TEZ and the five minesweeping trawlers of the 11th MCMS.

Northeast of South Georgia on Thursday 27 May HMS *Antrim* picks up Gen Moore and Brig Wilson before heading back to HMS *Fearless*, and the great liner continues on into Cumberland Bay East. Over the next 24hr, the Scots and Welsh Guards move to *Canberra* and the Gurkhas to *Norland*. On Friday, *Stromness* arrives to take on board more troops, together with ammunition and Rapiers from the newly-arrived transport *Lycaon*. When the transfers are complete, including the two No 825 NAS Sea Kings from *Queen Elizabeth 2* to *Canberra*, the Falklands-bound ships leave. *Queen Elizabeth 2* then heads back north on Saturday with the survivors. *Leeds Castle* follows her but only as far as Ascencion to take over as guardship; and in a week that sees 3 Cdo Bde moving out of San Carlos Water, 2 Para's victory at Goose Green and the battle for air supremacy being won, transports *Baltic Ferry* and *Nordic Ferry* approach the Falklands direct with helicopters and equipment for 5th Inf Bde.

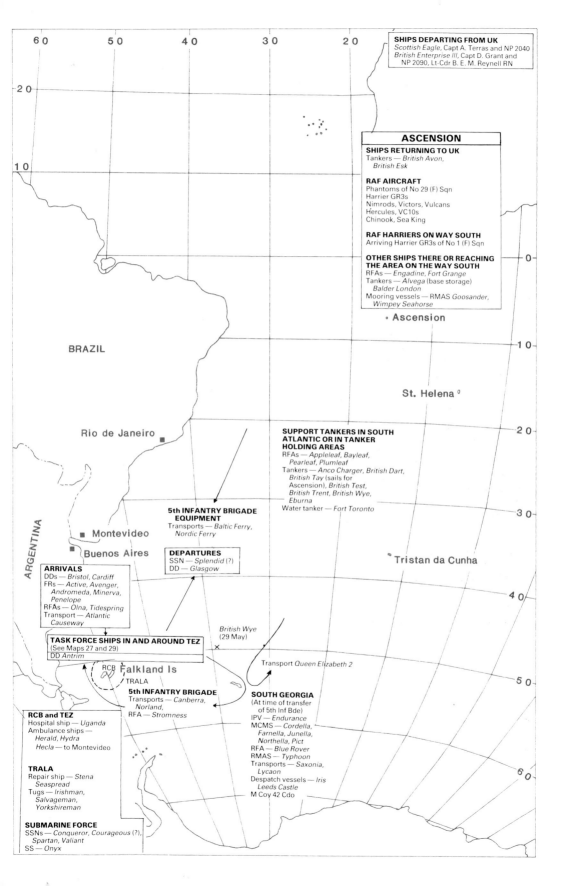

| 60 | 50 | 40 | 30 | 20 |

SHIPS DEPARTING FROM UK
Scottish Eagle, Capt A. Terras and NP 2040
British Enterprise III, Capt D. Grant and
NP 2090, Lt-Cdr B. E. M. Reynell RN

20

ASCENSION

SHIPS RETURNING TO UK
Tankers — *British Avon*,
British Esk

10

RAF AIRCRAFT
Phantoms of No 29 (F) Sqn
Harrier GR3s
Nimrods, Victors, Vulcans
Hercules, VC10s
Chinook, Sea King

RAF HARRIERS ON WAY SOUTH
Arriving Harrier GR3s of No 1 (F) Sqn

**OTHER SHIPS THERE OR REACHING
THE AREA ON THE WAY SOUTH**
RFAs — *Engadine, Fort Grange*
Tankers — *Alvega* (base storage)
Balder London
Mooring vessels — RMAS *Goosander,
Wimpey Seahorse*

0

∘ **Ascension**

10

BRAZIL

St. Helena ∘

**SUPPORT TANKERS IN SOUTH
ATLANTIC OR IN TANKER
HOLDING AREAS**
RFAs — *Appleleaf, Bayleaf,
Pearleaf, Plumleaf*
Tankers — *Anco Charger, British Dart,
British Tay* (sails for
Ascension), *British Test,
British Trent, British Wye,
Eburna*
Water tanker — *Fort Toronto*

20

■ Rio de Janeiro

**5th INFANTRY BRIGADE
EQUIPMENT**
Transports — *Baltic Ferry,
Nordic Ferry*

30

ARGENTINA

■ Montevideo

Tristan da Cunha ∘

■ Buenos Aires

DEPARTURES
SSN — *Splendid* (?)
DD — *Glasgow*

ARRIVALS
DDs — *Bristol, Cardiff*
FRs — *Active, Avenger,
Andromeda, Minerva,
Penelope*
RFAs — *Olna, Tidespring*
Transport — *Atlantic
Causeway*

40

British Wye
(29 May)
✕

TASK FORCE SHIPS IN AND AROUND TEZ
(See Maps 27 and 29)
DD *Antrim*

Transport *Queen Elizabeth 2*

RCB **Falkland Is**
/ TRALA

50

5th INFANTRY BRIGADE
Transports — *Canberra,
Norland,*
RFA — *Stromness*

SOUTH GEORGIA
(At time of transfer
of 5th Inf Bde)
IPV — *Endurance*
MCMS — *Cordella,
Farnella, Junella,
Northella, Pict*
RFA — *Blue Rover*
RMAS — *Typhoon*
Transports — *Saxonia,
Lycaon*
Despatch vessels — *Iris
Leeds Castle*
M Coy 42 Cdo

RCB and TEZ
Hospital ship — *Uganda*
Ambulance ships —
Herald, Hydra
Hecla — to Montevideo

TRALA
Repair ship — *Stena
Seaspread*
Tugs — *Irishman,
Salvageman,
Yorkshireman*

60

SUBMARINE FORCE
SSNs — *Conqueror, Courageous* (?),
Spartan, Valiant
SS — *Onyx*

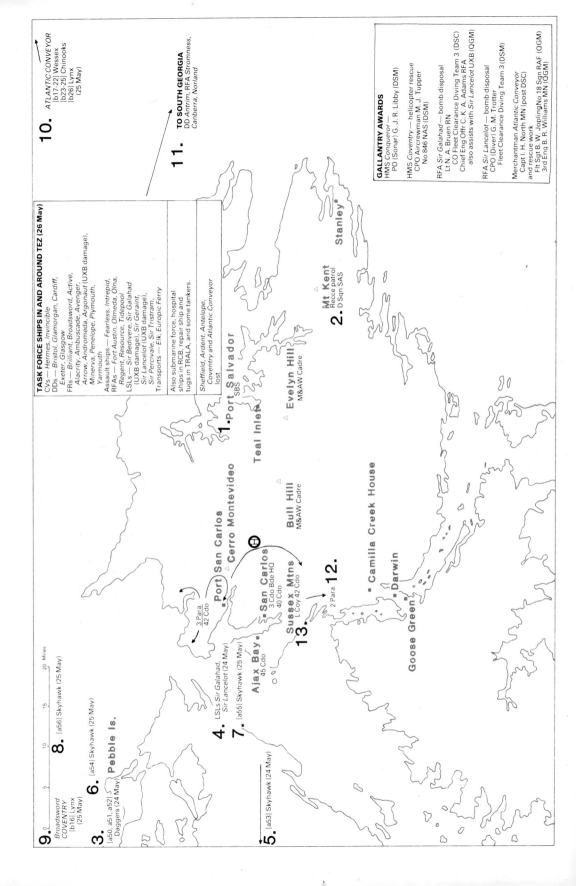

MAP 27 — WEEK NINE

Falkland Area Operations

24-26 May

As plans for the Darwin raid go ahead, Brig Thompson prepares to move towards Stanley — D Sqn SAS and then 42 Cdo are to fly to Mount Kent, and when *Atlantic Conveyor* arrives with her Chinooks, more of 3 Cdo Bde will be flown forward. A start is made when a SBS team goes ashore in Port Salvador to check Teal Inlet and a D Sqn patrol lands on Mount Kent, but the weather closes in stopping the rest of D Sqn joining them. Also 2 Para's artillery cannot be flown in, so the Darwin raid is cancelled. Then on Tuesday 25 May *Atlantic Conveyor* is lost and the planning has to start all over again. By then the battle for control of the air has almost been won, but the losses on both sides are heavy. In this, HMS *Broadsword* and HMS *Coventry* play a major role as missile trap and radar picket off Pebble Island.

Monday 24 May sees four more Argentine aircraft destroyed. That morning, four Grupo 6 Daggers come in low over Pebble Island, but under HMS *Broadsword's* direction, two No 800 NAS Sea Harriers bring three of them down with Sidewinder missiles [a50, a51, a52]. As this happens, more Daggers and Grupo 4 and 5 Skyhawks reach the anchorage from the south. LSLs *Sir Galahad* and *Sir Lancelot* each receive a UXB and *Sir Bedivere* is slightly damaged by a glancing hit, all believed to be from Skyhawks of Grupo 4. The three aircraft in this flight are damaged by the fierce AA, including claims by both HMS *Fearless* and HMS *Argonaut* Sea Cats, and on the way home, one crashes into King George Bay off West Falkland [a53]. Some of the crew of both LSLs are evacuated, but the bombs are later defused, although *Sir Lancelot* is not fully operational again for a long time.

Tuesday 25 May is Argentine National Day and the first target for Grupo 5 Skyhawks that morning is the two missile trap ships, but HMS *Coventry's* Sea Dart brings one of them down at long range north of Pebble Island and the sortie is abandoned [a54]. Then at midday four Grupo 4 aircraft reach San Carlos Water. One is blasted out of the sky by small arms fire and missiles — the claims received include one from HMS *Yarmouth* (Sea Cat) — although the pilot ejects safely [a55], and as the three survivors escape, a second aircraft is destroyed to the northeast of Pebble Island by another Sea Dart from HMS *Coventry* [a56].

In the afternoon, the tables are turned, first of all by four Skyhawks of Grupo 5 which reach HMS *Coventry* and HMS *Broadsword*. As the first pair approach, the CAP Sea Harriers are warned off, but HMS *Broadsword's* Sea Wolf system breaks contact and she is hit by a bomb which bounces up through her stern and out again badly damaging the Lynx helicopter on the way. The second pair now go for HMS *Coventry*, and just as HMS *Broadsword* prepares to fire Sea Wolf again, the Type 42 gets in the way and contact is broken for a second time. With little to stop them, the Skyhawks put three bombs into HMS *Coventry* at 15.20hrs. Within half an hour she has capsized and been abandoned with 19 men killed and 25 wounded. The survivors are picked up by HMS *Broadsword* and helicopters from San Carlos and she shortly sinks with her Lynx [b16]. Of the three Type 42 destroyers that first sailed south, two are now at the bottom and the third is damaged and soon to return.

As HMS *Coventry* goes down, and quite separate from the Skyhawk sorties, two Super Etendards of CANA 2 Esc approach the CVBG from the north having been refuelled on the way by a Hercules tanker. In their path and close together are the two carriers and transport *Atlantic Conveyor* at this time some 90 miles northeast of Stanley and heading in for San Carlos Water. Just after 16.30hrs, they launch two Exocets from a range of 30 miles, and in spite of attempts to decoy the missiles away by chaff fired by the warships including HMS *Ambuscade*, one of them hits *Atlantic Conveyor* and sets her uncontrollably ablaze. Little is known of the fate of the second Exocet.

HMS *Alacrity* and HMS *Brilliant* close in to help, but the order is soon given to abandon ship, and by the time the survivors are picked up, a total of 12 men have died including Capt North. Fortunately the Harriers have been flown off before the attack, but all the helicopters, apart from an airborne Chinook, and thousands of tons of stores including ammunition, Harrier spares and tents, have to be left on the burning ship. The tug *Irishman* goes to her aid and on Thursday takes the burnt-out hulk in tow, but *Atlantic Conveyor* soon sinks, taking with her six Wessex [b17-22], three Chinooks [b23-25] and a spare Lynx [b26].

Still on Tuesday 25 May as *Canberra* and *Norland* make their way to South Georgia, the two remaining merchantmen in the TEZ continue to support the landings. *Europic Ferry*, with her 2 Para stores, sails in to complete unloading, while *Elk* prepares to follow her with more vehicles and ammunition. Meanwhile to the north, the nuclear submarine HMS *Conqueror* on patrol has an aerial wrapped around her propeller, and on Tuesday in bad weather and under threat of aircraft attack, PO Libby dives to remove it.

With the loss of the *Atlantic Conveyor*, and with four Sea Kings already used for night missions and one for Rapier support, Brig Thompson has only six more plus five Wessex to move his troops towards Stanley. His staff meet on Wednesday morning (26 May) and, with new orders from Northwood, fresh plans are made. Goose Green is to be taken and held by 2 Para, and much of the rest of the Brigade will have to walk! Late that day, Lt-Col Jones leads 2 Para south on the path to Darwin, and on Thursday, 45 Cdo and 3 Para start their move overland to Teal Inlet while 42 Cdo waits a later move to Mount Kent. Still on Wednesday, L Coy 42 Cdo flies from Port San Carlos to Sussex Mountains to relieve 2 Para.

MAP 28

2 Para's Battle for Darwin and Goose Green

28 May

Late on Wednesday 26 May as some 500 men of 2 Para move south towards Darwin, there is much uncertainty about Argentine strength in the area. However by the time of the surrender, and after allowance is made for the near 50 killed (not the originally reported 250), there are over 1,000 POWs including the 12th Inf Regt and a coy from the 25th. With their approaches mined, the infantry are in well-prepared defensive positions, especially between Boca House and Darwin half way down the isthmus, and for support can call on 105mm artillery, AA guns later in the ground defence role, and attack aircraft from Stanley.

By early Thursday morning (27 May), 2 Para has marched the eight miles from Sussex Mountains and reached the holding position at Camilla Creek House where most lie up all day. Two patrols from C Coy probe forward towards either side of the isthmus to plot some of the enemy defences, but later pull back under fire. Early that afternoon, two Harrier GR3s attack Argentine positions with CBUs, and in a subsequent strafing run, one of them is hit (probably by 35mm Oerlikon fire) and crashes to the west of Goose Green [b27]. Sqn Ldr Iveson ejects and hides up before being rescued three days later.

That night, the three 105mm guns of 8 Bty RA and their ammunition are flown to Camilla Creek House by No 846 NAS Sea Kings, and HMS *Arrow* heads into Grantham Sound, opening fire from there under the control of a naval gunfire observer. A later turret fault is repaired and she remains on station supporting the paras advance towards Darwin, when with the threat of air attack at dawn, has to return to San Carlos Water. Meanwhile that same evening, 2 Para moves off the two miles to the start line with C (Patrol) Coy leading the way. Then with D Coy at first in reserve, A and B Coys wait on either side of Burntside Pond, the mortars to their rear, and the fire support company with its Milans initially across Camilla Creek from the forward Argentine positions. Early on Friday 28 May, the men of 2 Para prepare for a night attack against largely unknown forces across the open ground of the Goose Green area, five miles long and over a mile wide.

At 03.30hrs, A Coy moves off on the left and attacks Burntside House believed to be occupied by an Argentine platoon, but finds no-one there other than four unhurt civilians. Then at 04.10hrs, B Coy starts forward from the other side of Burntside Pond down the right flank with D Coy following them along the middle. With artillery support on both sides, B and D Coys are soon in confused action against a series of enemy trenches, and as they slowly

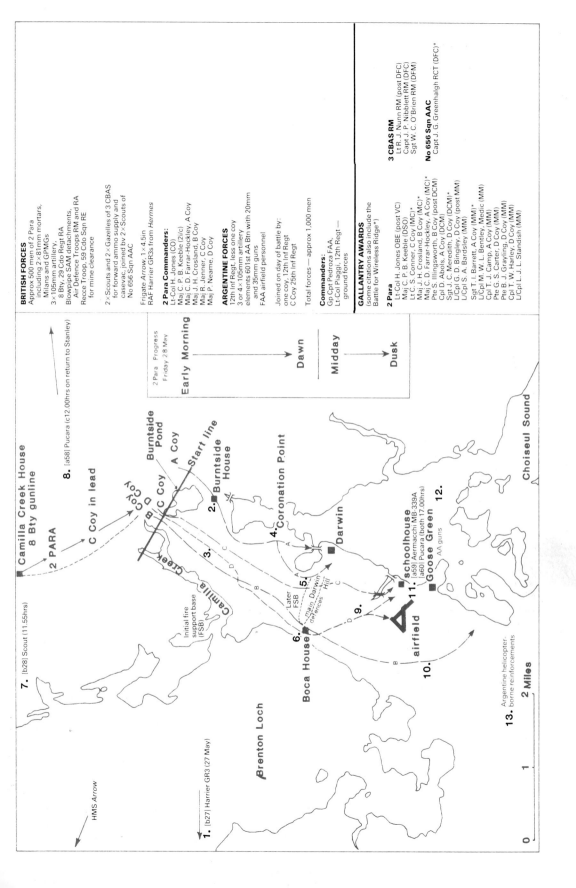

make progress, A Coy moves past unoccupied positions at Coronation Point. Then, leaving one platoon of A Coy to provide covering fire from the north side of Darwin, the remainder start to circle round the inlet to take the settlement. As dawn breaks, the attacks on both flanks bog down as B Coy comes up against the strongpoint of Boca House and A Coy finds that a small rise, later known as Darwin Hill, is the key to the Argentine defences. Not until midday will 2 Para break through.

As A Coy is hit and goes to ground, Lt-Col Jones and his Tac HQ come up, and another attempt to push forward is made which leads to two officers and an NCO being killed. He then moves off virtually on his own, and is soon shot and dying in an action which leads to the award of a Victoria Cross. Maj Keeble is called up from the rear, and leaving A Coy to slowly wrest Darwin Hill and pulling B Coy slightly back from Boca House, orders D Coy to move round them on the far right along the edge of the sea. Now in daylight, the battle continues with the Argentines helicoptering in their first reinforcements and flying more support missions. The first attack by Falklands based aircraft took place earlier when a Grupo 3 Pucara was hit, probably by a Blowpipe SAM, but limped back to Stanley. The next sortie by two more Pucaras catches two Royal Marine Scout helicopters on their way in to casevac Lt-Col Jones. Capt Niblett manages to evade them, but Lt Nunn is killed by cannon fire and goes down near Camilla Creek House [b28]. One of the Pucaras is later found to have crashed into high ground returning to Stanley [a58].

By midday, A Coy has taken and holds Darwin Hill, and B and D Coys have finally silenced Boca House. Then, still under fire, D and C Coys head towards the airfield and Goose Green while B Coy circles east to cut off the settlement. During the attack towards the schoolhouse, three men of D Coy are killed in an incident involving a white flag. Now into the late afternoon, aircraft from both sides come on the scene, starting with two MB-339s of CANA 1 Esc and two Pucaras of Grupo 3 which hit the school area. One of the Navy jets is brought down by a Royal Marine Blowpipe [a59], and minutes later one of the Pucaras drops napalm and the other is shot down by small arms fire [a60]. Then three Harrier GR3s bring much needed relief by hitting the AA guns at Goose Green with CBUs and rockets.

With evening approaching and the Argentines squeezed in towards Goose Green, more reinforcements arrive to the south by helicopter, while to the north, J Coy 42 Cdo is flown in to reinforce 2 Para but too late to join in the fighting. Two Argentine POWs are sent in to start negotiations which last most of the night, and next morning, Gp Capt Pedroza surrenders all his forces to Maj Keeble. British losses are 15 men from 2 Para, a Royal Engineer and the Marine pilot. Some 30 to 40 paras are wounded. Many of the 1,000 Argentine POWs including the FAA men sail on *Norland* to Montevideo in early June.

MAP 29 — WEEK NINE

Falkland Area Operations

27-30 May

As 2 Para fights the battle for Goose Green, 45 Cdo 'yomp' and 3 Para 'tab' across the rough, boggy ground towards Stanley by the northern route. Often in the dark and wet, and heavily laden, they move at a fast rate first for Teal Inlet. No 3 CBAS helicopters support 45 Cdo on the way and 3 Para is followed by No 4 Troop of The Blues and Royals with two Scimitars and two Scorpions. Starting on the morning of Thursday 27 May, Lt-Col Whitehead's 45 Cdo first moves by LCU from Ajax Bay to Port San Carlos before setting out on the 12-mile trek to New House, reaching there late that night.

After resting up they complete the eight miles to Douglas on Friday and dig in ready to move to Teal. Lt-Col Pike and 3 Para were to follow behind, but instead take a more southerly, direct route in two columns. After marching for 24hr they meet up on Friday a few miles short of Teal Inlet, and when darkness falls, complete the journey late that night and stay throughout Saturday. On Sunday, 45 Cdo pushes on to join them, but 3 Para and the light tanks are ordered to head for Mount Estancia as part of the plan to occupy the heights to the west of Stanley, and by the end of the day have

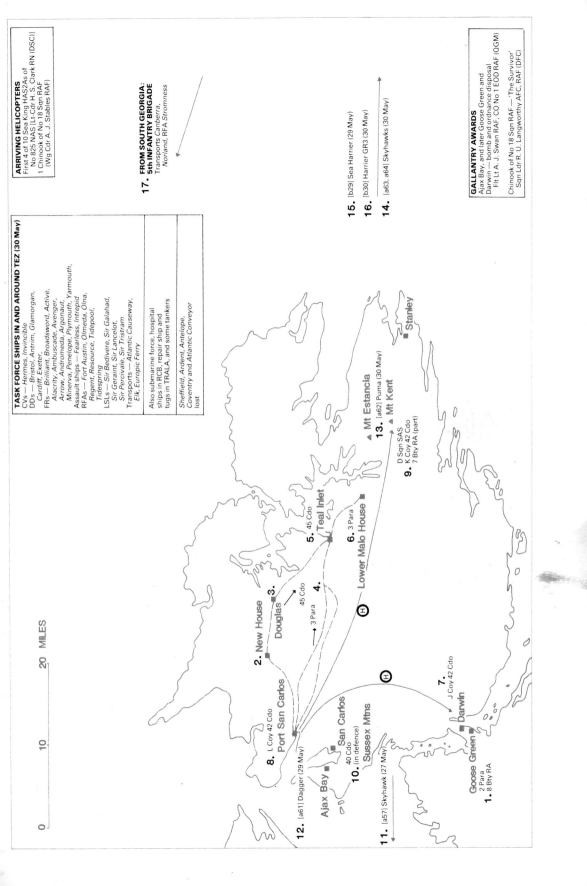

ARRIVING HELICOPTERS
First 4 of 10 Sea King HAS2As of No 825 NAS [Lt-Cdr H. S. Clark RN (DSC)]
1 Chinook of No 18 Sqn RAF (Wg Cdr A. J. Stables RAF)

17. **FROM SOUTH GEORGIA: 5th INFANTRY BRIGADE**
Transports *Canberra*, *Norland*, RFA *Stromness*

TASK FORCE SHIPS IN AND AROUND TEZ (30 May)
CVs — *Hermes*, *Invincible*
DDs — *Bristol*, *Antrim*, *Glamorgan*, *Cardiff*, *Exeter*,
FRs — *Brilliant*, *Broadsword*, *Active*, *Alacrity*, *Ambuscade*, *Avenger*, *Arrow*, *Andromeda*, *Argonaut*, *Minerva*, *Penelope*, *Plymouth*, *Yarmouth*,
Assault ships — *Fearless*, *Intrepid*
RFAs — *Fort Austin*, *Olmeda*, *Olna*, *Regent*, *Resource*, *Tidepool*, *Tidespring*
LSLs — *Sir Bedivere*, *Sir Galahad*, *Sir Geraint*, *Sir Lancelot*, *Sir Percivale*, *Sir Tristram*
Transports — *Atlantic Causeway*, *Elk*, *Europic Ferry*

Also submarine force, hospital ships in RCB, repair ship and tugs in TRALA, and some tankers

Sheffield, *Ardent*, *Antelope*, *Coventry* and *Atlantic Conveyor* lost

15. [b29] Sea Harrier (29 May)
16. [b30] Harrier GR3 (30 May)
14. [a63, a64] Skyhawks (30 May)

GALLANTRY AWARDS
Ajax Bay, and later Goose Green and Darwin — bomb and ordnance disposal
Flt Lt A. J. Swan RAF, CO No 1 EOD RAF (OGM)

Chinook of No 18 Sqn RAF — 'The Survivor'
Sqn Ldr R. U. Langworthy AFC, RAF (DFC)

0   10   20 MILES

2. New House
3. Douglas
5. 45 Cdo Teal Inlet
45 Cdo
4. 3 Para
6. 3 Para Lower Malo House
13. [a62] Puma (30 May) ▲ Mt Estancia
▲ Mt Kent
9. D Sqn SAS / K Coy 42 Cdo / 7 Bty RA (part)
■ Stanley
8. L Coy 42 Cdo Port San Carlos
12. [a61] Dagger (29 May)
Ajax Bay ■
San Carlos ■
40 Cdo (in defence)
10. Sussex Mtns
7. J Coy 42 Cdo
Darwin ■
11. [a57] Skyhawk (27 May)
Goose Green ■
1. 2 Para / 8 Bty RA

reached Lower Malo House. In the meantime, 45 Cdo stays put.

On Friday 28 May, with J Coy 42 Cdo flying down towards Darwin, the rest of the Commando prepares for the Mount Kent operation. K Coy is already at Port San Carlos, and is joined from Sussex Mountains by L Coy, after they in turn have been relieved by B Coy of 40 Cdo which has to stay in defence of the beachhead. That same night, D Sqn SAS finally completes its helicopter move below Mount Kent, but an attempt to follow them up with 42 Cdo Tac HQ, K Coy and three 105mm guns of 7 Bty over Saturday night is stopped by blizzards. Late on Sunday, No 846 NAS Sea Kings and the lone RAF Chinook manage to get in, but in the middle of an SAS fire-fight with Argentine troops, after which K Coy moves on to the summit. The Chinook is slightly damaged on the flight back, but support helicopter strength is increasing. The first No 825 NAS Sea Kings fly ashore from Atlantic Causeway on Saturday and join the other Navy, Marine and Army helicopters as well as the Chinook already flying from the Forward Operating Bases (FOBs) scattered around San Carlos Water.

Although there are few Argentine aircraft attacks between now and the second week in June, they nevertheless choose the afternoon of Thursday 27 May for their first strike against land targets, when two pairs of Grupo 5 Skyhawks bomb and strafe troop and supply positions. Coming in over the Brigade Maintenance Area at Ajax Bay, one pair kills six men of 45 Cdo and the Cdo Logistics Regt, wounds others and lands UXBs near the Field Dressing Station, which is where Flt Lt Swan later sleeps beside the bombs to reassure the staff and patients. The second pair hit San Carlos and kill one man each from 40 Cdo and the 59 Ind Cdo Sqn RE; but during the attacks, one of the Skyhawks is hit by 40mm Bofors fire from HMS Fearless or HMS Intrepid and crashes over West Falkland near Port Howard [a57].

More sorties take place over the weekend. Early on the morning of Saturday 29 May, Canberras of Grupo 2 carry out the first of a series of night time harrassing attacks on San Carlos Water, followed in June by raids on the Mount Kent area, and at midday when Daggers of Grupo 6 reach the anchorage, one is shot down by the defending Rapiers [a61]. On Sunday morning an Argentine Army Puma is lost near Mount Kent, possibly to its own forces [a62], and that afternoon, two A-4C Skyhawks are brought down in the first co-ordinated CANA/FAA mission. The plan is for two Super Etendards to launch the last airborne Exocet at the Task Force carriers, and for four Grupo 4 Skyhawks to finish off the target with bombs. Coming in from the south after tanker refuelling, the aircraft mistakenly release the missile from 20 miles at HMS Avenger then east of the Falklands. The Exocet is apparently deflected by chaff, and although the Super Etendards escape, two of the Skyhawks are destroyed by Sea Darts from HMS Exeter as they go in to attack, although HMS Avenger's 4.5in gun may have hit one of them [a63, a64].

As the Sea Harriers continue to fly CAP and drop bombs on Stanley airfield and the GR3s fly ground support from the carriers, a total of three are lost over these few days. Apart from the GR3 lost near Goose Green on Thursday, on Saturday afternoon a Sea Harrier of No 801 NAS slides off the deck of HMS Invincible as she turns into wind in heavy weather, although fortunately the pilot ejects and is rescued from the water [b29]. Then at midday on Sunday, the RAF finds itself down to just three GR3s. One of four aircraft over the Stanley area is hit by small arms fire from Argentine troops, and on the way back to HMS Hermes runs out of fuel [b30]. Sqn Ldr Pook parachutes into the sea and is soon rescued by a No 826 NAS Sea King.

Apart from all the shipping activity around South Georgia, Task Force warships continue to bombard Argentine positions and escort supply ships into and out of San Carlos Water, where only now are HMS Argonaut and LSL Sir Lancelot finally relieved of their UXBs. Elk goes in on the night of Thursday 27 May to continue unloading her ammunition, and over the weekend, HMS Argonaut and HMS Plymouth finally leave, with only HMS Yarmouth of the original escorts remaining for a few days more. And now 5th Inf Bde starts to arrive. HMS Fearless leaves San Carlos Water on Thursday to later meet HMS Antrim to the east of the TEZ, and with Gen Moore on board arrives back early on Sunday. When Brig Thompson returns to San Carlos from Teal Inlet to find his commander there, final plans are made to receive 5th Inf Bde, put 2 Para under Brig Wilson's command, and move 3 Cdo Bde HQ to the Inlet.

MAP 30 — WEEK 10

British Successes Against Argentine Forces and Task Force Movements

31 May-6 June

As the war approaches a speedy end this is a convenient place to summarise the British successes against Argentine sea and air forces. None of the 'scores' are official, some no doubt are open to argument, and of course only give a limited indication of the contribution made by each of the main front-line units. **All** squadron pilots receiving gallantry awards are also listed.

British ships and squadrons — Argentine ships sunk or damaged

HMS *Conqueror* — cruiser *General Belgrano* sunk

HMS *Alacrity* — fleet transport *Isla de los Estados* sunk

HMS *Brilliant* and *Yarmouth* — coaster *Monsunen* driven aground

HMS *Hermes*, No 800 NAS Sea Harriers — trawler *Narwal* sunk, fleet transport *Bahia Buen Suceso* damaged, transport *Rio Carcarana* damaged, patrol ship *Rio Iguaza* beached

HMS *Antelope*, No 815 NAS Lynx — *Rio Carcarana* destroyed

HMS *Antrim*, No 737 NAS Wessex, HMS *Brilliant*, No 815 NAS Lynx, HMS *Endurance* and HMS *Plymouth*, No 829 NAS Wasps — submarine *Santa Fe* disabled

HMS *Coventry* and HMS *Glasgow*, No 815 NAS Lynx — patrol vessel *Alferez Sobral* damaged

British forces — Argentine aircraft and helicopters destroyed

HMS *Hermes*, No 800 NAS Sea Harriers:
Lt-Cdr A. D. Auld RN (DSC) — 2 Daggers [a50, a51]
Lt-Cdr G. W. J. Batt RN (post DSC)
Lt-Cdr M. S. Blissett RN (MID) — Skyhawk [a36]
Lt-Cdr R. V. Frederiksen RN (MID) — Dagger [a38]

Lt M. Hale RN — Dagger [a49]
Flt Lt J. Leeming RAF — Skyhawk [a43]
Flt Lt D. H. S. Morgan RAF (DSC) — 2 Skyhawks [a67, a68]
Lt C. R. W. Morrell RN (MID) — 1½ Skyhawks [a42, a44]
Flt Lt R. Penfold RAF — Dagger [a7]
Lt D. A. Smith RN (MID) — Dagger [a52], Skyhawk [a69]
Lt-Cdr N. W. Thomas RN (DSC) — Skyhawk [a37]
plus 3 Pucaras [a2, a3, a4], 1½ Pumas [a45, a47], Agusta 109A [a46]

HMS *Invincible*, No 801 NAS Sea Harriers:
Flt Lt P. C. Barton RAF — Mirage [a5]
Lt W. A. Curtis RN (post MID) — Canberra [a8]
Lt S. R. Thomas RN (DSC), Mirage [a6], 2 Daggers (a39, a40)
Cdr N. D. Ward AFC RN (DSC) — Pucara [a35], Dagger [a41], Hercules [a65], plus ½ Puma [a47]

HMS *Ardent* — ½ Skyhawk [a44]
HMS *Brilliant* — 3 Skyhawks [a16, a17, a18]
HMS *Broadsword* — probably Dagger [a34]
HMS *Coventry* — Puma [a15], 2 Skyhawks [a54, a56]
HMS *Exeter* — 2 Skyhawks [a63, a64], Learjet [a66], Canberra [a70]
HMS *Fearless* or *Intrepid* — Skyhawk [a57]
Naval bombardment — Skyvan [a12]
Royal Marines — Puma [a1], Aermacchi [a59]

San Carlos Water defences — 3 Skyhawks [a48, a53, a55]

T Bty, 12 Air Defence Regt RA — Dagger [a61]
2 Para — Pucara [a60]
D Sqn SAS — 7 Pucaras [a20-a25, a33], 4 Mentors [a26-a29], Skyvan [a30]

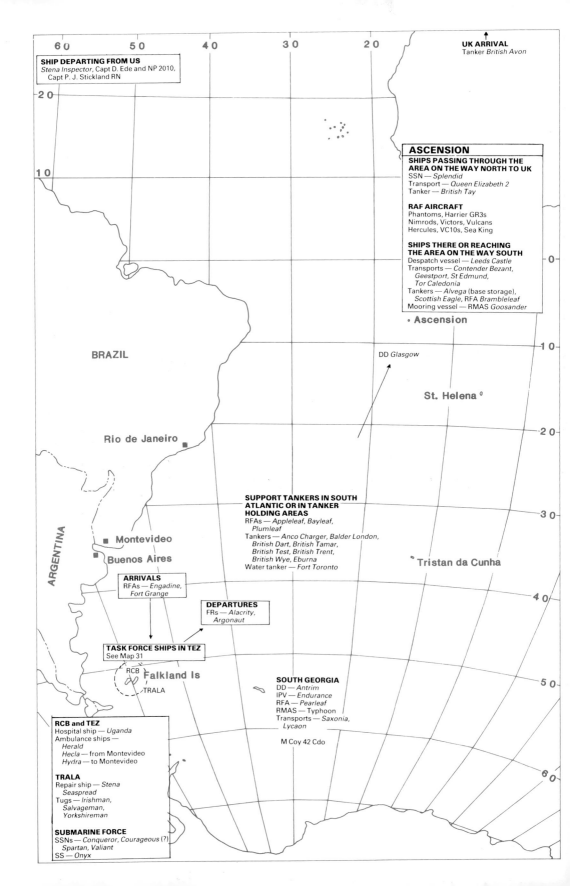

60   50   40   30   20

UK ARRIVAL
Tanker *British Avon*

SHIP DEPARTING FROM US
Stena Inspector, Capt D. Ede and NP 2010,
Capt P. J. Stickland RN

20

10

ASCENSION

**SHIPS PASSING THROUGH THE
AREA ON THE WAY NORTH TO UK**
SSN — *Splendid*
Transport — *Queen Elizabeth 2*
Tanker — *British Tay*

RAF AIRCRAFT
Phantoms, Harrier GR3s
Nimrods, Victors, Vulcans
Hercules, VC10s, Sea King

**SHIPS THERE OR REACHING
THE AREA ON THE WAY SOUTH**
Despatch vessel — *Leeds Castle*
Transports — *Contender Bezant,
   Geestport, St Edmund,
   Tor Caledonia*
Tankers — *Alvega* (base storage),
   Scottish Eagle, RFA *Brambleleaf*
Mooring vessel — RMAS *Goosander*

0

• Ascension

DD *Glasgow*

10

BRAZIL

St. Helena º

20

Rio de Janeiro ■

**SUPPORT TANKERS IN SOUTH
ATLANTIC OR IN TANKER
HOLDING AREAS**
RFAs — *Appleleaf, Bayleaf,
   Plumleaf*
Tankers — *Anco Charger, Balder London,
   British Dart, British Tamar,
   British Test, British Trent,
   British Wye, Eburna*
Water tanker — *Fort Toronto*

30

ARGENTINA

■ Montevideo

■ Buenos Aires

º Tristan da Cunha

40

ARRIVALS
RFAs — *Engadine,
Fort Grange*

DEPARTURES
FRs — *Alacrity,
Argonaut*

TASK FORCE SHIPS IN TEZ
See Map 31

RCB
Falkland Is
TRALA

50

SOUTH GEORGIA
DD — *Antrim*
IPV — *Endurance*
RFA — *Pearleaf*
RMAS — *Typhoon*
Transports — *Saxonia,
   Lycaon*

M Coy 42 Cdo

RCB and TEZ
Hospital ship — *Uganda*
Ambulance ships —
   Herald
   Hecla — from Montevideo
   Hydra — to Montevideo

TRALA
Repair ship — *Stena
   Seaspread*
Tugs — *Irishman,
   Salvageman,
   Yorkshireman*

SUBMARINE FORCE
SSNs — *Conqueror, Courageous* (?)
   Spartan, Valiant
SS — *Onyx*

60

No 1 (F) Sqn RAF Harrier GR3s — Chinook [a31], Puma [a32]
   Sqn Ldr J. J. Pook RAF (DFC)
   Wg Cdr P. T. Squire AFC RAF (DFC)

Task Force arrival and departure

British Avon is the first tanker to return to the UK to reload, and arrives at Portsmouth on Saturday 5 June with the special prisoner Lt-Cdr Astiz who is shortly flown back to Argentina as a POW. Next day, but across the Atlantic, a second repair ship Stena Inspector sets out from Charleston, South Carolina after conversion including the addition of a heavy machine shop.

Ascension

More ships pass by during the week on their way back to Britain including Queen Elizabeth 2, but aircraft, equipment and supplies are still urgently needed in the south. With a total of nine Harrier GR3s of No 1 (F) Sqn RAF now present, two fly direct to the TEZ on Tuesday 1 June and land on HMS Hermes, and another four, together with two No 3 CBAS Gazelles and the local RAF Chinook sail on Thursday with the helicopters already on board transport Contender Bezant. Two more GR3s fly on south the following week, but the ninth stays behind with fuel leaks. Wednesday night sees the launch of Operation 'Black Buck 6', the second successful Shrike raid against the Stanley radars, but this time the Vulcan has to divert to Rio de Janeiro on the way back.

South Atlantic

More ships of the original Task Force start to return north. Frigates HMS Alacrity and the damaged HMS Argonaut, after spending a short time in the TRALA with Stena Seaspread, follow over the weekend in the wake of HMS Glasgow bound for the UK. Going in the opposite direction, the three tugs stationed in the area make their way to South Georgia. By then, RFA Fort Grange has joined the CVBG to start replenishment operations and helicopter support ship Engadine is entering the TEZ on her way to San Carlos Water. Earlier in the week, Iris also reaches the TRALA with the scrap steel from South Georgia and then along with Dumbarton Castle continues her despatch duties between the Falklands, South Georgia and Ascension.

Carrying casualties of both sides, the Red Cross Box-Montevideo shuttle now starts in earnest. On Wednesday 2 June, as Hydra follows her north, Hecla arrives at the Uruguayan capital and by Sunday is back in the Box. In the meantime, Herald's Wasp helicopter is used to carry an International Red Cross team over from the Uganda to inspect the Argentine icebreaker Bahia Paraiso now being used in the hospital ship role.

South Georgia

As the only secure base where stores can be transferred between ships with little interference from Argentine aircraft, there are more arrivals from the TEZ. These include RFA Resource which calls in for replenishment herself, destroyer HMS Antrim returning this time as guardship, and RFA Pearleaf to take over as station tanker from the departed Blue Rover.

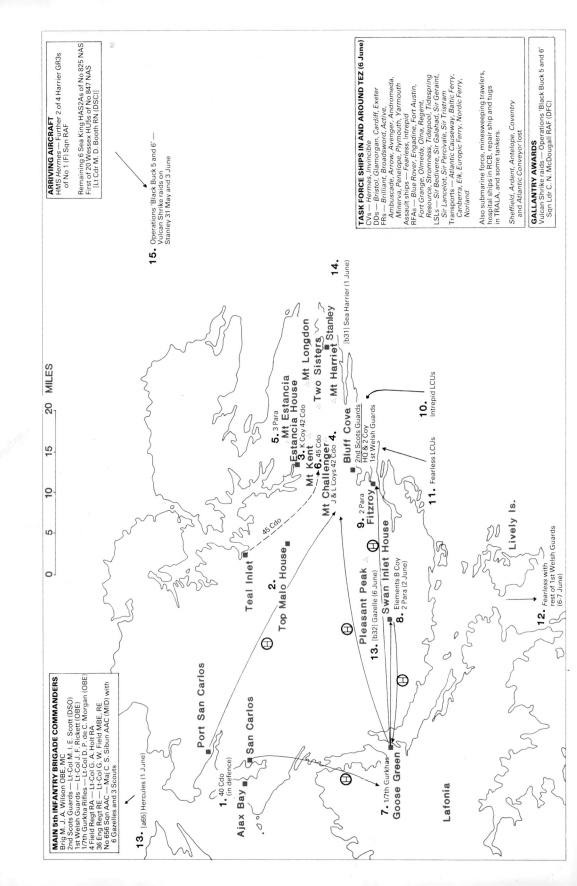

MAIN 5th INFANTRY BRIGADE COMMANDERS
Brig M. J. A. Wilson OBE, MC
2nd Scots Guards — Lt-Col M. I. E. Scott (DSO)
1st Welsh Guards — Lt-Col J. F. Rickett (OBE)
1/7th Gurkha Rifles — Lt-Col D. P. de C. Morgan (OBE)
4 Field Regt RA — Lt-Col G. A. Holt RA
36 Eng Regt RE — Lt-Col G. W. Field MBE, RE
No 656 Sqn AAC — Maj C. S. Sibun AAC (MID) with
6 Gazelles and 3 Scouts

ARRIVING AIRCRAFT
HMS *Hermes* — Further 2 of 4 Harrier GR3s
of No 1 (F) Sqn RAF

Remaining 6 Sea King HAS2As of No 825 NAS
First of 20 Wessex HU5s of No 847 NAS
[Lt Cdr M. D. Booth RN (DSC)]

15. Operations 'Black Buck 5 and 6' —
Vulcan Shrike raids on
Stanley 31 May and 3 June

TASK FORCE SHIPS IN AND AROUND TEZ (6 June)
CVs — *Hermes, Invincible*
DDs — *Bristol, Glamorgan, Cardiff, Exeter*
FRs — *Brilliant, Broadsword, Active,
Ambuscade, Arrow, Avenger, Andromeda,
Minerva, Penelope, Plymouth, Yarmouth*
Assault ships — *Fearless, Intrepid*
RFAs — *Blue Rover, Engadine, Fort Austin,
Fort Grange, Olmeda, Olna, Regent,
Resource, Stromness, Tidepool, Tidespring*
LSLs — *Sir Bedivere, Sir Galahad, Sir Geraint,
Sir Lancelot, Sir Percivale, Sir Tristram*
Transports — *Atlantic Causeway, Baltic Ferry,
Canberra, Elk, Europic Ferry, Nordic Ferry,
Norland*

Also submarine force, minesweeping trawlers,
hospital ships in RCB, repair ship and tugs
in TRALA, and some tankers.

*Sheffield, Ardent, Antelope, Coventry
and Atlantic Conveyor lost*

GALLANTRY AWARDS
Vulcan Shrike raids — Operations 'Black Buck 5 and 6'
Sqn Ldr C. N. McDougall RAF (DFC)

0   5   10   15   20   MILES

13. '(a65) Hercules (1 June)

Port San Carlos

1. 40 Cdo
(in defence)
San Carlos
Ajax Bay

Teal Inlet

2.
Top Malo House

45 Cdo

Mt Kent
3. K Coy 42 Cdo
Estancia House
5. 3 Para
Mt Estancia
△ Mt Longdon
△ Two Sisters
6. 45 Cdo
4. J & L Coys 42 Cdo
Mt Challenger
△ Mt Harrier
Stanley
14.
[b31] Sea Harrier (1 June)

Pleasant Peak △
13. [b32] Gazelle (6 June)

Swan Inlet House
Elements B Coy
8. 2 Para (2 June)

9. 2 Para
Fitzroy
Bluff Cove
2nd Scots Guards
HQ & 2 Coy
1st Welsh Guards
10.
Intrepid LCUs

11. Fearless LCUs

7. 1/7th Gurkhas
Goose Green

Lafonia

Lively Is.

12. *Fearless* with
rest of 1st Welsh Guards
(6-7 June)

THE APPROACH TO AND BATTLE FOR STANLEY

MAP 31 — WEEK 10

Falkland Area Operations

31 May-6 June

As Gen Moore assumes overall command, Brig Thompson is freed to concentrate on 3 Cdo Bde's move on Stanley by the northern route. But in the process he loses 40 Cdo for base defence, 2 Para, 29 Bty RA and The Blues and Royals to 5th Inf Bde, and the Cdo Logistics Regt now has to support both main units. The newly arriving 5th Infantry will move on Stanley from the southwest, by which time Forward Brigade Maintenance Areas will be established both at Teal Inlet and Fitzroy.

During a week when 3 Cdo Bde completes its moves forward, the first action comes on the morning of Monday 31 May when a small M & AW Cadre force helicopters in to attack an Argentine patrol at Top Malo House, and kills or captures all 17 in exchange for three marines wounded. By then, K Coy 42 Cdo is on the summit of Mount Kent, and stays through the week. Not so the rest of 42 Cdo. Over Monday night, L Coy (and the rest of 7 Bty RA) flies in from Port San Carlos, and marches to Mount Challenger, and over Wednesday night, J Coy moves there direct from Goose Green. By then 3 Para has completed its tab; securing Estancia House on Monday, and next day digging in, on and around Mount Estancia, before being joined by the six guns of 79 Bty RA. On Friday, 45 Cdo RM finishes its yomp from Teal Inlet and reaches a position below Mount Kent from where it can reinforce 3 Para or 42 Cdo in their exposed positions within range of the Argentine guns.

With 3 Cdo Bde on Mounts Estancia, Kent and Challenger, preparations are made for the coming Battle for Stanley. In increasingly foul and wintry weather, the three units start patrolling towards their objectives — 3 Para to Mount Longdon, 45 Cdo to Two Sisters, 42 Cdo to Mount Harriet. To complete 3 Cdo's move, Brigade HQ and the supplies needed converge on Teal Inlet. On Monday, the HQ staff fly in, followed by their Bandwagon snow vehicles and escorting tanks of No 3 Troop, although these continue on to join No 4 Troop at Estancia House before both move down to Bluff Cove. And to open up Teal as the forward base, HMS *Intrepid* arrives over Monday night with a LCU going in with the first supplies and accompanied by two LCVPs fitted with light minesweeping gear, followed on Tuesday night by LSL *Sir Percivale* as she and other LSLs start a delivery service from San Carlos Water.

Welcome reinforcements, including 5th Inf Bde now start arriving. The first transports reach San Carlos Water on Tuesday morning (1 June) and *Norland* lands the Gurkhas by LCU, *Baltic Ferry* her Scouts, and *Atlantic Causeway* the remaining No 825 NAS Sea Kings and some of the No 847 NAS Wessex. That same day, the frigate HMS *Penelope* picks up 2 Para's new CO after he parachutes into the sea from an extended-range Hercules, while *Canberra* reaches the CVBG. Heading on in, she offloads the two Guards battalions on Wednesday morning again using the hard-worked LCUs plus her two No 825 NAS Sea Kings. And on Thursday, *Nordic Ferry* arrives with the rest of the Gazelles, while *Canberra* leaves for the TRALA for the remaining days of the war.

Once they have landed, most of the 1/7th Gurkhas fly in the lone Chinook to Goose Green to relieve 2 Para, and to spend the next week patrolling into Lafonia. Now 5th Inf starts its push forward when on Wednesday 2 June, elements of B Coy 2 Para fly to Swan Inlet House in five Army Scouts and Maj Crosland makes his famous telephone call to find that Fitzroy and Bluff Cove are clear of the enemy. Later that day and the next, 2 Para is helicoptered the 35 miles from Goose Green to occupy the two settlements.

With 2 Para so far forward and lacking helicopter lift, Gen Moore decides to risk the assault ships on night runs from San Carlos Water with the two Guards units. Starting on Saturday night (5 June), HMS *Intrepid* carries the 2nd Scots Guards around the south of Lafonia and, off Lively Island, transfers them to her four LCUs. After a lengthy and rough passage they arrive at Bluff Cove early on Sunday to stay, while the three coys of 2 Para already there are ferried to Fitzroy by the same LCUs to join the rest of the battalion. That night it is the turn of HMS *Fearless* to bring round the 1st Welsh Guards. Reaching Lively Island, only her two LCUs are available to carry HQ and 2 Coy on to Bluff Cove. The rest have to return to San Carlos Water to try again on Monday night. Before then, a plan to improve communications links is thwarted. Early on Sunday morning as an AAC Gazelle flies forward with two Royal Signals to set up a relay station, it is accidentally shot down near Pleasant Peak by a Sea Dart fired by HMS *Cardiff*, and all four on board are killed [b32].

Back to Tuesday 1 June and the Task Force Harriers. Late that morning, a Grupo 1 Hercules on a reconnaissance mission is detected by the frigate HMS *Minerva* in San Carlos Water, and a vectored No 801 NAS Sea Harrier brings it down 50 miles north of Pebble Island using Sidewinder missiles and cannon fire [a65]. Then in the afternoon, the final Sea Harrier is lost when another No 801 NAS aircraft, on a sortie over Stanley, is hit by a Roland SAM [b31]. Flt Lt Mortimer bails out into the sea just to the south, but it is nine hours before he is found and rescued by a No 820 NAS Sea King. Next day, the first step is taken in extending Harrier operations when the Royal Engineers complete a Forward Operating Base at Port San Carlos, with two No 800 NAS Sea Harriers arriving on Saturday. Before then, early on Monday morning, the first Shrike attack has been made on the Stanley radars in Operation 'Black Buck 5', but the TPS-43 surveillance radar is only slightly damaged. A repeat Operation 'Black Buck 6' raid early on Thursday by the same Vulcan destroys a Skyguard AA radar, but on the return flight the bomber has to divert to Rio de Janeiro with refuelling difficulties, but is released a week later.

MAP 32 — WEEK 11 AND INTO WEEK 12

Task Force Movements

7-15 June

In just eight days, the war is brought to a close and the Argentines surrender their forces on West and East Falkland. But before they do, the FAA, in one last major effort damages frigate HMS *Plymouth*, sinks one of HMS *Fearless* LCUs, mortally damages LSL *Sir Galahad* (inflicting heavy casualties on the 1st Welsh Guards) and nearly puts paid to LSL *Sir Tristram*. Apart from the later hit on destroyer HMS *Glamorgan* by a land-based Exocet, these are virtually the last losses in ships or aircraft. But before the war is won, the Argentine troops defending Stanley in the mountains to the west have to be defeated by marines, paras and guardsmen in combat — often man against man, with rifle, bayonet, machine gun and grenade, supported by mortar and artillery, in the dark, in often atrocious weather and over tough terrain.

Over the night of Friday 11 June, the outer ring of defended heights will be taken — Mount Longdon by 3 Para, Two Sisters by 45 Cdo and Mount Harriet by 42 Cdo. Two nights later, over Sunday 13 June, the next line will fall — Wireless Ridge to 2 Para so soon after Goose Green, and Tumbledown Mountain to the 2nd Scots Guards. Meanwhile the 1/7th Gurkha Rifles stand by ready to attack Mount William and a depleted 1st Welsh Guards, reinforced by 40 Cdo, prepares to occupy Sapper Hill. In the event, the surviving Argentine troops stream back to Stanley where they still outnumber the British attackers. But throughout Monday 14 June, a surrender is negotiated, timed to take place from 21.00hrs local time. But still more ships, aircraft and supplies are needed.

Task Force departures and arrivals from Monday 7 June

During the week, four merchantmen head south. On Tuesday from Plymouth, *Astron-*

94

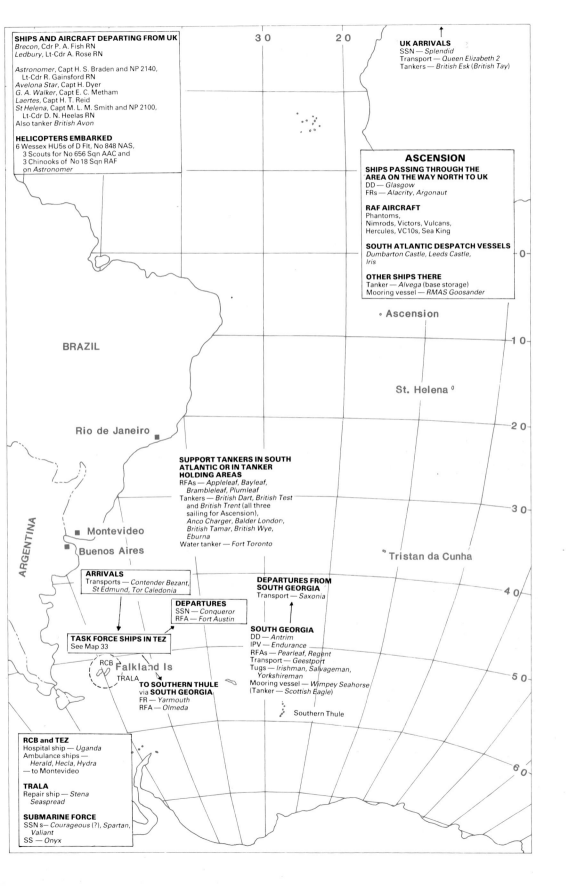

SHIPS AND AIRCRAFT DEPARTING FROM UK
Brecon, Cdr P. A. Fish RN
Ledbury, Lt-Cdr A. Rose RN

Astronomer, Capt H. S. Braden and NP 2140,
   Lt-Cdr R. Gainsford RN
Avelona Star, Capt H. Dyer
G. A. Walker, Capt E. C. Metham
Laertes, Capt H. T. Reid
St Helena, Capt M. L. M. Smith and NP 2100,
   Lt-Cdr D. N. Heelas RN
Also tanker *British Avon*

HELICOPTERS EMBARKED
6 Wessex HU5s of D Flt, No 848 NAS,
3 Scouts for No 656 Sqn AAC and
3 Chinooks of No 18 Sqn RAF
on *Astronomer*

30

20

UK ARRIVALS
SSN — *Splendid*
Transport — *Queen Elizabeth 2*
Tankers — *British Esk* (*British Tay*)

ASCENSION
**SHIPS PASSING THROUGH THE
AREA ON THE WAY NORTH TO UK**
DD — *Glasgow*
FRs — *Alacrity, Argonaut*

RAF AIRCRAFT
Phantoms,
Nimrods, Victors, Vulcans,
Hercules, VC10s, Sea King

SOUTH ATLANTIC DESPATCH VESSELS
*Dumbarton Castle, Leeds Castle,
Iris*

OTHER SHIPS THERE
Tanker — *Alvega* (base storage)
Mooring vessel — RMAS *Goosander*

0

∘ Ascension

10

St. Helena ∘

20

BRAZIL

Rio de Janeiro ▪

**SUPPORT TANKERS IN SOUTH
ATLANTIC OR IN TANKER
HOLDING AREAS**
RFAs — *Appleleaf, Bayleaf,
   Brambleleaf, Plumleaf*
Tankers — *British Dart, British Test*
   and *British Trent* (all three
   sailing for Ascension),
   *Anco Charger, Balder London,
   British Tamar, British Wye,
   Eburna*
Water tanker — *Fort Toronto*

30

Tristan da Cunha ∘

ARGENTINA

▪ Montevideo

▪ Buenos Aires

ARRIVALS
Transports — *Contender Bezant,
St Edmund, Tor Caledonia*

**DEPARTURES FROM
SOUTH GEORGIA**
Transport — *Saxonia*

40

DEPARTURES
SSN — *Conqueror*
RFA — *Fort Austin*

SOUTH GEORGIA
DD — *Antrim*
IPV — *Endurance*
RFAs — *Pearleaf, Regent*
Transport — *Geestport*
Tugs — *Irishman, Salvageman,
   Yorkshireman*
Mooring vessel — *Wimpey Seahorse*
(Tanker — *Scottish Eagle*)

TASK FORCE SHIPS IN TEZ
See Map 33

RCB
Falkland Is

TRALA

TO SOUTHERN THULE
via **SOUTH GEORGIA**
FR — *Yarmouth*
RFA — *Olmeda*

Southern Thule

50

RCB and TEZ
Hospital ship — *Uganda*
Ambulance ships —
   Herald, Hecla, Hydra
   — to Montevideo

TRALA
Repair ship — *Stena
   Seaspread*

SUBMARINE FORCE
SSN s — *Courageous* (?), *Spartan,
   Valiant*
SS — *Onyx*

60

omer sets out as a helicopter carrier and repair ship with a variety of helicopters and additionally equipped with 2×20mm Oerlikons, chaff launchers and a Unifoxer acoustic torpedo decoy. Leaving the same day is the ammunition ship *Laertes*, and two days later tanker *G. A. Walker*. Refrigerated stores ship *Avelona Star* sails at this time from Portsmouth loaded with food. Then on Sunday, cargo vessel *St Helena* sails from Portland after working up as a minesweeper support ship. Armed with 4×20mm Oerlikons, she accompanies 'Hunt' class mine countermeasures vessels HMS *Brecon* and HMS *Ledbury* — the first Navy minesweepers to leave for the Falklands. Next day, the reloaded tanker *British Avon* sails from Portland for a second voyage south.

Meanwhile, more ships return to the UK. By far the most publicised arrival occurs on Friday 11 June when *Queen Elizabeth 2* sails into Southampton with the survivors from HMS *Ardent*, HMS *Antelope* and HMS *Coventry* to be met by the Royal Yacht *Britannia* carrying HM Queen Elizabeth, The Queen Mother. The nuclear submarine HMS *Splendid* gets in to Devonport the next day. By then the tanker *British Esk* is back to reload, and as the surrender takes place, *British Tay* approaches British shores.

Ascension

There is no let up at this one and only advanced base (other than South Georgia), especially on the part of the RAF. On Tuesday 8 June, the last two Harrier GR3s fly direct to HMS *Hermes*, and on Friday, Operation 'Black Buck 7' is launched — the last Vulcan raid on Stanley and again using conventional bombs. The aircraft returns safely the next day. Also returning, but to the UK is the destroyer HMS *Glasgow* which passes through the area early in the week, followed by the frigates HMS *Alacrity* and HMS *Argonaut* around the time of the surrender.

South Atlantic

Tuesday 8 June sees the only non-belligerent casualty when two Grupo 2 Canberras mistakenly bomb the American-registered tanker *Hercules* then on passage to the northeast of the TEZ. On putting into Rio de Janeiro, a UXB is found that is too dangerous to disarm, and the ship has to be scuttled off Brazil in late July. Fortunately the FAA's attempts to hit the British lines of communications are unsuccessful as later in the week, tankers *British Test* and *British Trent* sail north for Ascension carrying the survivors from LSLs *Sir Galahad* and *Sir Tristram* respectively.

In the Falklands area itself, the hard-worked transport *Norland* heads out of San Carlos Water on Monday 7 June with 1,000 Argentine POWs bound for Montevideo, and gets in over the weekend. Aircraft and helicopter carrier *Contender Bezant* reaches the TEZ on Thursday with her Navy Sea King, Marine Gazelles, RAF Chinooks and four GR3s — too late to join in the fighting although the helicopters are needed to help in the clearing-up. Over the weekend, the transport *Tor Caledonia* reaches the TRALA to start offloading stores and, just after the surrender, the transport *St Edmund* reaches the CVBG. On the same day, Tuesday 15 June, the nuclear submarine HMS *Conqueror* leaves for the UK after her active eight weeks of patrols in the South Atlantic, while the frigate HMS *Yarmouth* and RFA *Olmeda* head in the opposite direction, first for South Georgia on their way to re-occupy Southern Thule. Well before then, on Monday 7 June, the first RFA to head south, *Fort Austin*, is returning north for England and Devonport.

South Georgia

This almost Antarctic island, still garrisoned by M Coy 42 Cdo and attended by HMS *Endurance*, sees more comings and goings. *Wimpey Seahorse* arrives to lay out moorings at various anchorages, the RFA *Regent* gets in from the TEZ to replenish from refrigerated stores ships *Saxonia* and the newly arrived *Geestport* and, at the time of the surrender, *Scottish Eagle* is heading there as base storage tanker. Well before then, RMAS tug *Typhoon* has left for the TRALA, as has ammunition ship *Lycaon*. Over the weekend, *Saxonia* leaves for the UK to reload after her three weeks at South Georgia.

MAP 33 — WEEK 11

Falkland Area Operations

7-13 June

The decision is now taken to use the LSLs to continue 5th Inf's move forward. *Sir Tristram* reaches Fitzroy on Monday 7 June to start unloading ammunition and, in San Carlos Water, *Sir Galahad* takes on board the rest of the 1st Welsh Guards from HMS *Fearless* before sailing around Lafonia to arrive on Tuesday morning (8 June). By now, only one LCU and a Mexeflote are left to complete offloading *Sir Tristram* and although by early afternoon Rapier SAMs and 16 Field Ambulance have gone ashore from *Sir Galahad*, plans to move the Guards to Bluff Cove to join the rest of the battalion have come to nothing. Worse still, the LSLs have been reported by enemy observers, and around 14.00hrs, five Skyhawks of Grupo 5 and five Daggers of Grupo 6 are coming in over the Falklands.

First to be attacked by the Daggers, but in Falkland Sound, is the frigate HMS *Plymouth* on her way to bombard an Argentine position on West Falkland. Hit by cannon fire and four UXBs, one of which detonates a depth charge, she is only slightly damaged. Shortly after, the Skyhawks reach Fitzroy. Three of them put two or more bombs into the crowded *Sir Galahad*, and the other two hit *Sir Tristram* with two UXBs, killing two crewmen. The ships catch fire and are soon abandoned, but by then the results for *Sir Galahad* are catastrophic with a total of 48 killed — five RFA crewmen, 32 guardsmen and 11 other Army personnel, with many more badly burned and wounded. *Sir Tristram* is later returned to the UK for repairs, but the burnt-out *Sir Galahad* is scuttled at sea as a war grave on 25 June.

As the FAA's last major effort continues, four Grupo 4 Skyhawks attack troops in the Fitzroy area later that afternoon and, minutes after, four Skyhawks of Grupo 5 arrive over Choiseul Sound to catch LCU F4 (belonging to HMS-*Fearless*) sailing from Goose Green to Fitzroy with 5th Inf Bde HQ vehicles. Hit by one bomb, which kills the coxswain, CSgt Johnston (post QGM) and five of the crew, she quickly sinks. Two No 800 NAS Sea Harriers overhead on CAP immediately dive to the attack and bring down three of the Skyhawks with Sidewinders [a67, a68, a69].

During the week, both Land Forces and 5th Inf HQs move to Fitzroy and 3 Cdo Bde's to Mount Kent, and although the *Sir Galahad* disaster causes delays, planning continues for the attack towards Stanley. In the first phase, 3 Cdo Bde will take Mount Longdon, Two Sisters and Mount Harriet, and if possible Tumbledown Mountain and Wireless Ridge. Otherwise these two plus Mount William will be assaulted in the second phase, and Sapper Hill and the ground south of Stanley in the third phase. As part of the build-up, 3 Cdo continues its reconnaissance patrols, and the special forces their covert operations, but with casualties. Only the previous week, a SBS sergeant is killed in an accidental clash with the SAS, and over on West Falkland, as the SAS keep a careful watch on the two large Argentine garrisons there, an observation post near Port Howard is surrounded on Thursday 10 June and Capt Hamilton is killed as he tries to fight his way out.

With seven of the eight infantry battalions and all five 105mm batteries forward, the first phase starts on the night of Friday 11 June, and by next morning 3 Cdo Bde is on Mount Longdon, Two Sisters and Mount Harriet, but during the night there are other losses. As the supporting warships shell Argentine positions in the mountains and near Stanley, a house in the capital is hit killing two women and mortally wounding a third in the first and last civilian deaths of the war. Then as the destroyer HMS *Glamorgan* retires out to sea after 45 Cdo's attack, a land-launched Exocet fired from Stanley hits her in the hangar area, badly damaging that part of the ship, killing 13 men and destroying her Wessex [b34].

The second phase is delayed until Sunday night (13 June), but by the morning, 2 Para has taken Wireless Ridge and 2nd Scots Guards are on Mount Tumbledown, but it is too late for the Gurkhas to assault Mount William in the dark. The movements during the week of the attacking battalions, including the Gurkhas (less C Coy at Goose Green) are covered by Maps 34 to 38. As for 40 Cdo and the 1st Welsh Guards, the badly depleted Guards stay at Bluff Cove until Friday 11 June when they are reinforced by A and C Coys 40 Cdo released from San Carlos defence (B Coy remains), and march that day to the south west of Mount Harriet to stay in reserve for the next two days.

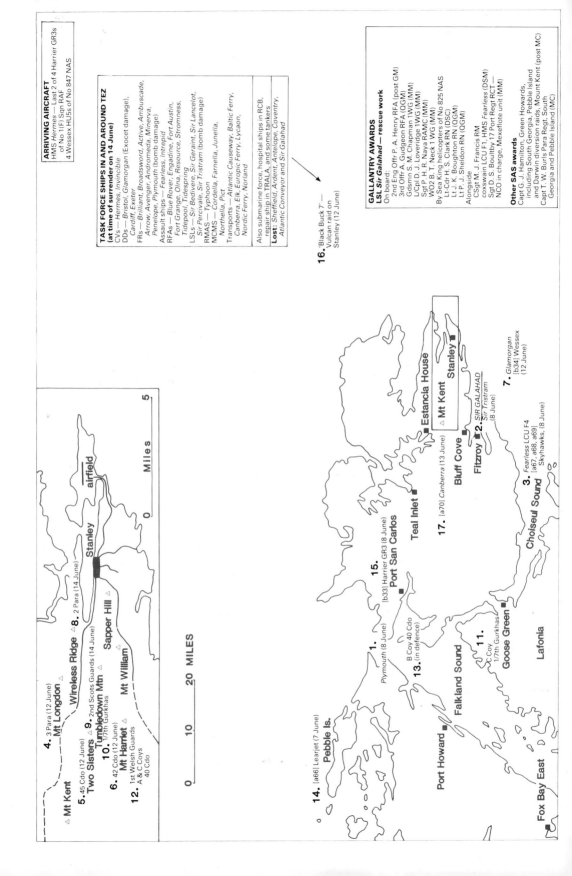

ARRIVING AIRCRAFT
HMS *Hermes* — Last 2 of 4 Harrier GR3s of No 1(F) Sqn RAF
4 Wessex HU5s of No 847 NAS

TASK FORCE SHIPS IN AND AROUND TEZ (at time of surrender on 14 June)
CVs — *Hermes, Invincible*
DDs — *Bristol, Glamorgan* (Exocet damage), *Cardiff, Exeter*
FRs — *Brilliant, Broadsword, Active, Ambuscade, Arrow, Avenger, Andromeda, Minerva, Penelope, Plymouth* (bomb damage)
Assault ships — *Fearless, Intrepid*
RFAs — *Blue Rover, Engadine, Fort Austin, Fort Grange, Olna, Resource, Stromness, Tidepool, Tidespring*
LSLs — *Sir Bedivere, Sir Geraint, Sir Lancelot, Sir Percivale, Sir Tristram* (bomb damage)
RMAS — *Typhoon*
MCMS — *Cordella, Farnella, Junella, Northella, Pict*
Transports — *Atlantic Causeway, Baltic Ferry, Canberra, Elk, Europic Ferry, Lycaon, Nordic Ferry, Norland*

Also submarine force, hospital ships in RCB, repair ship in TRALA, and some tankers
Lost: *Sheffield, Ardent, Antelope, Coventry, Atlantic Conveyor* and *Sir Galahad*

16. 'Black Buck 7' — Vulcan raid on Stanley (12 June)

GALLANTRY AWARDS
LSL *Sir Galahad* — rescue work
On board:
2nd Eng Offr P. A. Henry RFA (post GM)
3rd Offr A. Gudgeon RFA (QGM)
Gdsmn S. M. Chapman 1WG (MM)
L/Cpl D. J. Loveridge 1WG (MM)
Sgt P. H. R. Naya RAMC (MM)
WO2 B. T. Neck 1 WG (MM)
By Sea King helicopters of No 825 NAS
Lt-Cdr H. S. Clark RN (DSC)
Lt J. K. Boughton RN (QGM)
Lt P. J. Sheldon RN (QGM)
Alongside
CSgt M. J. Francis RM coxswain LCU F1, HMS *Fearless* (DSM)
Sgt D. S. Boultby 17 Port Regt RCT — NCO in charge, Mexeflote unit (MM)

Other SAS awards
Capt G. J. Hamilton, Green Howards, including South Georgia, Pebble Island and Darwin diversion raids, Mount Kent (post MC)
Capt T. W. Burls Para Regt, South Georgia and Pebble Island (MC)

Map labels:
△ Mt Kent
4. 3 Para (12 June) — Mt Longdon △
Wireless Ridge △ 8. 2 Para (14 June)
Stanley airfield
5. 45 Cdo (12 June) — Two Sisters △ 9. 2nd Scots Guards (14 June)
10. Tumbledown Mtn △ 1/7th Gurkhas
6. 42 Cdo (12 June) — Mt Harriet △ Sapper Hill
Mt William △
12. A & C Coys 40 Cdo — 1st Welsh Guards
0 10 20 MILES / 0 Miles 5

Estancia House
△ Mt Kent — Stanley
7. *Glamorgan* [b34] Wessex (12 June)
Teal Inlet
Bluff Cove
Fitzroy 2. SIR GALAHAD / *Sir Tristram* (8 June)
17. [a70] *Canberra* (13 June)
15. [b33] Harrier GR3 (8 June) — Port San Carlos
1. *Plymouth* (8 June)
13. B Coy 40 Cdo (in defence)
3. *Fearless* LCU F4 [a67, a68, a69] Skyhawks, (8 June)
Choiseul Sound
Falkland Sound
Port Howard
11. C Coy 1/7th Gurkhas
Goose Green
Lafonia
14. [a66] Learjet (7 June)
Pebble Is.
Fox Bay East

During this time, a battalion dispatch rider is mortally wounded by Argentine shellfire.

Even aside from the air strikes on Tuesday, there is little let-up during the week. On Monday morning (7 June), a reconnaissance Learjet of FAA Grupo 1 is shot down over Pebble Island by one of HMS *Exeter's* Sea Darts [a66]. The next day, the last two RAF Harrier GR3s from Ascension arrive on HMS *Hermes* and the fourth and last GR3 lost is damaged beyond repair when landing heavily at the Port San Carlos FOB with a partial engine failure [b33]. On Wednesday, RFA *Engadine* flies off her four Wessex HU5s of No 847 NAS to San Carlos Water to add to the helicopter lift, and early on Saturday morning, in Operation 'Black Buck 7', Stanley airfield is bombed by a Vulcan for the final time.

Sunday 13 June sees the last Argentine air raids. Late that morning, Skyhawks of FAA Grupo 5 conclude their successful war with an attack on 3 Cdo Bde's HQ on Mount Kent and 2 Para's on Mount Longdon, but without causing casualties. That evening, two Grupo 2 Canberras bomb Mount Kent, but as they turn away, one is brought down by a Sea Dart from HMS *Exeter* (or possibly HMS *Cardiff*) [a70]. All this time, RAF Harrier GR3s are hitting Argentine positions around Stanley and, on Sunday make their first successful laser-guided bomb attacks.

MAP 34 (overleaf)

3 Para's Approach to and Battle for Mount Longdon

11/12 June

After tabbing across East Falkland from Port San Carlos, securing Estancia House on Monday 31 May, and then on Tuesday 1 June moving Tac HQ and A Coy on to Mount Estancia, B Coy to the south of Mount Vernet and C Coy on to Mount Vernet itself, 3 Para prepares for its attack on Mount Longdon. On Thursday 3 June, A and B Coys set up patrol bases near Murrell Bridge and over the next week, D (Patrol) Coy and the other rifle coys intensively patrol towards their objective — at times penetrating Argentine positions and clashing with the enemy. Two members of D Coy are decorated for their reconnaissance patrols as well as for guiding in B Coy on the night of the attack. This takes place on Friday 11 June, after 3 Para moves from Murrell Bridge to the start line ('Freekick').

With minefields to the south, the Argentines on Wireless Ridge to the east, and given the long and narrow summit ridge of Mount Longdon, Lt-Col Pike decides to launch a silent attack from the west. With C Coy in reserve and fire support teams staying on the start line, the plan is for B Coy to take the length of the summit ('Fly Half' and 'Full Back') while A Coy occupies the northern spur ('Wing Forward') as a fire support base for the B Coy attack. Once Mount Longdon is secured, A and C Coys will, if possible, move on to Wireless Ridge. After a short delay, A and B Coys start off from 'Freekick' at 20.15hrs.

Argentine defenders

7th Inf Regt defending Mount Longdon and Wireless Ridge area, supported by snipers, heavy machine guns, mortars and artillery.

British forces

3 Para, including GPMGs, LAWs, MAWs, Milans and 81mm mortars. In support, 6×105mm artillery of 79 Bty, 29 Cdo Regt RA and frigate HMS *Avenger* with 1×4.5in. In reserve — 2 Para.

3 Para Commanders:

Lt-Col H. W. R. Pike I/C
Maj D. A. Collett, A Coy (Nos 1, 2 and 3 Platoons)
Maj M. H. Argue, B Coy (Nos 4, 5 and 6 Platoons)
Maj H. M. Osborne, C Coy
Maj P. P. Butler, D (Patrol) Coy

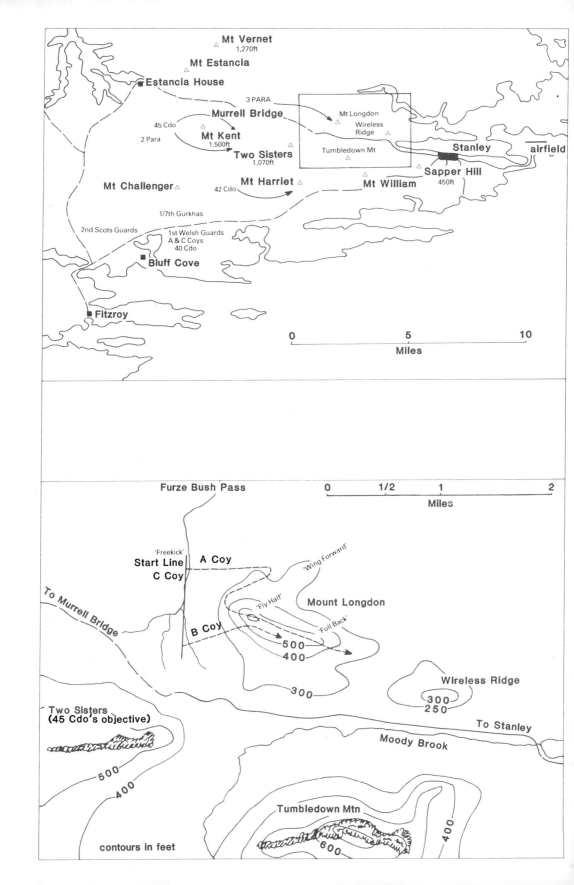

Mt Vernet
1,270ft

Mt Estancia

Estancia House

3 PARA

Murrell Bridge

Mt Longdon
Wireless Ridge

45 Cdo

2 Para

Mt Kent
1,500ft

Two Sisters
1,070ft

Tumbledown Mt

Stanley

airfield

Mt Challenger

42 Cdo

Mt Harriet

Mt William

Sapper Hill
450ft

1/7th Gurkhas

2nd Scots Guards

1st Welsh Guards
A & C Coys
40 Cdo

Bluff Cove

Fitzroy

0   5   10
Miles

Furze Bush Pass

0   1/2   1   2
Miles

'Freekick'   A Coy

Start Line
C Coy

'Wing Forward'

To Murrell Bridge

B Coy

'Fly Half'

Mount Longdon

'Full Back'

500
400

300

Wireless Ridge

300
250

Two Sisters
(45 Cdo's objective)

To Stanley

Moody Brook

500

400

Tumbledown Mtn

400

600

contours in feet

Gallantry awards
Approach to* and Battle for Mount Longdon by 3 Para:
Sgt I. J. McKay, B Coy (post VC)
Lt-Col H. W. R. Pike, MBE (DSO)
Maj M. H. Argue, B Coy (MC)
Maj D. A. Collett, A Coy (MC)
SSgt B. Faulkner, Regt Aid Post (DCM)
Sgt J. S. Pettinger D (Patrol) Coy* (DCM)
Pte R. J. de M. Absolon, D (Patrol) Coy* (post MM)
Cpl I. P. Bailey, B Coy (MM)
Sgt D. Fuller, B Coy (MM)

Capt W. A. McCracken RA, NGFO, 29 Cdo Regt RA (MC) (citation also includes Wireless Ridge).

As B Coy approaches Mount Longdon in the dark, on the left, one of No 4 Platoon's men steps on a mine and the alerted Argentines open fire at the start of a battle that stretches through to dawn, 10hr later. On the right, No 6 Platoon gets on to the western summit with little fighting, but the occupants of a bypassed bunker fire into them as they push through 'Fly Half' and later, when pinned down, they suffer a number of men killed mainly by sniper fire. Meanwhile Nos 4 and 5 Platoons, using anti-armour weapons against enemy bunkers, fight their way on to the western end, but as they attempt to move to the east come under heavy automatic fire. No 4 Platoon's commander is wounded, Sgt McKay takes over and, collecting some of his men and Cpl Bailey, moves in to knock out a heavy machine gun post. In an action which leads to the posthumous award of the Victoria Cross, Sgt McKay and one of the men are killed, but the enemy position is silenced.

Now a second heavy machine gun holds up B Coy HQ and No 5 Platoon. Sgt Fuller is put in charge of No 4 Platoon and, with support from No 5, tries to knock out this one, but without success. Maj Argue now pulls back both Nos 4 and 5 Platoons and calls down artillery and naval gunfire on the enemy positions, after which a left flanking attack is put in, making some progress. Before long, both they and the rest of B Coy find themselves under fire again and, having taken such heavy casualties, Lt-Col Pike brings B Coy to a halt half-way along the Longdon summit ridge.

Meanwhile, A Coy has moved from 'Freekick' towards 'Wing Forward', but has taken losses from the fire of the Argentine positions on the eastern end of the summit which are now holding up B Coy. With little hope of making progress, A Coy is pulled back to the western end of Mount Longdon, moved through B Coy, and with artillery and GPMG support, Nos 1 and 2 Platoons work their way along the eastern half of the summit, clearing the enemy positions with rifles, bayonets and grenades. Now the Argentines start withdrawing, and as soon as 'Full Back' is secured, No 3 Platoon moves down the slope facing Wireless Ridge. As dawn breaks, and with no possibility of exploiting forward, 3 Para starts digging in on Mount Longdon to spend the next two days under heavy and accurate artillery fire. Eighteen paras and an attached Royal Engineer have been killed in the attack with many more wounded, and three more paras and a REME craftsman are killed in the subsequent shelling.

MAP 35 (overleaf)

45 Commando's Approach to and Battle for Two Sisters

11/12 June

The 'yomp' by 45 Cdo from San Carlos Water via Teal Inlet ends to the west of Mount Kent on Friday 4 June and they spend the next week patrolling towards Two Sisters, leading to a number of bloody clashes with the Argentines.

On their second patrol, Lt Fox's Recce Troop reach the end of Two Sisters and, when discovered, fight their way out killing up to 13 of the enemy without loss. Later, Lt Stewart of X Coy breaks out in a similar action, and by

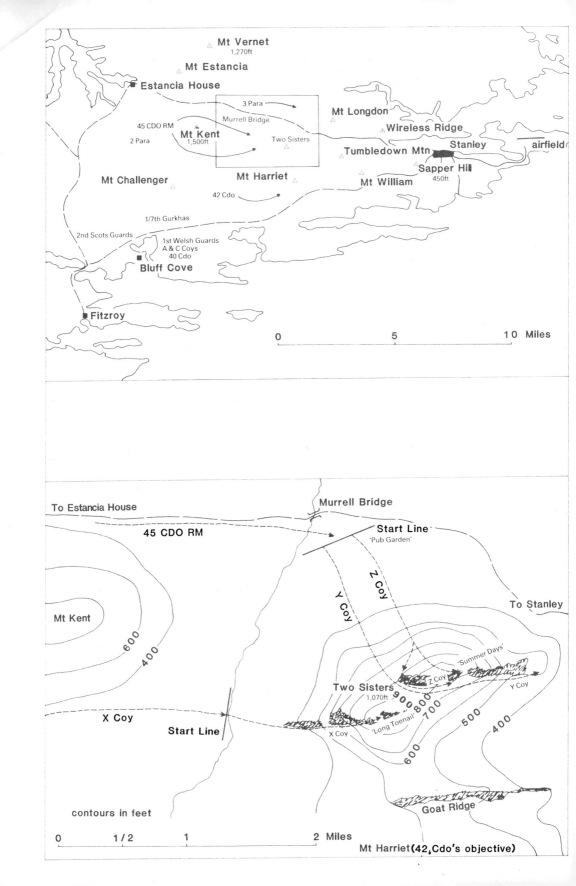

Mt Vernet
1,270ft

Mt Estancia

Estancia House

3 Para

Murrell Bridge

Mt Longdon

45 CDO RM

Wireless Ridge

2 Para

Mt Kent
1,500ft

Two Sisters

Stanley

airfield

Tumbledown Mtn

Mt Challenger

Mt Harriet

Sapper Hill
450ft

42 Cdo

Mt William

1/7th Gurkhas

2nd Scots Guards

1st Welsh Guards
A & C Coys
40 Cdo

Bluff Cove

Fitzroy

0   5   10 Miles

To Estancia House

Murrell Bridge

45 CDO RM

Start Line
'Pub Garden'

To Stanley

Z Coy

Y Coy

Mt Kent

600
400

'Summer Days'

Two Sisters
1,070ft

Z Coy

Y Coy

900 800 700

'Long Toenail'

500

400

X Coy

Start Line

X Coy

600

Goat Ridge

contours in feet

0   1/2   1   2 Miles

Mt Harriet (42 Cdo's objective)

Tuesday 8 June, 45 Cdo has reconnoitred the main Argentine positions towards the western end. Then over the next two days, Sgt Wassell and other men of the M & AW Cadre complete the picture by covering the eastern end and the ground between Two Sisters, Mount Harriet and Tumbledown Mountain, including Goat Ridge. Sadly these successes do not come without loss. Over Thursday night a Y Coy patrol accidentally fires on a supporting mortar group killing four men.

The night attack by 45 Cdo will also be silent without any preliminary artillery fire. Lt-Col Whitehead's plan is for X Coy to leave their start line at 21.00hrs and, having taken the southwest peak ('Long Toenail') around 2hr later, to set up a fire support base that includes 40 Cdo's Milan Troop. Z Coy will then assault the western part of the northeast peak ('Summer Days') and Y Coy the eastern part.

On Friday 11 June, 45 Cdo less X Coy leave their positions behind Mount Kent and, moving around the north side, reach the main start line ('Pub Garden') as planned. Meanwhile X Coy, marching down between Mounts Kent and Challenger, and heavily weighed down, especially by the Milans, arrive at the start line over 2hr late. After a short rest, they begin their move towards 'Long Toenail' at 23.00hrs.

Argentine defenders

4th Inf Regt defending Two Sisters and Mount Harriet area, supported by snipers, heavy machine guns, mortars and artillery.

British forces

45 Cdo RM, including GPMGs, LAWs, MAWs, Milans and 81mm mortars, and in support 6×105mm artillery of 8 Bty, 29 Cdo Regt RA and destroyer HMS *Glamorgan* with 2×4.5in. In reserve — 2 Para.

45 Cdo RM Commanders:

Lt-Col A. F. Whitehead RM, I/C
Capt I. R. Gardiner RM, X Coy (Nos 1, 2 and 3 Troops)
Maj R. J. Davis RM, Y Coy (Nos 4, 5 and 6 Troops)
Capt M. A. F. Cole RM, Z Coy (Nos 7, 8 and 9 Troops)

Gallantry awards

Approach to* and Battle for Two Sisters by 45 Cdo RM:
Lt-Col A. F. Whitehead RM (DSO)
Lt C. I. Dytor RM, Z Coy (MC)
Lt C. Fox RM, Recce Troop* (MC)
Lt D. J. Stewart RM, X Coy* (MC)
Cpl J. Burdett RM, Z Coy (DCM)

Cpl A. R. Bishop RM (MM)
Cpl D. Hunt RM, Z Coy (MM)
Mne G. W. Marshall RM* (MM)
Cpl H. Siddall RM, Y Coy (MM)

Bdr E. M. Holt RA, FOO Party, 29 Cdo Regt RA (MM)
Sgt J. D. Wassel RM, M&AW Cadre* (MM)
(citation includes other patrols)

X Coy heads across the open ground towards 'Long Toenail' led by No 1 Troop and, less than a mile short of the peak, No 3 Troop takes over the lead, but half way up is stopped by heavy machine gun fire and temporarily pulled back. The enemy positions are hit by Milans and some mortar fire, and now No 2 Troop pushes on to the summit under artillery fire. Reaching there, they are forced back by more shellfire, but shortly return driving off the Argentine machine gunners.

Soon after midnight, as X Coy continues its fight for 'Long Toenail', Z Coy, followed by Y Coy to their right, move off from 'Pub Garden' on their silent uphill approach. As the Argentines are still distracted by X Coy's attack, the other two companies go to ground until a flare near Z Coy leads to the right-hand No 8 Troop opening fire. The return enemy fire, including artillery and mortars, is so heavy — killing four men — that Lt Dytor leads his men of No 8 Troop forward in a charge towards the summit, followed by No 7 Troop in a firefight that still leaves them short of their objective.

On their right, Y Coy swings further right to come up alongside them, managing to knock out some of the machine guns holding up Z Coy. No 8 Troop is then able to advance towards the top covered by No 7 Troop, and goes on to clear the enemy positions on the southern side of their objective, while No 7 Troop goes on to do the same on the northern side. About 2½hr after crossing the start line, Z Coy has taken the western part of 'Summer Days'. During this time, No 9 Troop stays back in reserve after suffering casualties from mortars and artillery.

Y Coy now moves between the Two Sisters peaks and below Z Coy's No 8 Troop and heads for the eastern part of the northeast summit under heavy fire. Pushing on, and again using anti-armour weapons against enemy positions, all of Two Sisters is in 45 Cdo's hands before dawn. As they reorganise and dig in, heavy Argentine shelling starts. Lt-Col Whitehead prepares to move ahead towards Tumbledown Mountain, but is stopped by Brig Thompson. Thus 45 Cdo has now taken one of the main Argentine defences for the loss of three marines and a sapper of the Royal Engineers killed by shellfire and mortars.

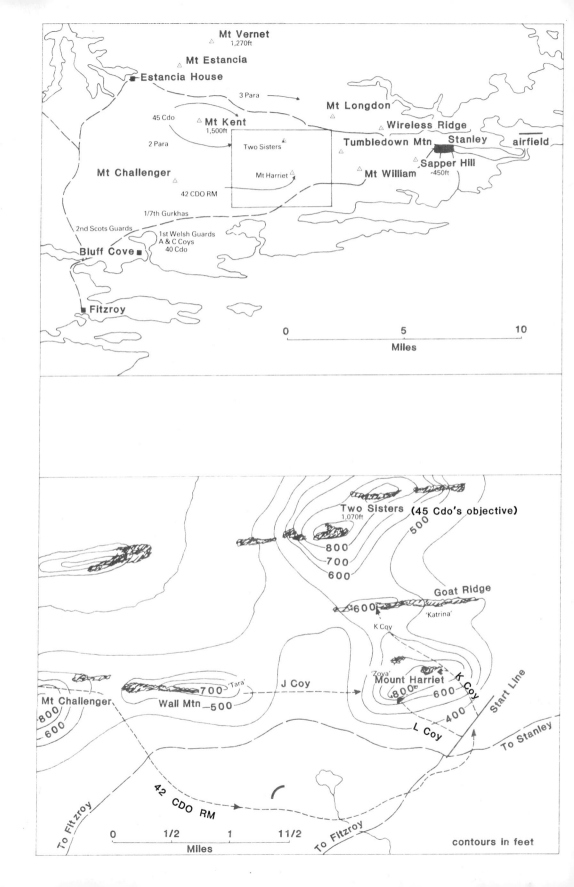

Mt Vernet
1,270ft

Mt Estancia

Estancia House

3 Para →

Mt Longdon

45 Cdo

Mt Kent
1,500ft

Wireless Ridge

Two Sisters

Tumbledown Mtn   Stanley   airfield

2 Para

Mt Challenger

Mt Harriet

Sapper Hill
~450ft

Mt William

42 CDO RM

1/7th Gurkhas

2nd Scots Guards

1st Welsh Guards
A & C Coys
40 Cdo

Bluff Cove

Fitzroy

0   5   10
Miles

Two Sisters (45 Cdo's objective)
1,070ft

500

800
700
600

Goat Ridge

600
'Katrina'

K Coy

'Zoya'
Mount Harriet   K Coy

800   600

Mt Challenger
800
600

700 'Tara'

J Coy

Wall Mtn 500

400

L Coy

Start Line

To Stanley

To Fitzroy

42 CDO RM

To Fitzroy

0   1/2   1   11/2
Miles

contours in feet

MAP 36

42 Commando's Approach to and Battle for Mount Harriet

11/12 June

Following K Coy's helicopter flight forward on to Mount Kent over the night of Sunday 30 May to join D Sqn SAS, the rest of 42 Cdo moves to Mount Challenger during that week, and are eventually joined by K Coy. From there, they push out a troop strength observation post to Wall Mountain, and plan for an attack on the heavily defended Mount Harriet. An advance direct from Wall Mountain across minefields and into Argentine machine guns is out of the question, and a left flanking move would risk overlapping 45 Cdo's assault on Two Sisters. Lt-Col Vaux therefore decides on a right hook taking him well south of the Fitzroy/Stanley track to come up behind the Argentines from the southeast. Finding an approach route through the extensive minefields and pinpointing enemy positions on this side of Mount Harriet calls for careful patrolling, and for his part in this Sgt Collins is decorated. As in the other battles and the approaches to them, men of the Royal Engineers play a key role in dealing with the minefields.

The final plan is to leave J Coy on Wall Mountain ('Tara') — both as a reserve and to create a diversion — and for K and L Coys to march from the western end of Wall Mountain and across the Fitzroy/Stanley track before swinging east and then up to the start line behind Mount Harriet ('Zoya'). Moving off at 20.30hrs, K Coy is to attack the eastern end, and 1hr later, L Coy the western end, after which 42 Cdo will move on to take Goat Ridge ('Katrina'). Unlike the other two attacks, this one is 'noisy' with Mount Harriet receiving a preliminary bombardment as part of the diversion plan.

On Friday 11 June, as 42 Cdo prepares to move off, Argentine shellfire kills one of the marines on Wall Mountain. Later, K and L Coys start off from Mount Challenger, with one of J Coy's troops going ahead to mark the route and drop off Milan sections, including one on the Stanley track in case any of the Argentine Panhard armoured cars should appear. They are also due to meet up with a Welsh Guards patrol assigned to secure 42 Cdo's start line. But there is a delay and H-hour is held up, although J Coy goes ahead and opens fire from Wall Mountain to simulate a large scale clash.

Argentine defenders

4th Inf Regt defending Two Sisters and Mount Harriet area, supported by snipers, heavy machine guns, mortars and artillery.

British forces

42 Cdo RM, including GPMGs, LAWs, MAWs, Milans and 81mm mortars, and in support 6×105mm artillery of 7 Bty, 29 Cdo Regt RA and frigate HMS *Yarmouth* with 2×4.5in. In reserve — 1st Welsh Guards with A and C Coys 40 Cdo.

42 Cdo RM Commanders:

Lt-Col N. F. Vaux RM, I/C
Maj M. J. Norman RM, J Coy
Capt P. M. Babbington RM, K Coy (Nos 1, 2 and 3 Troops)
Capt D. G. Wheen RM, L Coy (Nos 4, 5 and 6 Troops)

Gallantry awards

Approach to* and Battle for Mount Harriet by 42 Cdo RM:
Lt-Col N. F. Vaux RM (DSO)
Capt P. M. Babbington RM, K Coy (MC)
Sgt M. Collins RM, K Coy* (MM)
Cpl M. Eccles RM, K Coy (MM)
Cpl S. C. Newland RM, K Coy (MM)
Cpl C. N. H. Ward RM, K Coy (MM)

K Coy crosses the start line at 22.00hrs, and almost reaches the Argentine positions without being spotted. On the left, No 1 Troop engages the first enemy, and No 2 Troop to the right goes ahead to start clearing their part of K Coy's objective, during which time 42 Cdo suffers its only fatal casualty of the night. No 3 Troop now passes through No 2 Troop on to the summit, and with No 1 Troop below them to the south, start to work their way westwards bunker by bunker, but are held up by machine gun fire. It is at this time that three K Coy NCOs — Cpl Newland of No 1 Troop and Cpls Eccles and Ward of No 3 Troop — win the Military Medal for taking the enemy position.

While K Coy is fighting on the eastern end of the summit and coming under artillery fire, L Coy is making its way up towards the western end of Mount Harriet under heavy machine gun fire which opens up soon after they cross the start line. Milans are successful in knocking out these and other enemy sniper positions, but it takes a number of hours and casualties from artillery, before L Coy's half of the summit is taken while it is still dark. No 5 Troop is then sent forward to the next objective just to the north of the summit, but is initially held up until the enemy resistance crumbles under mortar and artillery fire.

With the arrival of dawn and with L Coy still fighting forward, K Coy is ordered on to Goat Ridge, by which time J Coy has moved directly across from Wall Mountain to join in the final securing of Mount Harriet, running through a minefield on the way. In successfully taking its objective, 42 Cdo has lost just one man killed.

MAP 37

2 Para's Approach to and Battle for Wireless Ridge

13-14 June

With 3 Para unable to exploit forward from Mount Longdon over Friday night, 2 Para, now commanded by Lt-Col Chaundler and transferred back to 3 Cdo Bde, are given the task two nights later. First helicoptering in from Fitzroy on to the western slopes of Mount Kent on Friday, 2 Para spends the night in reserve for the Longdon and Two Sisters attacks and, early next morning, marches to Furze Bush Pass and digs in. The battalion is also joined by No 3 Troop of The Blues and Royals, themselves back with 3 Cde Bde.

Lt-Col Chaundler's plan is divided into four 'noisy' phases using opening artillery fire. In phase one, D Coy is to attack the occupied feature ('Ring Diamond') northeast of Mount Longdon, while in phase two, A and B Coys will take 'Apple Pie'. Then from 'Rough Diamond', D Coy will go on in phase three to take the length of Wireless Ridge ('Blueberry Pie') from the west and with fire support from A and B Coys. In phase four, C (Patrols) Coy will swing to the east to take ring contour 100.

After 2 Para has finished marching that Sunday evening (13 June) from Furze Bush Pass, supporting fire is opened on 'Rough Diamond' at 21.15hrs, and 30min later, D Coy crosses its start line backed up by the supporting fire of four Scimitars and Scorpions.

Argentine defenders

7th Inf Regt defending (Mount Longdon and) Wireless Ridge area, supported by snipers, heavy machine guns, mortars and artillery.

British forces

2 Para, including GPMGs, LAWs, MAWs, Milans and 81mm mortars. In support No 3 Troop, The Blues and Royals with two Scorpions and two Scimitars, two bty's of 6×105mm artillery of 7 and 8 Btys, 29 Cdo Regt RA, mortars of 3 Para, and frigate HMS *Ambuscade* with 1×4.5in (and HMS *Yarmouth*, 2×4.5in).

2 Para Commanders:

Lt-Col D. R. Chaundler, I/C
Maj C. D. Farrar-Hockley, A Coy

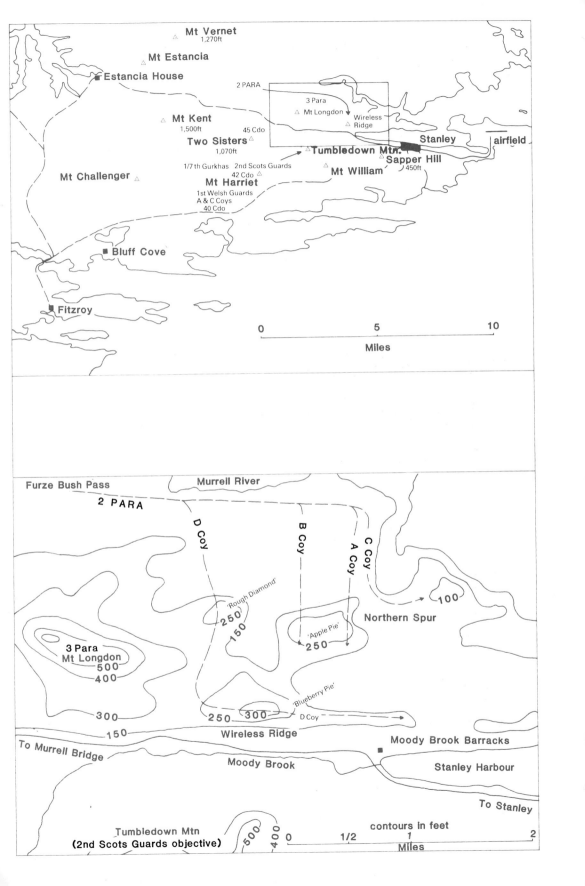

Mt Vernet
1,270ft

Mt Estancia

Estancia House

Mt Kent
1,500ft

2 PARA

3 Para
Mt Longdon
Wireless
Ride

45 Cdo

Two Sisters
1,070ft

Stanley   airfield

Tumbledown Mtn.
Sapper Hill
450ft

1/7th Gurkhas   2nd Scots Guards
42 Cdo

Mt William

Mt Challenger

Mt Harriet
1st Welsh Guards
A & C Coys
40 Cdo

Bluff Cove

Fitzroy

0   5   10

Miles

Furze Bush Pass   Murrell River

2 PARA

D Coy

B Coy

C Coy
A Coy

'Rough Diamond'
250
150

'Apple Pie'
250

Northern Spur
100

3 Para
Mt Longdon
500
400

300

250   300
D Coy

'Blueberry Pie'

150

Wireless Ridge

Moody Brook Barracks

To Murrell Bridge

Moody Brook

Stanley Harbour

To Stanley

Tumbledown Mtn
(2nd Scots Guards objective)

500
400

contours in feet

0   1/2   1   2

Miles

Maj J. H. Crosland, B Coy
Maj R. Jenner, C Coy
Maj P. Neame, D Coy

Gallantry Awards

Battle for Wireless Ridge by 2 Para (all citations include Goose Green):
Lt C. S. Connor, C Coy (MC)
Maj J. H. Crosland, B Coy (MC)
Maj C. D. Farrar-Hockley, A Coy (MC)
Sgt J. C. Meredith, D Coy (DCM)
Sgt T. I. Barrett, A Coy (MM)

Capt W. A. McCracken RA, NGFO, 29 Cdo Regt RA (MC) (citation also includes Mount Longdon)
Capt J. G. Greenhalgh RCT, No 656 Sqn AAC (DFC) (also includes Goose Green)

D Coy reaches 'Rough Diamond' to find the Argentines have withdrawn under the attacking fire, leaving behind a few dead, and, as the paras consolidate in the new position, it is their turn to come under defensive fire from the Argentine 155mm guns. Now from behind them to the east, A and B Coys cross their start line, but one man is killed by enemy shellfire. Then, as the two companies approach 'Apple Pie', the enemy breaks and withdraws under the weight of British artillery, mortar and GPMG fire, although they themselves are heavily shelled for the rest of the night. With 2 Para moving ahead so quickly, Lt-Col Chaundler gives C Coy the go-ahead to occupy ring contour 100, which it does without opposition.

From 'Rough Diamond', D Coy moves to the western end of Wireless Ridge and prepares to advance through its length, as the light tanks and supporting Milans and GPMGs join A and B Coys on 'Apple Pie' to pour in their fire from the left flank. D Coy takes the first half of the ridge without trouble, but the Argentines resist fiercely over the second half, often fighting from bunker to bunker. Then they break, and all of Wireless Ridge is in D Coy's hands, although not before one man has been killed by British artillery and another by Argentine small arms fire. As the men of 2 Para dig in and come under more defensive fire, the Argentines are heard regrouping in the dark in the vicinity of Moody Brook.

At dawn, a small group of Argentines counter-attack D Coy, but they are soon driven off with the help of mortars and the Royal Artillery's 105mm guns, by which time 2 Para has taken the whole feature at a cost of three men killed, considerably aided by the fire of the Scorpions and Scimitars and other supporting arms. From their positions, 2 Para sees the Argentines retreating towards Stanley in the morning light and press Brig Thompson to let them advance.

MAP 38

2nd Scots Guards' Approach to and Battle for Tumbledown Mountain

13/14 June

On the same night 2 Para continues 3 Cdo Bde's advance on Stanley from the west and north, 5th Inf Bde starts its attacks against the main Argentine defences towards the southwest of the capital — 2nd Scots Guards aiming for Tumbledown and 1/7th Gurkhas for Mount William. Before then, the Marine's M & AW Cadre has built up a picture of the area to the west of Tumbledown.

First of all, on the morning of Sunday 13 June, the Scots Guards move by helicopter from their positions at Bluff Cove to the western end of Goat Ridge for a detailed reconnaissance and briefing. By now, Lt-Col

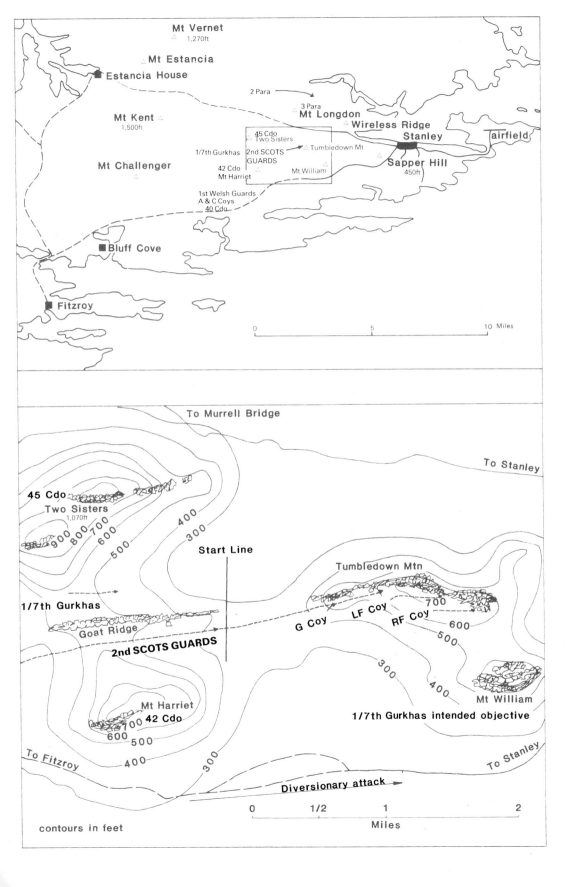

Mt Vernet
△ 1,270ft

△ Mt Estancia
■ Estancia House

2 Para →

3 Para
Mt Longdon

Wireless Ridge
Stanley

airfield

Mt Kent △
1,500ft

45 Cdo
△ Two Sisters

1/7th Gurkhas   2nd SCOTS
GUARDS   △ Tumbledown Mt

Mt Challenger
△

42 Cdo
Mt Harriet   △ Mt William

Sapper Hill
450ft

1st Welsh Guards
A & C Coys
40 Cdo

■ Bluff Cove

■ Fitzroy

0   5   10 Miles

To Murrell Bridge

To Stanley

45 Cdo
Two Sisters
1,070ft
900 800 700 600
500
400
300

Start Line

Tumbledown Mtn

1/7th Gurkhas

Goat Ridge

2nd SCOTS GUARDS

G Coy   LF Coy   RF Coy
700
600
500

Mt Harriet
700 42 Cdo
600 500

300
400
Mt William

1/7th Gurkhas intended objective

To Fitzroy
400

300

To Stanley

Diversionary attack →

0   1/2   1   2

Miles

contours in feet

Scott has decided that an attack across the open southern slopes of Mount Tumbledown would be far too hazardous, and instead opts for a 'silent' assault from the west along the line of the summit ridge. Preceded by a diversionary raid along the Fitzroy/Stanley track, in phase one, G Coy will take the western end of the mountain. In phase two, Left Flank (LF) Coy will pass through them before tackling the summit area. Finally, Right Flank (RF) Coy will move around LF Coy to secure the eastern end. Led in from Goat Ridge by men of the M & AW Cadre, G Coy is followed to the start line by LF and RF Coys. The diversion starts on schedule at 20.30hrs, and 30min later, G Coy moves forward into the bitterly cold night.

Argentine defenders

5th Marine Inf Btn defending Tumbledown Mountain, Mount William and Sapper Hill, supported by snipers, heavy machine guns, mortars and artillery.

British forces

2nd Scots Guards, including GPMGs, LAWs, MAWs, Milans and 81mm mortars. In support No 4 Troop, The Blues and Royals with two Scorpions and two Scimitars, up to five btys each of 6×105mm artillery, mortars of 42 Cdo RM and 1/7th Gurkha Rifles, and frigate HMS *Active* with 1×4.5in gun (and HMS *Avenger*, 1×4.5in gun).

2nd Scots Guards Commanders:

Lt-Col M. I. E. Scott, I/C
Maj I. E. Dalzell-Job, G Coy (Nos 7, 8 and 9 Platoons)
Maj J. P. Kiszley, LF Coy (Nos 13, 14 and 15 Platoons)
Maj S. Price, RF Coy (Nos 1, 2 and 3 Platoons)

Gallantry Awards

Battle for Tumbledown Mountain by 2nd Scots Guards:
Lt-Col M. I. E. Scott (DSO)
Maj J. P. Kiszley, LF Coy (MC)
Lt R. A. D. Lawrence, RF Coy (MC)
Gdsmn J. B. C. Reynolds, LF Coy (post DCM)
WO2 W. Nicol, LF Coy (DCM)
Sgt R. W. Jackson, RF Coy (MM)
Gdsmn A. S. Pengelly, RF Coy (MM)

Capt S. M. Drennan AAC, No 656 Sqn AAC (DFC)
Cpl J. A. Foran RE, 9 Para Sqn RE (MM)
Sgt R. H. Wrega RE, 9 Para Sqn RE (MM)

The diversionary attack along the Stanley track goes in as planned by a small assault group led by the light tanks. Reaching the enemy positions, one Guardsman and a Royal Engineer are killed in a fire-fight that lasts for 2hr,

and more are wounded withdrawing through a minefield, but the diversion does its job. By now, in phase one, G Coy has crossed the start line with No 7 Platoon and Coy HQ occupying the first half of their objective and Nos 8 and 9 Platoons the second half. Secured by 22.30hrs, the positions are used to support LF Coy who come through to face heavy fire from snipers and GPMGs.

In this second phase, LF Coy's No 13 Platoon fights for the high crags on the left and No 15 Platoon lower down on the right, while No 14 Platoon follows in reserve with Coy HQ. As they push forward under increasing mortar and artillery bombardment, two men are killed and a third mortally wounded by snipers. Anti-armour weapons are only partially successful against the Argentine bunkers, but No 13 Platoon makes some progress with grenades. However, only after 3hr, at 02.30hrs, can artillery fire be brought down on the enemy positions in front of the stalled No 15 Platoon, who with Coy HQ are now able to attack forward and up, overcoming the defences — often in hand-to-hand fighting. Eventually, after a 7hr struggle, just a few men of LF Coy reach the summit.

Now in phase three, RF Coy is able to come up, although the battle is far from over. With No 1 Platoon giving covering fire, No 2 and Lt Lawrence's No 3 Platoon continue the assault, again using the MAWs and LAWs, but also moving forward in small groups taking positions with grenades and bayonets. Eventually, around 08.15hrs and well after dawn, Mount Tumbledown is in the hands of the Scots Guards after fighting probably the best Argentine unit and losing eight men and the Royal Engineer.

1/7th Gurkha Rifles

Leaving C Coy to garrison Goose Green, the Gurkhas moved towards Stanley. On Monday 7 June, D Coy sails around to the Fitzroy/Bluff Cove area in the Falklands coaster *Monsunen* — now back in British hands after being taken over by the Royal Navy at Darwin. Over the next two days, the rest of the battalion helicopters in, and then moves to an area south of Mount Challenger in reserve, in time for the 3 Cdo Bde assaults. In preparation for their attack on Mount William, they again helicopter forward on Sunday 13 June to a position just south of Two Sisters. As the Scots Guards battle for Mount Tumbledown, the Gurkhas march along the line of Goat Ridge and just to the north of Tumbledown, ready for their assault. On the way they suffer casualties from Argentine shellfire. As dawn approaches and the Guards have still not secured Tumbledown, it appears the Gurkhas will have to make a daylight assault on Mount William.

VICTORY

MAP 39

Falklands, Surrender and Aftermath

As dawn breaks on Monday 14 June, and the Scots Guards complete the capture of Mount Tumbledown, 2 Para on Wireless Ridge see the Argentinians streaming back to Stanley as the British artillery shells their positions at will. The British forces now edge forward. Under Brig Thompson, 2 Para moves off along the Stanley road followed later by 3 Para; 42 Cdo shortly flies forward from Mount Harriet and marches towards Stanley; and 45 Cdo 'yomp' from Two Sisters for Sapper Hill, so that by nightfall all of 3 Cdo Bde is close to the capital. As for 5th Infantry Bde, the Gurkhas are ready to make a daylight attack on Mount William, but the Argentinians disappear and D Coy moves on to the summit that morning without any opposition. Meanwhile the Welsh Guards are delayed by minefields on their way to Sapper Hill, but then fly in with A and C Coys 40 Cdo to face slight enemy resistance just as 45 Cdo shows up.

2 Para is the first unit to reach the outskirts of Stanley, but halts as surrender negotiations get underway. These last for much of the day and as they proceed British forces are ordered not to fire on the apparently demoralised enemy. However, even now Gen Menendez has 8,000 troops in the Stanley area including the largely intact 3rd, 6th and 25th Inf Regts, still well supplied with food and small arms ammunition, but with little left for their remaining artillery and with all the high ground taken.

Although ordered by Galtieri that morning to continue the fight, Menendez decides to negotiate, and a small British team led by Lt-Col Rose of the SAS helicopters in. A surrender document covering enemy forces both on West and East Falkland is agreed at the end of the afternoon, and that evening, Gen Moore flies to Stanley for the official signing. Timed to take effect from 21.00hrs local time, the actual signing takes place at 21.30hrs or half an hour into the 15th, Zulu time. First into Stanley next morning is 2 Para, followed by 3 Para and 42 Cdo, whose men of J Coy, last there with NP 8901, later hoist the Governor's flag over Government house. With 3 Cdo Bde staying in the Stanley area, most of 5th Infantry Bde returns to Fitzroy, although the Gurkhas go to Goose Green where they later lose a man killed on battlefield clearance duties.

With the surrender of the Argentinians around Stanley, and their transfer to the airfield as a POW camp, steps are taken to deal with the forces on West Falkland and far away on Southern Thule. Still on Tuesday 15 June, B Coy 40 Cdo crosses over to Port Howard by ship and helicopter to take the surrender of the 5th Inf Regt, and HMS *Avenger's* Lynx lands a small party at Fox Bay to deal with the 8th Regt, after which all the POWs move to San Carlos. To retake Southern Thule in Operation 'Keyhole', the frigate HMS *Yarmouth* and RFA *Olmeda* reach South Georgia from the TEZ on Thursday 17 May to pick up men of M Coy 42 Cdo under the command of Capt Nunn RM, some of whom have already left with HMS *Endurance* and the tug *Salvageman*. Arriving off the bleak shores on Saturday, HMS *Endurance's* Wasp lands a small group near the Argentine base, and when HMS *Yarmouth* arrives (with *Olmeda*) to provide gunfire support on Sunday 20 June, the tiny remaining garrison on Southern Thule surrenders without a shot being fired.

Needing food and shelter for his own men, a priority for Gen Moore is to ship home the POWs, with the exception of around 500 senior officers and technicians held as a guarantee against the junta fighting on. Both *Canberra* and *Norland* load a thousand POWs at San Carlos Water before heading for Stanley. There, *Canberra* takes on board a further 3,000, leaving for Argentina on Friday 18 June to be escorted into Puerto Madryn next day by the destroyers *Santisima Trinidad* and *Comodoro Py*. *Norland* sails from Stanley on Friday with a total of 2,000 POWs to arrive off the same port two days later, and many of the

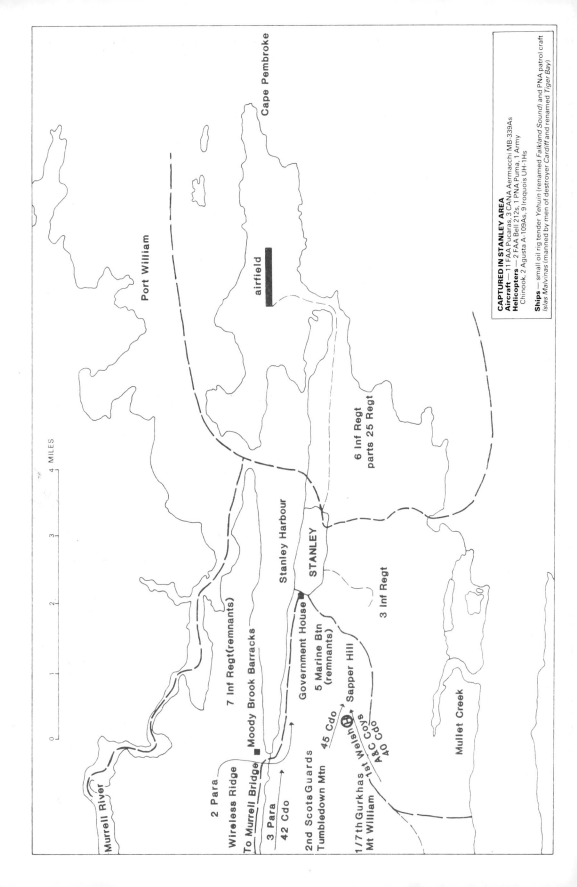

Port William

Cape Pembroke

airfield

Murrell River

2 Para
Wireless Ridge
To Murrell Bridge ■ Moody Brook Barracks
3 Para
42 Cdo
2nd Scots Guards
Tumbledown Mtn
45 Cdo
1/7th Gurkhas 1st Welsh
Mt William A&C Coys
40 Cdo

7 Inf Regt(remnants)

Government House
5 Marine Btn
(remnants)
Sapper Hill

Stanley Harbour

STANLEY

3 Inf Regt

6 Inf Regt
parts 25 Regt

Mullet Creek

0   1   2   3   4 MILES

CAPTURED IN STANLEY AREA
Aircraft — 11 FAA Pucaras, 3 CANA Aermacchi MB-339As
Helicopters — 2 FAA Bell 212s, 1 PNA Puma, 1 Army
Chinook, 2 Agusta A-109As, 9 Iroquois UH-1Hs

Ships — small oil rig tender *Yehuin* (renamed *Falkland Sound*) and PNA patrol craft
Islas Malvinas (manned by men of destroyer *Cardiff* and renamed *Tiger Bay*)

remaining Argentinians follow in the ice-breaker *Bahia Paraiso*. The 'specials' return on *St Edmund* a month later.

Even with their losses during the fighting, the Argentinians leave behind considerable amounts of war material including artillery and armoured cars, missile and radar systems, and aircraft and helicopters in various states of repair, some of which return to the UK for evaluation or integration into the Services. Apart from recovering the two Falklands coasters *Forrest* and *Monsunen* for local duties, the Royal Navy takes over two other small craft.

As the Task Force ships start entering Port William and Stanley Harbour, the mine-sweeping trawlers move in to successfully sweep a field of contact mines laid off Cape Pembroke. On land, the situation is far worse as, apart from the Army having to clear all the battlefield litter and discarded ordnance, the Royal Engineers have to deal with the extensive and mainly unmarked minefields especially around Stanley. (There are doubts if the work will ever be finished.) As for the islands themselves, the British Government is committed to their defence in a policy often referred to as 'Fortress Falklands'. If great and continuous expenditure and large, permanent garrisons are to be avoided, facilities for the rapid reinforcement of the garrison by air will be essential. A first step comes on 24 June when an extended range Hercules lands at Stanley airfield. Then in October, after its enlargement and redesignation as RAF Stanley, the airport can be used by Phantom fighters. But this is still not enough. A major airfield and associated installations are therefore constructed near Pleasant Peak. Completed in 1985, Mount Pleasant airport is able to handle long-range, wide-bodied jet transports capable of reinforcing the Falklands at short notice.

MAP 40

The Main Task Force Returns Home

By the time of the surrender, a number of ships are already well on their way north or have reached the UK, including the nuclear submarine HMS *Splendid*, destroyer HMS *Glasgow*, frigates HMS *Alacrity* and HMS *Argonaut*, RFA *Fort Austin*, some of the BP tankers and *Queen Elizabeth 2* to her great welcome. Although more ships will soon follow, a first priority is to start getting the land forces home as soon as *Canberra* and *Norland* have played their part in taking the large number of Argentinian POWs back to their homeland.

First to leave are 3 Cdo Bde and the paras with 5th Inf Bde staying on (most of 2nd Scots Guards moving to West Falkland) until the arrival of the first garrison troops, 1st Battalion, The Queen's Own Highlanders who reach the Falklands in mid-July on *Norland*:

3 Commando Brigade

40, 42 and Z Coy 45 Cdo on *Canberra*, departing on 25 June from Falklands and arriving Southampton on 11 July.

45 Cdo including X and Y Coy on RFA *Stromness*, leave the Falklands in late June and arrive at Ascension on 7-8 July and fly home by VC10, landing near Arbroath on 8-9 July.

M Coy 42 Cdo on *Nordic Ferry*, depart from South Georgia on 8 July, arrive at Ascension and fly to RAF St Mawgan.

2 and 3 Para on *Norland* depart from the Falklands on 25 June, arriving at Ascension on 5 July and fly by VC10 to Brize Norton on 6 July.

5th Infantry Brigade

2nd Scots and 1st Welsh Guards on *Norland*, leave the Falklands around 19 July. They arrive at Ascension and fly by VC10 to Brize Norton on 29 July.

1/7th Gurkha Rifles leave the Falklands on 18 July on *Uganda*, and arrive at Southampton on 9 August.

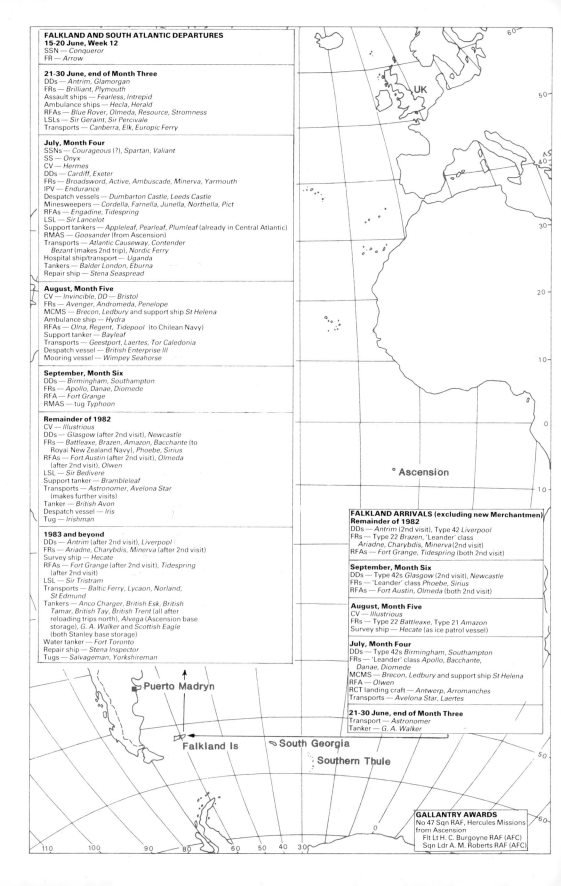

FALKLAND AND SOUTH ATLANTIC DEPARTURES
15-20 June, Week 12
SSN — *Conqueror*
FR — *Arrow*

21-30 June, end of Month Three
DDs — *Antrim, Glamorgan*
FRs — *Brilliant, Plymouth*
Assault ships — *Fearless, Intrepid*
Ambulance ships — *Hecla, Herald*
RFAs — *Blue Rover, Olmeda, Resource, Stromness*
LSLs — *Sir Geraint, Sir Percivale*
Transports — *Canberra, Elk, Europic Ferry*

July, Month Four
SSNs — *Courageous* (?), *Spartan, Valiant*
SS — *Onyx*
CV — *Hermes*
DDs — *Cardiff, Exeter*
FRs — *Broadsword, Active, Ambuscade, Minerva, Yarmouth*
IPV — *Endurance*
Despatch vessels — *Dumbarton Castle, Leeds Castle*
Minesweepers — *Cordella, Farnella, Junella, Northella, Pict*
RFAs — *Engadine, Tidespring*
LSL — *Sir Lancelot*
Support tankers — *Appleleaf, Pearleaf, Plumleaf* (already in Central Atlantic)
RMAS — *Goosander* (from Ascension)
Transports — *Atlantic Causeway, Contender Bezant* (makes 2nd trip), *Nordic Ferry*
Hospital ship/transport — *Uganda*
Tankers — *Balder London, Eburna*
Repair ship — *Stena Seaspread*

August, Month Five
CV — *Invincible*, DD — *Bristol*
FRs — *Avenger, Andromeda, Penelope*
MCMS — *Brecon, Ledbury* and support ship *St Helena*
Ambulance ship — *Hydra*
RFAs — *Olna, Regent, Tidepool* (to Chilean Navy)
Support tanker — *Bayleaf*
Transports — *Geestport, Laertes, Tor Caledonia*
Despatch vessel — *British Enterprise III*
Mooring vessel — *Wimpey Seahorse*

September, Month Six
DDs — *Birmingham, Southampton*
FRs — *Apollo, Danae, Diomede*
RFA — *Fort Grange*
RMAS — tug *Typhoon*

Remainder of 1982
CV — *Illustrious*
DDs — *Glasgow* (after 2nd visit), *Newcastle*
FRs — *Battleaxe, Brazen, Amazon, Bacchante* (to Royal New Zealand Navy), *Phoebe, Sirius*
RFAs — *Fort Austin* (after 2nd visit), *Olmeda* (after 2nd visit), *Olwen*
LSL — *Sir Bedivere*
Support tanker — *Brambleleaf*
Transports — *Astronomer, Avelona Star* (makes further visits)
Tanker — *British Avon*
Despatch vessel — *Iris*
Tug — *Irishman*

1983 and beyond
DDs — *Antrim* (after 2nd visit), *Liverpool*
FRs — *Ariadne, Charybdis, Minerva* (after 2nd visit)
Survey ship — *Hecate*
RFAs — *Fort Grange* (after 2nd visit), *Tidespring* (after 2nd visit)
LSL — *Sir Tristram*
Transports — *Baltic Ferry, Lycaon, Norland, St Edmund*
Tankers — *Anco Charger, British Esk, British Tamar, British Tay, British Trent* (all after reloading trips north), *Alvega* (Ascension base storage), *G. A. Walker* and *Scottish Eagle* (both Stanley base storage)
Water tanker — *Fort Toronto*
Repair ship — *Stena Inspector*
Tugs — *Salvageman, Yorkshireman*

FALKLAND ARRIVALS (excluding new Merchantmen)
Remainder of 1982
DDs — *Antrim* (2nd visit), Type 42 *Liverpool*
FRs — Type 22 *Brazen*, 'Leander' class *Ariadne, Charybdis, Minerva* (2nd visit)
RFAs — *Fort Grange, Tidespring* (both 2nd visit)

September, Month Six
DDs — Type 42s *Glasgow* (2nd visit), *Newcastle*
FRs — 'Leander' class *Phoebe, Sirius*
RFAs — *Fort Austin, Olmeda* (both 2nd visit)

August, Month Five
CV — *Illustrious*
FRs — Type 22 *Battleaxe*, Type 21 *Amazon*
Survey ship — *Hecate* (as ice patrol vessel)

July, Month Four
DDs — Type 42s *Birmingham, Southampton*
FRs — 'Leander' class *Apollo, Bacchante, Danae, Diomede*
MCMS — *Brecon, Ledbury* and support ship *St Helena*
RFA — *Olwen*
RCT landing craft — *Antwerp, Arromanches*
Transports — *Avelona Star, Laertes*

21-30 June, end of Month Three
Transport — *Astronomer*
Tanker — *G. A. Walker*

GALLANTRY AWARDS
No 47 Sqn RAF, Hercules Missions from Ascension
Flt Lt H. C. Burgoyne RAF (AFC)
Sqn Ldr A. M. Roberts RAF (AFC)

UK

Ascension

Puerto Madryn

Falkland Is   South Georgia

Southern Thule

Some ships will sadly not be returning — the destroyers HMS *Coventry* and HMS *Sheffield*, the frigates HMS *Antelope* and HMS *Ardent*, the LSL *Sir Galahad* and the *Atlantic Conveyor* — but by the end of August, most of the others have left the Falklands area (some to later make a second trip) to be replaced by a smaller number of destroyers and frigates and other vessels mostly on their first journey south. Amongst these are the four merchantmen, two minesweepers and their support ship *St Helena* — all of which sailed from the UK before the surrender. The MCM ships HMS *Brecon* and HMS *Ledbury* arrive in early July to relieve the five minesweeping trawlers, and spend the next five weeks hunting for any ground mines laid by the Argentines, none of which are found.

Of the major warships, the assault ships HMS *Fearless* and HMS *Intrepid* set sail a week and a half after the surrender, and arrive at Portsmouth on 14 July after first unloading marines and Sea Kings of No 846 NAS at Devonport. As for the carriers, until the arrival of the RAF Phantoms at Stanley only their Harriers can provide much of the air defence still needed by the Falklands. Following the surrender, HMS *Invincible's* first priority is to sail well clear to the north, escorted by the frigate HMS *Andromeda* in order to change a main engine. HMS *Hermes* remains behind until HMS *Invincible* is back, and on 4 July sails with her escort HMS *Broadsword* for Portsmouth, arriving on 21 July to another great welcome. Well before then, on 2 July, Adm Woodward is relieved as Task Group commander by Rear-Adm Reffell flying his flag on the destroyer HMS *Bristol*.

But there is no relief for HMS *Invincible* which has to await the arrival of the newly-commissioned sister ship HMS *Illustrious* carrying reformed No 809 NAS Sea Harriers and the first airborne early warning Sea King helicopters. HMS *Illustrious* reaches the Falk-

lands on 27 August, and after a day's vertrep, HMS *Invincible* is at last able to head north on 28 August accompanied by HMS *Bristol* and later RFA *Olna*, arriving at Portsmouth on 17 September to be met by Her Majesty The Queen. After 166 days at sea, HMS *Invincible* claims the record for the longest continuous carrier operations ever. The Sea Harriers and most of the Royal Navy, Royal Marine and Army Air Corps helicopters go back to the UK with the returning ships.

As for the RAF, mainly based at or flying to Ascension, the few Vulcan bombers fly home by the time of the surrender and the last Nimrod MR2s continue operating from Ascension until August. But even then, there is little let-up for the other aircraft. VC10s maintain the air link between the UK and Ascension, returning with many of the troops from there. Hercules transports fly south regularly and from late June are landing at Stanley. (By then, two members of No 47 Sqn have earned gallantry awards for their air-drop missions.) For many more months, Victor tankers and later Hercules conversions refuel the extended-range Nimrods and Hercules deep into the South Atlantic and on to the Falklands. On the island itself, a number of Harrier GR3s of No 1(F) Sqn, once again fitted with Sidewinder missiles for air defence, are based at Stanley, but in October No 29(F) Sqn Phantoms fly down from Ascension to the newly opened RAF Stanley to start taking over from them.

Finally there is the question of the last resting place for those British dead not buried or lost at sea. The policy has long been for those killed on active service to remain in the country where they fall, but many families choose to bring their men home and in October the LSL *Sir Bedivere* leaves the Falklands carrying over 60 back to the UK. However, another 16, including Lt-Col H. Jones VC, stay in the Falklands.

Appendix 1   British Gallantry Awards

Victoria Cross — Posthumous

Lt-Col H. Jones OBE, CO 2nd Battalion The
  Parachute Regiment
Sgt I. J. McKay, 3rd Battalion The Parachute
  Regiment

Royal Navy, Royal Marines, Royal Fleet Auxiliary and Merchant Navy

Distinguished Service Order

Capt M. E. Barrow RN, CO HMS *Glamorgan*
Capt J. J. Black MBE, RN, CO HMS *Invincible*
Capt W. R. Canning RN, CO HMS *Broadsword*
Capt J. F. Coward RN, CO HMS *Brilliant*
Capt P. G. V. Dingemans RN, CO HMS *Intrepid*
Cdre S. C. Dunlop CBE, RFA, CO RFA *Fort
  Austin*
Lt-Cdr B. F. Dutton QGM, RN, CO Fleet
  Clearance Diving Team No 1
Capt E. S. J. Larken RN, CO HMS *Fearless*
Capt C. H. Layman MVO, RN, CO
  HMS *Argonaut*
Capt L. E. Middleton ADC, RN, CO
  HMS *Hermes*
Capt D. Pentreath RN, CO HMS *Plymouth*
Capt P. J. G. Roberts RFA, CO RFA *Sir Galahad*
Lt-Cdr I. Stanley RN, Flt Cdr, No 737 NAS,
  HMS *Antrim*
Lt-Col N. F. Vaux RM, CO 42 Cdo RM
Lt-Col A. F. Whitehead RM, CO 45 Cdo RM
Cdr C. L. Wreford-Brown RN, CO
  HMS *Conqueror*
Capt B. G. Young RN, CO HMS *Antrim*

Distinguished Service Cross — Posthumous

Lt-Cdr G. W. J. Batt RN, No 800 NAS,
  HMS *Hermes*
Capt I. H. North, MN, CO *Atlantic Conveyor*
Lt-Cdr J. M. Sephton RN, HMS *Ardent*
Lt-Cdr J. S. Woodhead RN, HMS *Sheffield*

Distinguished Service Cross

Lt-Cdr A. D. Auld RN, CO No 800 NAS,
  HMS *Hermes*
Lt A. R. C. Bennett RN, No 846 NAS
Lt-Cdr M. D. Booth RN, CO No 847 NAS
Cdr P. J. Bootherstone RN, CO HMS *Arrow*

Lt N. A. Bruen RN, CO Fleet Clearance Diving
  Team No 3
Lt-Cdr H. S. Clark RN, CO No 825 NAS
Cdr C. J. S. Craig RN, CO HMS *Alacrity*
Lt-Cdr J. A. Ellerbeck RN, Flt Cdr, No 829 NAS,
  HMS *Endurance*
Fleet CPO (Diver) M. G. Fellows BEM, Fleet
  Clearance Diving Team No 1
Capt G. R. Green RFA, CO RFA *Sir Tristram*
Lt R. Hutchings RM, No 846 NAS
Capt D. E. Lawrence RFA, CO RFA *Sir Geraint*
Lt-Cdr H. J. Lomas RN, No 845 NAS
Lt K. P. Mills RM, RM Detachment
  HMS *Endurance*
Sub-Lt P. T. Morgan RN, HMS *Argonaut*
Cdr A. Morton RN, CO HMS *Yarmouth*
Lt N. J. North RN, No 846 NAS
Capt A. F. Pitt RFA, CO RFA *Sir Percivale*
Lt-Cdr N. W. Thomas RN, Nos 899/800 NAS,
  HMS *Hermes*
Lt S. R. Thomas RN, No 801 NAS,
  HMS *Invincible*
Lt-Cdr S. C. Thornewill RN, CO No 846 NAS
Cdr N. J. Tobin RN, CO HMS *Antelope*
Cdr N. D. Ward AFC, RN, CO No 801 NAS,
  HMS *Invincible*
Cdr A. W. J. West RN, CO HMS *Ardent*

Military Cross

Capt P. M. Babbington RM, 42 Cdo RM
Maj C. P. Cameron RM, CO 3 CBAS
Lt C. I. Dytor RM, 45 Cdo RM
Lt C. Fox RM, 45 Cdo RM
Lt D. J. Stewart RM, 45 Cdo RM

Distinguished Flying Cross — Posthumous

Lt R. J. Nunn RM, 3 CBAS

Distinguished Flying Cross

Capt J. P. Niblett RM, 3 CBAS

Air Force Cross

Lt-Cdr D. J. S. Squier RN, CO No 826 NAS,
  HMS *Hermes*
Lt-Cdr R. J. S. Wykes-Sneyd RN, CO No 820
  NAS, HMS *Invincible*

Distinguished Conduct Medal

Cpl J. Burdett RM, 45 Cdo RM

George Medal — Posthumous

2nd Eng Offr P. A. Henry RFA, RFA *Sir Galahad*

George Medal

AB (Radar) J. E. Dillon, HMS *Ardent*

Distinguished Service Medal — Posthumous

PO MEM(M) D. R. Briggs, HMS *Sheffield*
Cpl Aircrewman M. D. Love RM, No 846 NAS

Distinguished Service Medal

Clr Sgt M. J. Francis RM, coxswain LCU F1,
    HMS *Fearless*
Ldg Aircrewman P. B. Imrie, No 846 NAS
Sgt R. J. Leach RM, RM Detachment,
    HMS *Endurance*
PO J. S. Leake, HMS *Ardent*
Sgt W. J. Leslie RM, HMS *Broadsword*
PO (Sonar) G. J. R. Libby, HMS *Conqueror*
Chief MEM(M) M. D. Townsend,
    HMS *Argonaut*
CPO (Diver) G. M. Trotter, Fleet Clearance
    Diving Team No 3
CPO Aircrewman M. J. Tupper, No 846 NAS
LS (Radar) J. D. Warren, HMS *Antelope*

Military Medal

Acting Cpl A. R. Bishop RM, 45 Cdo RM
Sgt T. Collings RM
Sgt M. Collins RM, 42 Cdo RM
Cpl M. Eccles RM, 42 Cdo RM
Cpl D. Hunt RM, 45 Cdo RM
Mne G. W. Marshall RM, 45 Cdo RM
Cpl S. C. Newland RM, 42 Cdo RM
Cpl H. Siddall RM, 45 Cdo RM
Cpl C. N. H. Ward RM, 42 Cdo RM
Sgt J. D. Wassell RM, M & AW Cadre RM

Distinguished Flying Medal

Sgt W. C. O'Brien RM, 3 CBAS

Queen's Gallantry Medal — Posthumous

Clr Sgt B. Johnston RM, coxswain LCU F4,
    HMS *Fearless*

Queen's Gallantry Medal

Chief Eng Offr C. K. A. Adams RFA, RFA *Sir
    Galahad*
Lt J. K. Boughton RN, No 825 NAS
MEA(M) 1 K. Enticknapp, HMS *Ardent*
3rd Offr A. Gudgeon RFA, RFA *Sir Galahad*

PO Medical Asst G. A. Meager, HMS *Sheffield*
Lt P. J. Sheldon RN, No 825 NAS
3rd Eng B. R. Williams MN, *Atlantic Conveyor*

Army

Distinguished Service Order

Maj C. N. G. Delves, Devonshire & Dorsets, CO
    D Sqn, 22 SAS Regt
Maj C. P. B. Keeble, 2 Para
Lt-Col H. W. R. Pike MBE, CO 3 Para
Lt-Col M. I. E. Scott, CO 2nd Scots Guards

Distinguished Service Cross

WO2 J. H. Phillips, 49 EOD Sqn RE

Military Cross — Posthumous

Capt G. J. Hamilton, Green Howards, D Sqn 22
    SAS Regt

Military Cross

Maj M. H. Argue, 3 Para
Capt T. W. Burls, Parachute Regt, D Sqn 22 SAS
    Regt
Maj D. A. Collett, 3 Para
Lt C. S. Conner, 2 Para
Maj J. H. Crosland, 2 Para
Maj C. D. Farrar-Hockley, 2 Para
Maj J. P. Kiszely, 2nd Scots Guards
Lt R. A. D. Lawrence, 2nd Scots Guards
Capt W. A. McCracken, 29 Cdo Regt RA
Capt A. J. G. Wight, Welsh Guards

Distinguished Flying Cross

Capt S. M. Drennan AAC, No 656 Sqn AAC
Capt J. G. Greenhalgh RCT, No 656 Sqn AAC

Distinguished Conduct Medal — Posthumous

Pte S. Illingsworth, 2 Para
Gdsmn J. B. C. Reynolds, 2nd Scots Guards

Distinguished Conduct Medal

Cpl D. Abols, 2 Para
SSgt B. Faulkner, 3 Para
Sgt J. C. Meredith, 2 Para
WO2 W. Nicol, 2nd Scots Guards
Sgt J. S. Pettinger, 3 Para

Conspicious Gallantry Medal — Posthumous

SSgt J. Prescott, 49 EOD Sqn RE

Military Medal — Posthumous

Pte R. J. de M. Absolon, 3 Para
L/Cpl G. D. Bingley, 2 Para

Military Medal

Cpl I. P. Bailey, 3 Para
L/Cpl S. A. Bardsely, 2 Para
Sgt T. I. Barrett, 2 Para
L/Cpl M. W. L. Bentley, 2 Para
Sgt D. S. Boultby, 17 Port Regt RCT
Cpl T. Brookes, Royal Signals
Cpl T. J. Camp, 2 Para
Pte G. S. Carter, 2 Para
Gdsmn S. M. Chapman, 1st Welsh Guards
Cpl J. A. Foran, 9 Para Sqdn RE
Sgt D. Fuller, 3 Para
Pte B. J. Grayling, 2 Para
Cpl T. W. Harley, 2 Para
Bdr E. M. Holt, 29 Cdo Regt RA
Sgt R. W. Jackson, 2nd Scots Guards
L/Cpl D. J. Loveridge, 1st Welsh Guards
Sgt J. G. Mather, SAS
Sgt P. H. R. Naya, 16 Field Ambulance RAMC
WO2 B. T. Neck, 1st Welsh Guards
Gdsmn A. S. Pengelly, 2nd Scots Guards
L/Cpl L. J. L. Standish, 2 Para
Sgt R. H. Wrega, 9 Para Sqn RE

Royal Air Force

Distinguished Service Cross

Flt Lt D. H. S. Morgan RAF, Nos 899/800 NAS,
    HMS *Hermes*

Distinguished Flying Cross

Wg Cdr P. T. Squire AFC, RAF, CO No 1 (F) Sqn
    RAF
Sqn Ldr R. U. Langworthy AFC, RAF, No 18 Sqn
    RAF
Sqn Ldr C. N. McDougall RAF, Vulcan aircrew
Sqn Ldr J. J. Pook RAF, No 1 (F) Sqn RAF
Flt Lt W. F. M. Withers RAF, Vulcan aircrew

Air Force Cross

Wg Cdr D. Emmerson RAF, Nimrod aircrew
Sqn Ldr R. Tuxford RAF, Victor aircrew
Flt Lt H. C. Burgoyne RAF, No 47 Sqn RAF
Sqn Ldr A. M. Roberts RAF, No 47 Sqn RAF

Queen's Gallantry Medal

Flt Lt A. J. Swan RAF, CO No 1 EOD Unit RAF
Flt Sgt B. W. Jopling, No 18 Sqn RAF

Appendix 2   British Ships Lost and Damaged

Saturday 1 May

HMS *Alacrity* — slightly damaged by bomb
near misses.

HMS *Arrow* — slightly damaged by cannon
fire.

HMS *Glamorgan* — slightly damaged by bomb
near misses, all off Stanley by Daggers of FAA
Grupo 6.

Tuesday 4 May

HMS *Sheffield* — mortally damaged southeast
of Falklands by Exocet missile fired by Super
Etendard of CANA 2 Esc. Burns out and sinks in
tow on Monday 10 May.

Wednesday 12 May

HMS *Glasgow* — moderately damaged off
Stanley by UXB dropped by A-4B Skyhawks of
FAA Grupo 5. Bomb passes through hull but
damage takes some days to repair and she
shortly returns to UK.

Friday 21 May

HMS *Antrim* — seriously damaged in Falkland
Sound outside San Carlos Water by UXB
dropped by Daggers of FAA Grupo 6. UXB
removed but damage takes some days to
repair.

HMS *Broadsword* — slightly damaged outside
San Carlos Water by cannon fire from Daggers
of Grupo 6.

HMS *Argonaut* — slightly damaged outside San Carlos Water by rockets and cannon fire from Aermacchi MB-339A of CANA 1 Esc, and then seriously damaged by two UXBs dropped by A-4B Skyhawks of FAA Grupo 5. Removing the UXBs and carrying out repairs takes a number of days and although declared operational, she soon sails for the UK.

HMS *Brilliant* — slightly damaged outside San Carlos Water by cannon fire from Daggers of Grupo 6. (Different attack from *Broadsword*.)

HMS *Ardent* — badly damaged in Grantham Sound by bombs (hits, UXBs and near misses) dropped by Daggers of Grupo 6, then mortally damaged by bombs from A-4Q Skyhawks of CANA 3 Esc off North West Island. Sinks the following evening.

Sunday 23 May

HMS *Antelope* — damaged in San Carlos Water by two UXBs dropped by A-4B Skyhawks of Grupo 5. One of the bombs explodes that evening while being defused and she catches fire and sinks next day.

Monday 24 May

RFA *Sir Galahad* — damaged by UXB and out of action for some days.

RFA *Sir Lancelot* — damaged by UXB and not fully operational for almost three weeks.

RFA *Sir Bedivere* — slightly damaged by glancing bomb, all in San Carlos Water probably by A-4C Skyhawks of FAA Grupo 4.

Tuesday 25 May

HMS *Broadsword* — damaged north of Pebble Island by bomb from A-4B Skyhawk of Grupo 5 bouncing up through her stern and out again to land in the sea.

HMS *Coventry* — sunk in same attack by three bombs.

Atlantic Conveyor — mortally damaged northeast of Falklands by Exocet missile fired by Super Etendard of CANA 2 Esc. Burns out and later sinks in tow.

Tuesday 8 June

HMS *Plymouth* — damaged in Falkland Sound off San Carlos Water by four UXBs from Daggers of FAA Grupo 6.

RFA *Sir Galahad* — mortally damaged off Fitzroy by bombs from A-4B Skyhawks of Grupo 5 and burns out. Later in June towed out to sea and sunk as a war grave.

RFA *Sir Tristram* — badly damaged in same attack and abandoned, but later returned to UK and repaired.

LCU F4 (HMS *Fearless*) — sunk in Choiseul Sound by bomb from A-4B Skyhawk of Grupo 5.

Saturday 12 June

HMS *Glamorgan* — damaged off Stanley by land-based Exocet missile.

Appendix 3   British Aircraft Lost

Thursday 22 April

[b1, b2] — Two Wessex HU5s of C Flt, No 845 NAS, RFA *Tidespring* crash on Fortuna Glacier, South Georgia in bad weather. All crew rescued.

Friday 23 April

[b3] — Sea King HC4 of No 846 NAS embarked on HMS *Hermes* crashes into sea at night in bad weather southwest of Ascension (20.15hrs). Pilot rescued but PO Aircrewman Casey lost.

Tuesday 4 May

[b4] — Sea Harrier of No 800 NAS, HMS *Hermes* shot down over Goose Green by

radar-controlled, 35mm Oerlikon fire (13.10hrs). Lt Taylor RN killed.

Thursday 6 May

[b5, b6] — Two Sea Harriers of No 801 NAS, HMS *Invincible* lost in bad weather, presumably by collision, southeast of Falklands (09.00hrs). Lt Curtiss and Lt-Cdr Eyton-Jones RN lost.

Wednesday 12 May

[b7] — Sea King HAS5 of No 826 NAS, HMS *Hermes* ditches in sea with engine failure east of Falklands (14.35hrs). All crew rescued.

Monday 17 May

[b8] — Sea King HAS5 of No 826 NAS, HMS *Hermes*, then to the east of Falklands, hits the sea late at night because of altimeter problems (22.30hrs). All crew rescued.

18/19 May

[b9] — Sea King HC4 of No 846 NAS deliberately destroyed by its crew near Punta Arenas, southern Chile around this date.

Wednesday 19 May

[b10] — Sea King HC4 of No 846 NAS, then embarked on HMS *Hermes*, crashes into sea northeast of Falklands, believed at the time due to a bird strike, although this is now open to doubt (19.15hrs). Of 30 men on board, the aircrewman, 18 men of the SAS, a member of the Royal Signals and the only RAF man killed in the war are all lost. The two pilots are saved.

Friday 21 May

[b11, b12] — Two Gazelles of C Flt, 3 CBAS shot down by small arms fire near Port San Carlos (c08.45hrs). Pilot Sgt Evans RM killed in the first incident and pilot Lt Francis RM and crewman L Cpl Griffin RM in the second.

[b13] — Harrier GR3 of No 1(F) Sqn RAF shot down over Port Howard, West Falkland probably by Blowpipe SAM (09.35hrs). Flt Lt Glover ejects and, injured, is taken prisoner-of-war.

[b14] — Lynx HAS2 of No 815 NAS destroyed in bombing attack on HMS *Ardent* in Grantham Sound by Daggers of FAA Grupo 6 (14.40hrs).

Sunday 23 May

[b15] — Sea Harrier of No 800 NAS, HMS *Hermes* crashes into sea northeast of Falklands shortly after take-off and explodes (19.55hrs). Lt-Cdr Batt RN killed.

Tuesday 25 May

[b16] — Lynx HAS2 of No 815 NAS lost when HMS *Coventry* sunk north of Pebble Island in bombing attack by A-4B Skyhawks of FAA Grupo 5 (15.20hrs).

[b17-b22] — Six Wessex HU5s of No 848 NAS D Flt.

[b23-b25] — Three Chinook HC1s of No 18 Sqn RAF.

[b26] — Lynx HAS2 of No 815 NAS, all destroyed by fire when *Atlantic Conveyor* hit to the northeast of Falklands by Exocet from Super Etendard of CANA 2 Esc.

Thursday 27 May

[b27] — Harrier GR3 of No 1(F) Sqn RAF shot down over Goose Green probably by 35mm Oerlikon fire (13.35hrs). Sqn Ldr Iveson ejects to the west, hides up and is later rescued.

Friday 28 May

[b28] — Scout of B Flt, 3 CBAS shot down near Camilla Creek House, north of Goose Green by Pucaras of FAA Grupo 3 (11.55hrs). Pilot Lt Nunn RM is killed.

Saturday 29 May

[b29] — Sea Harrier of No 801 NAS, HMS *Invincible* — ready for take-off — slides off the deck as the carrier turns into wind to the east of Falklands (15.50hrs). Lt-Cdr Broadwater RN ejects and is safely picked up.

Sunday 30 May

[b30] — Harrier GR3 of No 1(F) Sqn RAF damaged near Stanley by small arms fire from Argentine troops. Runs out of fuel short of *Hermes* and Sqn Ldr Pook RAF ejects to be picked up to east of the Falklands (12.20hrs).

Tuesday 1 June

[b31] — Sea Harrier of No 801 NAS, HMS *Invincible* shot down south of Stanley by Roland SAM (14.40hr). Flt Lt Mortimer RAF ejects and is later rescued from the sea.

Sunday 6 June

[b32] — Gazelle of No 656 Sqn AAC accidentally shot down west of Fitzroy by Sea Dart SAM fired by HMS *Cardiff* (01.10hrs).

Pilot, SSgt Griffin, crewman L Cpl Cockton and two Royal Signals passengers killed.

Tuesday 8 June

[b33] — Harrier GR3 of No 1(F) Sqn RAF lands heavily at Port San Carlos with partial engine failure, and is damaged beyond repair (12.00hrs). Wg Cdr Squire escapes unhurt.

Saturday 12 June

[b34] — Wessex HAS3 of No 737 NAS destroyed when HMS *Glamorgan* hit by land-based Exocet off Stanley (03.35hrs).

Appendix 4 Argentine Aircraft Lost

Saturday 3 April

[a1] — Puma SA330L of CAB 601 shot down at Grytviken, South Georgia by Royal Marine small arms fire.

Saturday 1 May

[a2, a3, a4] — One Pucara of FAA Grupo 3 destroyed and two more damaged and not repaired at Goose Green by CBUs dropped in attack by No 800 Sea Harriers flown by Lt-Cdr Frederiksen, Lt Hale and Lt McHarg RN (08.25hrs). Lt Jukic killed in the destroyed aircraft.

[a5] — Mirage IIIEA of FAA Grupo 8 shot down north of West Falkland by Flt Lt Barton RAF in No 801 NAS Sea Harrier using Sidewinder (16.10hrs). Lt Perona ejects safely.

[a6] — Mirage IIIEA of FAA Grupo 8 damaged in same incident north of West Falkland by Lt Thomas RN in No 801 NAS Sea Harrier using Sidewinder. Then shot down over Stanley by own AA defences and Capt Cuerva killed (16.15hrs).

[a7] — Dagger A of FAA Grupo 6 shot down over East Falkland by Flt Lt Penfold RAF in No 800 NAS Sea Harrier using Sidewinder (16.40hrs). Lt Ardiles killed.

[a8] — Canberra B62 of FAA Grupo 2 shot down north of Falklands by Lt Curtiss RN in No 801 NAS Sea Harrier using Sidewinder (17.45hrs). Lts Ibanez and Gonzalez eject but are not rescued.

Sunday 2 May

[a9] — Lynx HAS 23 of CANA 1 Esc embarked on ARA *Santisima Trinidad* lost in flying accident probably to north of Falklands.

[a10] — Alouette III of CANA 1 Esc lost on board ARA *General Belgrano* when she is torpedoed and sunk to south west of Falklands.

Monday 3 May

[a11] — Aermacchi MB-339A of CANA 1 Esc crashes into ground near Stanley approaching airfield in bad weather (16.00hrs). Lt Benitez killed.

[a12] — Skyvan of PNA damaged by naval gunfire at Stanley on the night of 3-4 May and not repaired.

Sunday 9 May

[a13, a14] — Two A-4C Skyhawks of FAA Grupo 4 lost and Lt Casco and Lt Farias killed. Possibly damaged by Sea Darts from HMS *Coventry* or crashed in bad weather, with one aircraft found on South Jason Island.

[a15] — Puma SA330L of CAB 601 shot down over Choiseul Sound by Sea Dart fired by HMS *Coventry* (16.10hrs). Crew of three lost.

Wednesday 12 May

[a16, a17, a18] — Two A-4B Skyhawks of FAA Grupo 5 shot down off Stanley by Sea Wolf fired by HMS *Brilliant* and third aircraft hits sea trying to evade missile (13.45hrs). All three pilots, Lt Bustos, Lt Ibarlucea and Lt Nivoli killed.

[a19] — A-4B Skyhawk of FAA Grupo 5 shot down over Goose Green by own AA fire (14.25hrs). Lt Gavazzi killed.

Saturday 15 May

[a20-a25] — Six Pucaras of FAA Grupo 3,

[a26-a29] — Four T-34C Mentors of CANA 4 Esc,

[a30] — Skyvan of PNA, all destroyed or put out of action at Pebble Island in raid by D Sqn SAS (early morning).

Friday 21 May

[a31] — Chinook CH-47C of CAB 601 destroyed on ground near Mount Kent by Flt Lt Hare RAF in No 1 (F) Sqn Harrier GR3 using 30mm cannon (08.00hrs).

[a32] — Puma SA330L of CAB 601 badly damaged on ground near Mount Kent in same attack by Sqn Ldr Pook and Flt Lt Hare RAF in No 1 (F) Sqn Harrier GR3s using 30mm cannon (08.00hrs). Destroyed on 26 May in same position by Sqn Ldr Pook using CBUs.

[a33] — Pucara of FAA Grupo 3 shot down over Sussex Mountains by Stinger SAM fired by D Sqn SAS (10.00hrs). Capt Benitz ejects safely.

[a34] — Dagger A of FAA Grupo 6 shot down near Fanning Head by Sea Cat fired by HMS *Argonaut* or HMS *Plymouth*, or more likely, Sea Wolf from HMS *Broadsword* (10.30hrs). Lt Bean killed.

[a35] — Pucara of FAA Grupo 3 shot down near Darwin by Cdr Ward RN in one of three Sea Harriers of No 801 NAS using 30mm cannon (12.10hrs). Major Tomba ejects.

[a36, a37] — Two A-4C Skyhawks of FAA Grupo 4 shot down near Chartres, West Falkland by Lt-Cdr Blissett and Lt-Cdr Thomas RN in No 800 NAS Sea Harriers using Sidewinders (13.05hrs). Lt Lopez and Lt Manzotti killed.

[a38] — Dagger A of FAA Grupo 6 shot down near Teal River Inlet, West Falkland by Lt-Cdr Frederiksen RN in No 800 NAS Sea Harrier using Sidewinder (14.35hrs). Lt Luna ejects.

[a39, a40, a41] — Two Dagger As of FAA Grupo 6 shot down north of Port Howard, West Falkland by Lt Thomas and a third by Cdr Ward RN In No 801 NAS Sea Harriers using Sidewinders (14.50hrs), Maj Piuma, Capt Donaldille and Lt Senn all eject.

[a42] — A-4Q Skyhawk of CANA 3 Esc shot down near Swan Island in Falkland Sound by Lt Morell RN in No 800 NAS Sea Harrier using Sidewinder (15.12hrs). Lt-Cdr Philippi ejects.

[a43] — A-4Q Skyhawk of CANA 3 Esc shot down in same incident by Flt Lt Leeming RAF in No 800 NAS Sea Harrier using 30mm cannon (15.12hrs). Lt Marquez is killed.

[a44] — A-4Q Skyhawk of CANA 3 Esc damaged over Falkland Sound by small arms fire from HMS *Ardent* and again in same incident as above by Lt Morrell using 30mm cannon. Unable to land at Stanley with undercarriage problems and Lt Arca ejects (15.30hrs).

Sunday 23 May

[a45] — Puma SA330L of CAB 601 flies into ground near Shag Cove House, West Falkland attempting to evade Flt Lt Morgan RAF in No 800 NAS Sea Harrier (10.30hrs). All crew escape.

[a46] — Agusta A-109A of CAB 601 in same incident destroyed on ground by Flt Lt Morgan and Flt Lt Leeming RAF in No 800 NAS Sea Harriers using 30mm cannon (10.30hrs).

[a47] — Puma SA330L of CAB 601 also in same incident damaged on ground by Flt Lt Morgan with 30mm cannon (10.30hrs). Then believed shortly destroyed by Lt Cdr Gedge and Lt Cdr Braithwaite RN In No 801 NAS Sea Harriers with more cannon fire.

[a48] — A-4B Skyhawk of FAA Grupo 5 shot down over San Carlos Water by unknown SAM 13.50hrs). Claims that day include those from HMS *Broadsword* (Sea Wolf), HMS *Antelope* (Sea Cat) and land-based Rapiers and Blowpipe. Lt Guadagnini killed.

[a49] — Dagger A of FAA Grupo 6 shot down over Pebble Island by Lt Hale RN in No 800 NAS Sea Harrier using Sidewinder (16.00hrs). Lt Volponi killed.

Monday 24 May

[a50, a51, a52] — Two Dagger A's of FAA Grupo 6 shot down north of Pebble Island by Lt-Cdr Auld and a third by Lt D. Smith RN in No 800 NAS Sea Harriers using Sidewinder (11.15hrs). Maj Puga and Capt Diaz eject, but Lt Castillo killed.

[a53] — A-4C Skyhawk of FAA Grupo 4 damaged over San Carlos Water by ship and ground-based air defences and crashes into King George Bay, West Falkland on flight home

(13.30hrs). Claims that day include those from HMS *Argonaut* and *Fearless* Sea Cats and Rapier and Blowpipe SAMs. Lt Bono lost.

Tuesday 25 May

[a54] — A-4B Skyhawk of FAA Grupo 5 shot down north of Pebble Island by Sea Dart fired by HMS *Coventry* (09.30hrs). Lt Palaver killed.

[a55] — A-4C Skyhawk of FAA Grupo 4 destroyed over San Carlos Water by a variety of weapons, the claims including small arms fire, HMS *Yarmouth's* Sea Cat, and Rapier and Blowpipe SAMs (12.30hrs). Lt Lucero ejects.

[a56] — A-4C Skyhawk of FAA Grupo 4 damaged over San Carlos Water in same attack, and then brought down northeast of Pebble Island by Sea Dart fired by HMS *Coventry* (12.45hrs). Lt Garcia killed.

Thursday 27 May

[a57] — A-4B Skyhawk of FAA Grupo 5 damaged over San Carlos Water by 40mm Bofors from either HMS *Fearless* or HMS *Intrepid*, and crashes near Port Howard (17.00hrs). Lt Velasco ejects.

Friday 28 May

[a58] — Pucara of FAA Grupo 3 crashes into high ground returning to Stanley from Goose Green attack (c10.00hrs). Lt Giminez killed.

[a59] — Aermacchi MB-339A of CANA 1 Esc shot down at Goose Green by Blowpipe SAM fired by Royal Marine Air Defence Troop (17.00hrs). Lt Miguel killed.

[a60] — Pucara of FAA Grupo 3 shot down at Goose Green by small arms fire from 2 Para (17.10hrs). Lt Cruzado ejects and becomes POW.

Saturday 29 May

[a61] — Dagger A of FAA Grupo 6 shot down over San Carlos Water by Rapier SAM (12.00hrs). Lt Bernhardt killed.

Sunday 30 May

[a62] — Puma SA330L of CAB 601 lost in the morning in uncertain circumstances near Mount Kent — possibly to own forces fire.

[a63, a64] — A-4C Skyhawks of FAA Grupo 4 shot down east of Falklands by Sea Darts fired by HMS *Exeter*, although 4.5in gunfire from HMS *Avenger* may have hit one (14.35hrs). Lt Vazquez and Lt Castillo killed.

Tuesday 1 June

[a65] — Hercules C130E of FAA Transport Grupo 1 shot down 50 miles North of Pebble Island by Cdr Ward RN in No 801 NAS Sea Harrier using Sidewinder and 30mm cannon (10.45hrs). Crew of seven killed.

Monday 7 June

[a66] — Learjet 35A of FAA Photo-Reconnaissance Grupo 1 shot down over Pebble Island by Sea Dart fired by HMS *Exeter* (09.05hrs). Wg Cdr de la Colina and crew of four killed.

Tuesday 8 June

[a67, a68, a69] — Two A-4B Skyhawks of FAA Grupo 5 shot down over Choiseul Sound by Flt Lt Morgan RAF and a third by Lt D. Smith RN in No 800 NAS Sea Harriers using Sidewinders (16.45hrs). Lt Arraras, Lt Bolzan and Ensign Vazquez killed.

Sunday 13 June

[a70] — Canberra B62 of FAA Grupo 2 shot down west of Stanley by Sea Dart fired by HMS *Exter* (10.55hrs). Pilot, Capt Pastran ejects safely but Capt Casado is killed.

Postwar — Captured at Stanley

[a71-a81] — 11 Pucaras of FAA Grupo 3

[a82-a83] — Two Bell 212s of FAA Grupo 7

[a84-a86] — Three Aermacchi MB-339As of CANA 1 Esc

[a87] — Puma SA330L of PNA

[a88] — Chinook CH-47C of CAB 601

[a89-a90] — Two Agusta A-109A Hirundos of CAB 601

[a91-a99] — Nine Iroquois UN-1H's of CAB 601

Unknown Date

[a100] — Pucara of FAA Grupo 4 reported lost over the sea on reconnaissance mission from Comodoro Rivadavia.

Bibliography

General and Political

Cawkwell Mary, *The Falkland Story 1592-1982*, Anthony Nelson, 1983

Coll, Alberto R. and Arend, Anthony C., editors, *The Falklands War: Lessons for Strategy, Diplomacy and International Law*, George Allen and Unwin, 1985

Daynes, John A., *The Forces Postal History of the Falkland Islands and the Task Force*, The Forces Postal History Society, 1983

Fox, Robert, *Antarctica and the South Atlantic: Discovery, Development and Dispute*, British Broadcasting Corporation, 1985

Goebel, Julius, *The Struggle for the Falkland Islands: A Study in Legal and Diplomatic History*, Yale University Press, 1982

Hastings, Max and Jenkins, Simon, *The Battle for the Falklands*, Michael Joseph, 1983

HMSO, *Falkland Islands Review: Report of a Committee of Privy Counsellors* (The Franks Report), 1983

HMSO, *The Falklands Campaign: The Lessons*, 1982

HMSO, *The Falkland Islands: The Facts*, 1982

HMSO, Foreign and Commonwealth Office, *The Disputed Islands, The Falklands Crisis: A History and Background*

HMSO, House of Commons, *The Falklands Campaign: A Digest of Debates in the House of Commons 2 April – 15 June 1982*, 1982

Headland, Robert, *The Island of South Georgia*, Cambridge University Press, 1984

Middlebrook, Martin, *Task Force: The Falklands War, 1982* (Revised edition), Penguin Books, 1987

Smith, John, *74 Days, An Islander's Diary of the Falklands Occupation*, Century Publishing, 1984

Strange, Ian J., *The Falklands Islands*, 3rd edition, David and Charles, 1983

Sunday Express Magazine Team, *War in the Falklands: The Campaign in Pictures*, Weidenfeld and Nicolson, 1982

Sunday Times Insight Team, *The Falklands War: The Full Story*, Andre Deutsch, 1982

Way, Peter, editor, *The Falklands War in 14 parts*, Marshall Cavendish, 1983

Whitakers Almanac, 1983

Military and Combined Operations

Arthur, Max, *Above All, Courage: The Falklands Front Line: First-hand Accounts*, Sidgwick and Jackson, 1985

Fox, Robert, *Eyewitness Falklands: A Personal Account of the Falklands Campaign*, Methuen, 1982

Jolly, Rick, *The Red and Green Life Machine: A Diary of the Falklands Field Hospital*, Century, 1983

Kitson, Linda (The Official War Artist), *The Falklands War: A Visual Diary*, Michael Beazley, 1982

McGowan, Robert and Hands, Jeremy, *Don't Cry for Me Sergeant Major*, Futura, 1983

Perrett, Bryan, *Weapons of the Falklands Conflict*, Blandford Press, 1982

Supplement to *The London Gazette*, 8 October 1982 (British gallantry awards)

Aviation, including Naval

Braybrook, Roy, *Battle for the Falklands (3), Air Forces*, Osprey 'Men-at-Arms' Series, 1982

Braybrook, Roy, *British Aerospace: Harrier and Sea Harrier*, Osprey Publishing, 1984

Burden, Rodney A., Draper, Michael I., Rough, Douglas A., Smith, Colin R. and Wilton, David L. *Falklands: The Air War*, British Aviation Research Group, 1986

Ethell, Jeffrey and Price, Alfred, *Air War: South Atlantic, Sidgwick and Jackson, 1984*

Land Forces, including Marines

Fowler, William, *Battle for the Falklands (1), Land Forces*, Osprey 'Men-at-Arms' Series, 1982

Frost, Maj-Gen John, *2 PARA, Falklands: The Battalion at War*, Buchan and Enright, 1983

Gander, Terry, *Encyclopaedia of the Modern British Army*, Patrick Stephens, 2nd edition, 1982

Geraghty, Tony, *This is the SAS: A Pictorial History of the Special Air Service Regiment*, Arms and Armour Press, 1982

HMSO, *The British Army in the Falklands 1982*, 1983

Keegan, John, *World Armies*, MacMillan, 1983

Ladd, James D., *SBS: The Invisible Raiders: The History of the Special Boat Squadron from World War 2 to the Present*, Arms and Armour Press, 1983

McManners, Capt Hugh, Royal Artillery, *Falklands Commando*, William Kimber, 1984

Strawson, John, *A History of the SAS Regiment*, Secker and Warburg, 1984

Thompson, Julian, *No Picnic: 3 Commando Brigade in the South Atlantic: 1982*, Secker and Warburg, 1985

Vaux, Nick, *March to the South Atlantic: 42 Commando Royal Marines in the Falklands War*, Buchan and Enright, 1986

Weeks, Col John, *Jane's Pocket Book: Armies of the World*, Janes, 1981

Naval and Maritime

Beaver, Paul, *Modern Combat Ships 2, 'Invincible' Class*, Ian Allan, 1984

BP Shipping Ltd, *Operation Corporate: BP Shipping Ltd's Involvement in the Falkland Island Crisis 1982*, 1982

Brown, David, *The Royal Navy and the Falklands War*, Leo Cooper, 1987

Director of Naval Air Warfare, *Flight Deck, The Fleet Air Arm Quarterly: Falklands Edition*, Ministry of Defence, 1982 (Journal)

English, Adrian and Watts, Anthony, *Battle for the Falklands (2), Naval Forces*, Osprey 'Men-at-Arms' Series, 1982

Hill, Rear-Adm J. R., RN, *The Royal Navy: Today and Tomorrow*, Ian Allan, 1982

Gavshon, Arthur and Rice, Desmond, *The Sinking of the 'Belgrano'*, Secker and Warburg, 1984

Jane's Fighting Ships, 1981/82

Koburger, Jnr, Charles W., *Sea Power in the Falklands*, Praeger, 1983

Lockett, Andrew, Munro, Neil and Wells, David, editors, *HMS Endurance 1981-82 Deployment: A Season of Conflict*, Andrew Lockett, 1983

Marriot, Leo, *Modern Combat Ships 3, Type 42*, Ian Allan, 1985

Meyer, Cdr C. J., OBE, RN, *Modern Combat Ships 1, 'Leander' Class*, Ian Allan, 1984

P & O Steam Navigation Company, *P & O in the Falklands; A Pictorial Record, 5th April – 25th September 1982*, 1982

Preston, Anthony, *Sea Combat off the Falklands*, Willow Books, 1982

Ross, P. J. (editor), *HMS Invincible: The Falklands Deployment 2nd April – 17th September 1982*, privately printed, 1983

Royal Fleet Auxiliary Service, *The RFA in the Falklands* (Journal)

Speed, Keith, *Sea Change: The Battle for the Falklands and the Future of Britain's Navy*, Ashgrove Press, 1982

Tinker, Hugh, compiled by, *A Message from the Falklands: The Life and Gallant Death of David Tinker, Lt RN*, Junction Books, 1982

Villar, Capt Roger, *Merchant Ships at War: The Falklands Experience*, Conway Maritime Press, 1984

Index